T0341743

POWER AND LOSS IN SOUTH AFRICAN JOURNALISM

POWER AND LOSS IN SOUTH AFRICAN JOURNALISM

News in the age of social media

Glenda Daniels

WITS UNIVERSITY PRESS

Published in South Africa by:
Wits University Press
1 Jan Smuts Avenue
Johannesburg 2001

www.witspress.co.za

First published 2020

http://dx.doi.org.10.18772/12020075997

978-1-77614-599-7 (Paperback)
978-1-77614-603-1 (Hardback)
978-1-77614-600-0 (Web PDF)
978-1-77614-601-7 (EPUB)
978-1-77614-602-4 (Mobi)

Project manager: Inga Norenius
Copyeditor: Monica Seeber
Proofreader: Alison Lockhart
Indexer: Sanet le Roux
Cover design: Triple M
Typesetter: Newgen
Typeset in 10 point Minion Pro

This book is dedicated to Margaret and Ivan

CONTENTS

TABLES AND FIGURES

PREFACE

I approached this work from my many selves, but one gaze was fixed. I believe that journalism in the public interest is critical to the deepening of democracy, and that finding and revealing the truth is becoming tougher and more dangerous in the world of social media. Indeed, social media, where misinformation is proliferating unchecked, is killing journalism.

One of my selves is that of an academic. From this position, I experimented with and deployed diverse theoretical frameworks to make sense of power and loss in the media in the twenty-first century. These theories were radical democracy blended with psychoanalytical concepts, decolonisation theory, black consciousness and feminist theory. I have deliberately simplified political and philosophical concepts for accessible reading.

Another self is that of a journalist. This relates to my history as a journalist and my writing on media matters these days, as well as my methods and techniques in gathering information – through research, interviewing, observation and 'connecting the dots'.

A further self is that of an activist, advocating for better media ethics, diversity, freedom, access to information, feminist emancipation and transparency. For two chapters I also used surveys, one on job losses and the other on the anti-feminist backlash in the media.

The idea for this book first percolated in 2007 and, like coffee, it became stronger as it was left to brew. I also write about my personal tug-of-war with social media – the idea was not to examine social media and technology and their effects but, rather, to look at different aspects of journalism and to examine how it was changing in terms of power and loss – for instance, the power journalism evinced in the investigation of corruption and the loss it suffers through the harrassment of journalists (this is dealt with more deeply in chapter 1 and, indeed, throughout the book). All the chapters show how social media and technology have profoundly affected the news media landscape in South Africa, which mirrors the international situation but has its own nuances.

In 2007, when I worked in a print media newsroom in Rosebank, Johannesburg, and social media began to gain traction, I had reservations about the possible downsides. I knew I could not write then about my misgivings, which were based on instinct and feelings, not on fact. No one could know for sure that social media would become toxic platforms for divisive and polarising politics. Nor that journalists, particularly women, would be attacked online; community print media would die and find new life on Facebook; or that there would be further marginalising of the poor who could not afford smartphones and data. I didn't know that job losses in journalism would be a bloodbath of lost skills, expertise and diversity. It was too early to research this back in 2007, and I needed to 'show' rather than 'tell'. It was also too early in 2011, when I was working in another newsroom, also in Rosebank, and where we were hauled off to a seminar and told to sing the new mantra of 'digital first'– and even given T-shirts that said 'digital first', and encouraged to sign up to Twitter if we hadn't already.

By 2018, amassing data from the news media landscape to make sometimes suggestive, sometimes definitive and sometimes reflective findings had become easier. The conundrums the craft of journalism faces are worse than most imagined they would become. For example, by 2019 the calls to regulate and tax Facebook and Google had become louder around the world but not in South Africa. Many governments and nongovernmental organisations internationally, especially in the UK, US, Canada and Australia, have instituted commissions of inquiry into the state of news media. These inquiries are reaching similar conclusions and a new regime of tax reform is necessary for the giants Google and Facebook that are now gobbling up journalism.

Lurking in every chapter of this book is how the power of social media, and the issues that arise from it – misinformation, mal-information, disinformation and propaganda – have overtaken journalism. Audiences consume media in new ways. Media companies and their management executives seem to be unimaginative in dealing with such crises – apart from laying off staff and making senior and skilled journalists redundant in order to cut their bills. They chase innovation but seem to show few results; they chase clicks, metrics and search engine optimisation and efficient algorithms that can replace human journalists. All the while, something valuable is getting lost – fact-based, ethical journalism that is in the public interest.

Times quickly change. My first book, an academic monograph, *Fight for Democracy: The ANC and the Media in South Africa*, featured a political struggle as the (ANC) wrestled with the media for ideological hegemony instead of recognising the separate role it had in a democracy. In this book, the ANC does not dominate every chapter. In fact, it hardly features at all. The ruling party appears to have enough of its own problems, mainly of its own making. For instance, a few months before the national election in May 2019, the ANC was blaming 'sabotage' for the electricity blackouts. Subsequently, the ANC-led government's newly minted president, Cyril Ramaphosa, was 'shocked' at what was going wrong. The ANC urged its disastrous behemoth, the power entity Eskom, to provide electricity, despite knowing that in the past decade this entity, through cadre deployment, lacked technical expertise. In the 'new era' since 2018 under President Ramaphosa there appeared to be a commitment to end the scourge of corruption, and perhaps the ruling party recognised that news in the public interest was valuable. Nevertheless, although Ramaphosa mentioned just about everything else in his two-hour State of the Nation speech in February 2019, he said not a word about the contribution that journalism, particularly investigative journalism, has played, for instance, in outing the 'Zupta' crooks. He asked us to 'watch this space' for action against the corrupt, for growth in the economy and for combating violence against women – among at least 20 other issues.

News media in the public interest includes digging hard to find the truth, such as why South Africa is having power blackouts in an age when all techno optimists and determinists are cheering the Fourth Industrial Revolution. Public interest journalism includes investigative journalism, and the space for women journalists to bring diversity to news and tell their stories without fear of being 'trolled'. Public interest journalism includes local communities having access to media that focuses on their own voices and issues, rather than relying on national news, which often has little bearing on their day-to-day realities. Public interest journalism needs diversity in the content of stories and the gender composition of newsrooms.

MY FACEBOOK STORY IN A LITTLE MORE DETAIL

This was long before the idea of 'surveillance capitalism' emerged, and the knowledge that media technology companies were using data for profit (they continue to do so).

It was 2007. I was working in *The Times* newsroom, in Rosebank, Johannesburg, managing editor of the *Business Times* supplement (of the *Sunday Times*). Neither the print version of *The Times* nor the *Business Times* supplement exists today. It was a desk job, the most boring I'd had in an otherwise stimulating career as a journalist since 1990. Often, I would look up from my computer. There were interesting things happening around me. For example, the online news video section was starting up. Lots of excitement there. One day, I noticed that every time I looked up from my desk, a few metres away from me a colleague was smiling at her computer screen. Her work must be more interesting than mine, I thought. But that wasn't hard. It was the same the next day. She was smiling. I had to ask. Was it 'a biggie', 'cracker', 'funny one'?

She replied, 'It's not a story, it's Facebook. I'm connecting with friends.' She smiled again at her screen, while talking to me. 'I'm happy to put you on. Please can I? Send me a pic of you.' The next day, she was smiling at her screen again. She asked if I had a pic for Facebook. I didn't, but might have one the next day, I said. That year, as I was working in that newsroom, I was also thinking about the topic and research question for my PhD. It was to be on the role of the media in a democracy. I was to register the following year. I wondered about the power of social media: would it overtake journalism, would it replace journalism, would it kill journalism? Would it potentially serve democracy, enabling more participation in the media space? Would it be news for free that would be wonderful for audiences but kill journalism? Shouldn't I be researching this area? I soon realised that it was too early to do that. Time would tell. I declined my friend's offer to 'put me on' Facebook. I thought about privacy issues. At the time I didn't think, and nor did anyone else, that data would be consumed and analysed for nefarious purposes, but I did wonder whether social media would become an addictive platform for narcissistic exhibitionism. Today, I see social media mainly as an attention-seeking obsession, with participants giving opinions not necessarily based on facts. Many seem to believe that they are 'activists', merely by having opinions.

About ten years later, in 2018 at my Wits media studies undergraduate classes, I noticed a trend: there were more and more doctors' notes for extensions on essays, but these notes were not for 'flu' and 'tummy bugs'. They were from psychiatrists. I asked my class why there were so many depression and anxiety disorders today, compared to five years ago. For the first time ever, in all my teaching years, everyone appeared to participate. In unison, in a loud chorus, they responded 'social media addiction'.

There are more than 1.7 billion Facebook users. I remain unsubscribed. I have had doubts and misgivings about my limited social media use. For example, in addition to having no Facebook profile at all, I have limited Twitter, LinkedIn and WhatsApp use. People have said that they were 'trying to find me' and could not. They asked, 'How can you be a journalist and not be on Facebook?' 'How can you market your work if you are not on Facebook?' 'You missed out on this fight between so-and-so on the land debate. It was so lit.' And so forth. I was even told, 'You not being on Facebook isn't going to stop it.'

I did have a fear of missing out but it was a small one. I stuck to my initial misgivings. I didn't know that being 'on' Facebook would have consequences worse than I had imagined. Instead of creating more diversity, social media conglomerates have displaced mainstream media conglomerates. We may have leapt from the frying pan into the fire: instead of enabling democracy, social media like Facebook has thrown it into disarray.

About half of the population in South Africa uses the internet, according to the technology research organisation World Wide Worx. Many people do not have smartphones. It requires expensive data to be engaged in social media, which has become a loud echo chamber of polarised political views, divisive rhetoric, binary oppositions and many falsities, rumour, disinformation and propaganda. This is known as 'fake news'. According to Massachusetts Institute of Technology research in 2018, 'fake news' spreads more quickly than fact-based news.

Facebook was created to 'connect' people, by enabling them to share their photos, issues, news and views, said its founder, Mark Zuckerberg. That sounds so warm and fuzzy. Then Facebook became a spy and started selling data. It exercised enormous power without responsibility. Facebook has had unintended consequences, unimagined by most. It has affected the workings of democracy. For example, during the 2016 election in the US, Cambridge Analytica, the internet technology services management company, harvested and sold data from 50 million profiles and decisively influenced Donald Trump's victory.

There were also unintended consequences for journalism. Advertising abandoned print and went online, transferring to technology media companies such as Facebook and Google. The business of the mainstream media started to collapse. The structural crisis in journalism began. Previously, people had mainly been readers and viewers of news. Now they were also makers of news. But this also meant that the unscrupulous, enabled by the internet, could produce 'news' that was both more 'instant' and 'diverse'. Without analysis this may sound an ideal way to deepen democracy. The unintended consequences have been serious. Democracy has been weakened.

The public began to conflate Facebook social media with journalism, and trust in journalists began to erode. Even with 'trust' there is a paradox. Over the past five years, 'complete trust and confidence in journalism' has increased, but so has 'no trust and confidence'. According to research on trust and confidence in journalism conducted in 2018 by the South African survey Futurefact, 'no trust' has, however, grown to a lesser extent than 'complete trust'. It is hard to make something of that. Futurefact's research showed that complete trust and confidence in journalists has increased each year from 2012 to 2017 and over the past five years, it has increased by 37 per cent. There are, accordingly, more people who are not ambivalent about their complete trust in journalists and if we combine 'complete' with 'some trust and confidence', then 73 per cent of the respondents leaned in favour of feeling positive towards journalists, with varying degrees of intensity.

More than ten years ago, after declining an invitation for 'help' to be put on Facebook, I also wondered whether I would one day publish reflections and analysis about journalism's power and loss. This book is about that.

ACKNOWLEDGEMENTS

A big thank you to those, especially journalists, who gave their time to be interviewed for this book. For many it was the first time, they said, that they had had the opportunity to reflect on their own craft of the trade. They were quite unaccustomed to being on the other end of the interview.

Thank you to Wits University's School of Languages, Literature and Media for granting my one-year sabbatical leave from 2018 to 2019, which provided a break from teaching to enable me to write. Thank you also to the university for the Anderson Capelli sabbatical grant, which allowed for some travel. As a rated scholar with the National Research Foundation I also received an incentive grant which contributed towards costs of research.

To the South African National Editors' Forum a not-for-profit organisation whose members are editors, senior journalists and journalism educators, and where I am a council member, your commitment to media freedom and diversity inspires me to continue to do service work in the public interest. The research, findings and views in this book, however, are my own and not the organisation's.

This work has been enhanced by various fruitful collaborations. The chapter on the anti-feminist backlash and glass ceiling for women in media emanated from research with Gender Links and was supported by the Media Development and Diversity Agency. A further collaboration was an international one, with the New Beats project based in Melbourne, Australia. Here, I was allowed to adapt the project's online job losses survey for South African conditions. It is a continuation of my work on 'State of the Newsroom South Africa'. The survey had a weighty 158 respondents, South African journalists and editors who had left the newsroom, and were now part of the precarious 'gig' economy, from which the chapter on job losses is derived. The completed international New Beats research will be published in a book in 2020.

I would like to acknowledge a handful of academic colleagues who have influenced my work in a variety of ways: through their generosity with ideas, discussions on black consciousness, decoloniality, feminism and media freedom. They have also become supportive friends over the years and their calls for collaborations on different research projects have always been welcome. They are Tendayi Sithole, Bruce Mutsvairo, Julie Reid, Viola Milton, Ylva Rodny-Gumede, Kate Skinner, Sarah Chiumbu, Dale McKinley, Tawana Kupe, Ufuoma Akpojivi, Dina Ligaga, Pier Paolo Frassinelli, Colin Chasi and Winston Mano. I am grateful to Ferial Haffajee for her strong and generous friendship and for allowing me to use her Twitter trolling story to talk about cyber misogyny, 'whenever and for whatever you want'. Then there are 'veterans' in the journalism industry whom I should acknowledge as they inspire me and influence my reflections and advocacy work; they include Joe Thloloe, Ray Louw, Guy Berger, Mathatha Tsedu, Barbara Ludman, Mondli Makhanya, Janet Heard, Judy Sandison, Amina Frense and Latiefa Mobara.

It was excellent to work with the experienced copy editor Monica Seeber who, besides eagle-eye editing and cutting overly long quotes, also encouraged me to insert my voice into this book. It was also good to work with Helen Grange who did fact checking and made corrections on the first draft. Thanks also to Vanessa Malila, who checked the reference style.

Wits University Press's Roshan Cader and Veronica Klipp had faith in this book from the start. I am grateful for their patience with the process and for the advice.

To Nigel, thanks for your love and support, and also for reading and commenting on this work. My children, Alexandra and Ashok, you continue to inspire me with your critical thinking on issues of feminism and activism, #MeToo, #FeesMustFall and the social justice policy paths you pursue in your studies.

Finally, I am also fortunate to be learning every day and all the time, from my students in Media Studies where I teach media and politics, democracy, media freedom, issues in the South African newsroom, gender, diversity and decoloniality – from first-years to PhDs.

ACRONYMS AND ABBREVIATIONS

AIP	Association of Independent Publishers
ANC	African National Congress
ANN7	African News Network 7
BCCSA	Broadcasting Complaints' Commission of South Africa
COO	chief operating officer
CPJ	Committee to Protect Journalists
CWU	Communication Workers Union
EFF	Economic Freedom Fighters
Icasa	Independent Communications Authority of South Africa
ICT	Information and Communication Technologies
LGBTIQ	lesbian, gay, bisexual, transgender/transsexual, intersex and queer/ questioning
LRA	Labour Relations Act
MAT	Media Appeals Tribunal
MDDA	Media Development and Diversity Agency
MMA	Media Monitoring Africa
Mwasa	Media Workers Association of South Africa
NGO	non-governmental organisation
NPA	National Prosecuting Authority
PDMTTT	Print and Digital Media Transformation Task Team
PIC	Public Investment Corporation
PR	public relations
R2K	Right2Know
SABC	South African Broadcasting Corporation

Sanef	South African National Editors' Forum
SARS	South African Revenue Service
SAUJ	South African Union of Journalists
WAN-IFRA	World Association of Newspapers and News Publishers
WIN	Women in the News

1

Power and Subjection in the Media Landscape

Wherever there is power, there is resistance and yet, or rather consequently, this resistance is never in a position of exteriority in relation to power.
Michel Foucault, *The History of Sexuality*

Power is quirky, slippery and paradoxical. It shifts and slides, depending on where you are standing, your position and your gaze. It can press upon you from the outside, from above. It can be horizontal among equals, and it can be internal, as when we subject ourselves to compliance. It can enable insecurities, trauma and passionate attachments.

Corruption in South Africa meant that the poor lost power. Then the power of investigative media kicked in, not overnight but over ten years of true stories, of exposés which helped bring about the fall of a president in January 2018 while his corrupt business cronies fled the country.

But it has not all been power to journalism. 'Traditional' journalism, print and broadcast, has lost power through thousands of job losses in the industry. Women have lost voice through a backlash against feminism. Community media has become even more financially unsustainable, and has lost power.

In South Africa, the state has power, the ruling (ANC) has power, the judiciary has power, the Constitution has power, 'the people' have power, the corrupt have power.

The media have power,[1] but it can be lost when jobs are lost in newsrooms, when credibility is lost, women's voices are lost, local voice is lost, diversity is lost. The internet and social media have power, generating 'fake news' – which then gains power too. It is against this matrix of power tangents that public interest journalism contributes to a deeper democracy.

The years 2017–2019 were spectacular for investigative journalism in South Africa, particularly in relation to the #GuptaLeaks,[2] which reverberated in myriad ways, although the first really big break had come ten years earlier in 2009, by the investigative journalist Mandy Rossouw, with the exposure in the *Mail & Guardian* of the cost and the funding of work at the president's homestead in Nkandla. Taxpayers' money had been used for the personal gain of the president. After the euphoria at investigative journalism's role in bringing down the president in 2018, a more sober and realistic assessment of journalism was needed in 2019, as job losses mounted up. Mentorships in newsrooms came to an end, subs' desks were decimated, training dried up. Women journalists experienced death and rape threats, vile forms of cyber misogyny.

This book weaves together the threads, using the tools of radical democracy, feminist and decolonial theory to show the contribution journalism has made to a deeper and more inclusive democracy. I examine power losses in journalism in terms of job losses, of diversity of voice, of women – and black women in particular – but I also highlight green shoots, or re-significations: how media can change from normative liberal reporting to include fresher decolonial, black consciousness and feminist perspectives.

Although the current volume is a scholarly work there is also an advocacy element to it – a fierce argument for public interest and not-for-profit journalism. I also call for more freedom of the press, more diversity in journalism, more community and independent media start-ups that are not hamstrung by greedy monopolies. The international context and rationale for the book are that regimes all over the world (including the 'free world', the West) are clamping down on media freedom as well as closing down media outlets in favour of entertainment news, and women journalists are being trolled and threatened. The analysis of the media freedom organisation Freedom House is that 'across the world, freedom of the press is atrophying'.[3]

In 2018, Freedom House recorded that the muzzling of journalists and independent news media was at its worst in 13 years, exemplified by the murder of Jamal Khashoggi at the Saudi Arabian consulate in Istanbul in October 2018.[4] The Committee to Protect Journalists (CPJ) also calculated that the number of journalists jailed for their work was at the highest level since the 1990s. In the Philippines, the editor of *Rappler*, Maria Ressa, was detained (subsequently released) in February 2019, on charges of 'cyber libel' (in reality, for exposing government corruption). The deterioration exists in all quarters: the president of Russia, Vladimir Putin, has so thoroughly throttled his country's news media that Freedom House's scorers rated Venezuela freer. Strongmen such as Daniel Ortega of Nicaragua and Viktor Orban of Hungary have flexed censorious muscles. Donald Trump demonises the news media as the 'enemy of the people' (but the US's strong First Amendment and independent courts have so far prevented him from acting on these outbursts). His rhetoric has encouraged autocrats in other countries, who passed laws outlawing 'fake news' and quickly set about persecuting political opponents.

This book's focus is on power and loss in journalism, using the voices of journalists themselves. It follows my 2012 book *Fight for Democracy: The ANC and the Media in South Africa*, which ended with the Zuma regime coming to power. It uses psychoanalytical concepts: the ticklish subject of Zuma's rule (Zuma seen by journalists as the master signifier of corruption), and then the interpellation (naming, hailing, labelling and shaming) of journalists as the enemy and agents of 'white monopoly capital'. In the new times of digitisation and social media there is not enough political analysis of journalism using a balance of the forces of power and loss, although there are many works on media, transformation and freedom.

Yes please, but no thanks. By this seeming contradiction I mean two things. First, my work, like all such works, also builds upon what has been offered before. Second, here in the global South, you can centre the gaze of Africa, feminism and black consciousness while also including theorists from the global North who espouse social justice in an interconnected world which is also full of divisions. Why add to these divisions, and in an intellectually infantile way? In the same way that Achille Mbembe, in *On the Postcolony*,[5] wrote that to think is to experiment, here too I experiment with a blend of theories and methods.

There are immensely important recent contributions to the analysis of the news media, of journalism and media companies in our southern part of the world, which I add to. The method in this book, as explained in the Preface, is a multiple one, ranging from the theoretical and conceptual (mainly of 'power' and 'loss'), and surveys of job losses by retrenched journalists, through contacting over 20 media organisations.[6] In partnership with Gender Links and the South African National Editors' Forum (Sanef), I use another survey method to highlight sexist practices and the bullying of women journalists in newsrooms and by political parties. I also include a collection of stories from print media over the period of a year to discuss the 'Afro' debate in schools and how this was covered. Finally, the interview method is used in chapters 4 and 5 to discuss the demise of the community media. This book also marks the first time that a book is written about journalism using the voices of journalists themselves.

I cite the contributions of researchers from the global South who have informed and inspired my work. So, even though I parachute into the media landscape at a particular point in time, from the Jacob Zuma era to that of the Cyril Ramaphosa regime, I do not land without the energies, theoretical contributions and historical backgrounds of other works.

THE CONTRIBUTION TO THIS FIELD OF SCHOLARS FROM THE GLOBAL SOUTH

This chapter introduces the topic and the rationale for research, and explains the conceptual tools deployed to the analysis of power and subjection vis-à-vis the news media, within the media itself, and the media's relationship with the ANC and the state. A large part of the chapter provides a media landscape: the news media in South Africa, the legal and political framework and the existing owner-ship structures. It therefore has two sections. The first is theory. The other is the media landscape, which sets the scene for the other chapters, mainly to elaborate on journalism's losses, and some gains of power.

There are new reflections in research by scholars in the global South about the importance of research for communications, journalism and media studies that is not Eurocentric but, instead, a gaze that is African, black, feminist, and with a decolonial perspective. Some theorists (Chela Sandoval, for example, with whom I concur) do not believe in 'academic apartheid',[7] but would rather support what Francis Nyamnjoh calls 'epistemological conviviality' and 'interconnectedness of theory'.[8] This work embraces rather than shuns, especially if freedom, equality and social justice are the principles – for, as Viola Milton warned in her inaugural lecture, this kind of shunning, or centrism could become just another bigotry.[9] For the obvious marriage of black consciousness with decolonial theorising, I found Tendayi Sithole's 2016 work on Steve Biko inspiring.[10] My question is: this book deconstructs news media politics, power and loss, so what is the relevance of decolonial theory? I like the starting point of Pier Paolo Frassinelli: 'So why is it important?'[11] Frassinelli explains simply that Western theories have the habit (I call this the sneaky ideological unconscious conscious in operation) of claiming to embrace the whole of humanity, as though Europe is the centre of the universe. One meaning, therefore, of decoloniality is seeing the world from where we are, as Sabelo Ndlovu-Gatsheni has explained well.[12] There are, of course, some issues that are particular to this continent, and some particular to South Africa, and of course even within South Africa one area differs from the next (for example, I live in Houghton where the garbage is collected spot on time, next to Yeoville where it isn't). Scholars must theorise, and are, with increasing regularity, theorising with particularities rather than universalities. This point has been noted by Helge Rønning and Tawana Kupe: that the African media carries contradictions that have roots in the colonial period when newspapers and broadcasting mainly served the needs of the colonial administrators.[13] To bring this down to a concrete example: in their discussions about the Ebola crisis and responses to it, Winston Mano and Viola Milton ask: What about an African response to a uniquely African crisis?[14]

Moving on, but from another angle and still related to the importance of decolonial theory, Colin Chasi argues that because life is characterised by violence it is worthwhile noting that the African moral philosophy of ubuntu says people should seek 'the beautiful, great and good'.[15] He contends that 'over, against and within the violence that defines the condition of being human, ubuntu is open to the varied uses of cooperation and violence in pursuit for the beautiful, great and good'. But he also warns, 'don't separate Africans from other humanities, we are human and all things human are possible for Africans'. Violent communication is not alien to ubuntu; indeed Chasi writes that nothing human is alien to Africans.

Although all the chapters in this book parachute, in a sense, straight into the media landscape from the Zuma years onwards, this work on power and loss in the news media has built upon the valuable theorising from a variety of critical anti-racist, anti-media monopolies, ubuntu and people's voices perspectives from the global South. These include the work of Herman Wasserman and Arnold de Beer,[16] which is critical about the lens that the mainstream media uses in telling stories. On the ownership of media, examination of the structures of concentration and lack of diversity, Keyan Tomaselli's work is important,[17] as is Lynette Steenveld's.[18] Guy Berger has also been one of the first to start theorising about media in the post-apartheid period.[19] And lastly, but far from least (in fact also regarded as one of the first media studies theorists in South Africa) Pieter Fourie's volumes of *Media Studies* remain as pertinent as they ever were, especially as they deploy South African examples to illustrate theories.[20]

In chapter 2, I examine the tensions between the ANC, the media and the state, looking closely at the words of these players on the role of journalism and how they have differently exercised their power in relation to one another: how, for instance, police have attacked journalists out on assignments; the trumped-up charges against the investigative journalist Jacques Pauw (after the publication of his book exposing the corruption at the South African Revenue Service [SARS]); the 'SABC 8' saga; and the tug-of-war between editorial independence and the loud barking voice of power. This part of my book is also inspired by the work of Mbembe – based in the global South and one of the world's most renowned scholars on Frantz Fanon – on what has happened to elites after the political structures of colonialism have been removed, what remains, and what elites do with the power.

That leads to the next chapter, where I show that there is an excess in how the new power elites behave by discussing the corrupt relationship between former president Zuma and the Guptas, what the #GuptaLeaks showed and what role investigative journalism played. The chapter analyses state capture and how it crept into the body politic, and lauds the contribution investigative journalism has made in recent years to the deepening of democracy. But rather than revisiting the stories of corruption themselves, chapter 3 examines the contribution of journalism from the perspective of the journalists themselves, and then it goes on to the media and loss of credibility. At the time of writing, the public is still confused about whether the Cato Manor hit-squad stories were true or false, as media organisations and journalists turned against one another, fighting for credibility. We do know that more than 35 stories on the SARS 'rogue unit' were false. Journalists were deployed, or deliberately allowed themselves to be used, as pawns in political factions. The concepts of ideology, interpellation and excess were useful to make sense of what happened in journalism here.

The professional journalist workforce has been halved over the past decade, according to research and to unionists who helped calculate this figure (which they also said was conservative). Thousands of journalists have lost their jobs through retrenchments, dismissals (sometimes due to not being on the same political page as the owner) and a 'digital first' approach, though companies provided little or no training for digitisation. Chapter 4 shines the spotlight on the media companies and the impact on newsrooms, through what journalists who lost their jobs say about the process of retrenchments – as well as their reflections on journalism today. The replacement of journalists by content producers has negatively affected the quality of newspapers and broadcasting because of a lack of context in stories. The online Job Losses Survey 2018, which I conducted, found that there were no longer mentorships for entrants into the profession, and there was no union involvement for support. There are serious questions about the future of journalism, critical to this book on journalism's power and losses. Harry Dugmore's 2018 report on 'the sustainability of the news industry and journalism in South Africa in a time of digital transformation and political uncertainty' is the most recent and important contribution to examining the sustainability and future of journalism.[21]

With the internet, online news and social media entering the media space, it was believed there would be a levelling of the playing fields between the races and the classes. However, with government not delivering on the broadband roll-out it promised more than ten years ago, and community newspapers' move to online, in particular re-grouping on Facebook, the irony is that even fewer people can access their local news. Ten years ago there were 575 community newspapers; the Association of Independent Publishers (AIP) said in interviews for this chapter that the number today may be less than 275. (The commercial sector, separate from the AIP's umbrella of community newspapers, is dominated by Caxton, and has more than 500 local newspapers, but the content carries more advertising than editorial. They are not dealt with in this book.) Chapter 5 examines diversity and the survival of the sector, and asks questions about the meaning of 'local'. Are the majority of voices really local? What did a content analysis of the newspapers show? Are community newspapers gaining or losing power in the digital age? Here, I build upon the work of Jane Duncan,[22] and of Sarah Chiumbu who argued in 2016 that despite the end of apartheid South Africa remains a country deeply divided along class, race and gender lines, with persistent inequalities laid by colonialism.[23] The demise of community media attests to this. As Chiumbu conceptualised the Marikana miners as Fanon's damned of the earth, I posit, in this chapter on community media, and in the next, that women journalists are also damned for daring to occupy the public space of journalism and for speaking out. Some of the hailings and shamings or interpellations against women by populist nationalist politicians have been 'bitch', 'whore', 'slut' and 'presstitude'.

The most recent research on women in the newsroom, *Glass Ceilings: Women in South African Media Houses 2018*,[24] showed that while the numbers of men and women have evened out, men hold the senior positions, and sexism, male domination and a male superiority complex in the newsroom (and in the media in general) is as common as in society generally. Chapter 6 covers some of the findings in detail: the increased salary gap between men and women of the same experience, the new threat of cyber misogyny. The chapter also reveals how women feel undermined in the newsroom, shafted for promotions, and how decisions appear to be made outside – for example, in bars after work or at soccer or golf on weekends, in an old boys' network or club. This chapter shows the dangers of social media for women journalists in the public space of journalism. Other scholars who have written on women in the newsroom include Lizette Rabe in her work for Sanef in 2006 with the first Glass Ceilings reports,[25] and Ylva Rodny-Gumede[26] and Pat Made and Colleen Lowe Morna.[27] But here are signs of new thinking in the mainstream media itself. The next chapter reveals the old, the colonial lenses of the traditional school, in contrast to the new decolonial gazes.

Is it even possible to analyse and write about what we are experiencing as we are experiencing it? In the first part of chapter 7, which tells the story of the 'Afro saga' at Pretoria Girls High School, in 2016, and how the mainstream media covered it, it was possible to do this. The second part of the chapter, about possible 'decolonial greenshoots' in the media, is suggestive, not definitive, because it is too early to tell. In this part of the book, the question is whether the media had the power to think and act beyond the norms of everyday mainstream culture and thinking. In this chapter, I started with some preconceived imaginings that the media would not be attentive or empathetic to the girls, that the media would put on its usual Western gaze. But the findings were different from my expectations. It then became an example of how the media can turn its gaze around from the old ways of being and seeing.

REFLECTIONS: POWER, LOSS AND REIMAGINING

In chapter 8 I have used a quote on power by Oriana Fallaci: 'True power does not need arrogance, a long beard and a barking voice. True power strangles you with silk ribbons, charm and intelligence.'[28] This ties up the findings on power and loss in journalism from the previous chapters: the media landscape and freedom, the fights between the state, government and the media, intra-power losses as in the media clash about the *Sunday Times* false stories; the traumatic power losses from the job-loss bloodbath; community newspapers going online (but the poor finding it harder to access local news). Finally, the anti-feminist backlash witnessed in the Glass Ceilings 2018 research saw loss of voice from women but also new militancy. It made findings about the silky power of social media and about the loud voices of authority, which were ultimately weak and vicious. The concepts in this book include power, loss, trauma, ambivalence, master and floating signifiers, passionate attachment, diversity, plurality, feminism and backlash.

'Can the subaltern speak?' asked Gayatri Spivak.[29] The media is the opposite of the subaltern – it has power. But here I ask: Can the journalists speak? They are full of power, unlike the subaltern, but they do not talk about how they work, nor do they defend themselves much or publicise their pain, such as that from retrenchment by the media companies. Here, however, they do. This book speaks about them, for them, and through them – but it also regards them critically, where they have failed.

Is there enough empathy and love from the media for women, for black women in particular, and for black consciousness? Although the media's passionate attachment to uncovering corruption has made an enormous contribution to democracy, there are some blind spots. Here, in the final analysis, the concept of 'decolonial love' is used as a political technology, as borrowed from decolonial theorist Chela Sandoval in *Methodology of the Oppressed* as a body of knowledge, arts, practices and procedures for re-forming the self and the world.[30] This book, besides dealing with the normative role of the media in tackling corruption by holding power to account, gazes on diversity of thinking (celebrating the Afro hairstyle stories in chapter 7) and gender (chapter 6) which – together with class (chapter 5), it could be argued – are the biggest blind spots in the media today. The mainstream media, of course, as it loses advertising and revenue, presses its own power down on the newsroom, and squeezes it, closing down the spaces for diversity, feminism and access for the poor to thrive.

The method of research in this book is not rigid. It is based on politico-philosophical concepts tied to power and also on standard journalistic techniques of research – gathering information through interviews. My experience of media, having worked as a journalist in newsrooms for many years, also counted, a form of self-reflexivity and just a bit of autoethnography, for otherwise it would be too self-indulgent. Both qualitative and quantitative methods were deployed. Online survey methods were used for the chapters on job losses and the backlash against feminism. All graphs and tables are author-generated for the former chapter but for the latter the graphs were generated by Gender Links. For background information I draw on my publications *State of the Newsroom, South Africa, 2013: Disruptions and Transitions* and *State of the Newsroom, South Africa, 2014: Disruptions Accelerated*.

THE PARADOXICAL NATURE OF POWER AND THE DECOLONIAL TURN

Power in the twenty-first century is not just a top-down vertical or pyramidical structure, with white heterosexual males at the top. As Sandoval depicts, today's forces of power circulate horizontally too, with many sides and deviations.[31] But in postmodern, postcolonial and neoliberal gazes these conflagrations of power presuppose more equality and more democracy – which is misleading because not everyone has the same access. Indeed, even more divisions, suspicions and antagonisms have emerged in the world in the twenty-first century. We can translate this meta-ideological analysis of the world to our local context, or the subject of this book directly to news media in South Africa. The media believes it is acting for the people, and for the underclasses, the most robbed by corruption, yet it is they who are the most suspicious of the media. Power and losses bind this book through every chapter via the issues it tackles. 'To be dominated by a power external to oneself is a familiar agonising form that power takes. To find, however, that what "one" is, one's very formation as a subject, is in some sense dependent upon that very power, is quite another,' as Judith Butler says.[32]

The key words in Butler's theories of subjection are 'reflexivity', 'passionate attachments', 'loss' and 'norms'. Using Michel Foucault's theorising, she writes that 'norms' are not fixed, and 'turns' can be unpredictable. She theorises that no subject emerges without a psychical and passionate attachment to norms – the very same norms that oppress or subjugate it. This happens through a turn: described variously as a reflexive turn, sometimes a violent turn or a melancholic turn towards the voice of authority. The subject is thus produced by a turn towards the voice of power that is hailing, naming or shaming. Then, agency can emerge in the form of shunning the bullying voice. Turns can take unpredictable paths and trajectories. For Butler, the process of subjection is a process of becoming subordinated by power, with power and through power. One can turn one's back against the shaming and hailing and voices of power, or one can succumb to the ideological interpellations.

THE MEDIA LANDSCAPE IN SOUTH AFRICA

Media regulation and freedom

The overarching law is the Constitution. It provides for freedom of expression and the right to information, but also protects human dignity, and does not allow hate speech or racism, among other undesirables in a progressive society.

Print and online media are governed by co-regulation with the Press Council of South Africa, which is so constituted that there are equal numbers of public and media representatives, six of each. It also has a retired judge and an ombudsman. Not all newspapers, however, subscribe to this voluntary system. Independent Newspapers pulled out of the Press Council in 2016 and set up its own ombudsman, and *The New Age*, which briefly became *Afro Voice* before it folded in June 2018, did the same.

Changes from self-regulation to co-regulation came about after the Press Freedom Commission inquiry in 2011, instituted by the industry itself but after pressure from the ruling party for statutory regulation of the print media via a Media Appeals Tribunal (MAT). The ANC first mooted a MAT at its Polokwane conference in December 2007, and then again at its Mangaung conference in December 2012. It resolved that there was a need for Parliament to conduct an inquiry into the desirability and feasibility of a MAT (within the framework of the country's Constitution) empowered to impose sanctions on the media. Even though this threatening and vague 'tribunal' remains a resolution, there was no active pursuit of it in 2018–2019.

Broadcasters are regulated via the Independent Communications Authority of South Africa (Icasa) and the Broadcasting Complaints' Commission of South Africa (BCCSA).

Media freedom trends

Media freedom all over the world is under threat: violence against journalists; jailing of journalists; politicians shouting 'fake news' at facts that don't suit them; corporations putting the squeeze on the newsrooms when they don't make profits; lack of diverse voices. In August 2018, more than 300 news publications across the US committed to a *Boston Globe* coordinated effort to run editorials promoting the freedom of the press in light of Donald Trump's frequent attacks on the media such as calling journalists 'enemies of the American people'.

In South Africa the danger to media freedom is due to the threat of a MAT and the Protection of State Information Bill (the Secrecy Bill). The Secrecy Bill and the resolution for a MAT have negative implications for the newsroom and for journalists. In different ways, these two pieces of proposed legislation would impede the free flow of information and allow for surveillance of citizens and journalists – by means of tapping phones, for example.

The Secrecy Bill

In 2018 Cyril Ramaphosa said he had to attend to the Protection of State Information Bill left on his desk by his predecessor, Jacob Zuma. According to the campaign for the free flow of information by Right2Know (R2K), the Bill overreaches into the public's right to know and criminalises journalism. The definition of 'national security matters' is not consistent with international law, or law in other countries, because it includes the exposure of economic, scientific or technological secrets, which is too broad. The criminal penalties in the law are severe, disproportionate and excessive. Each of the Secrecy Bill offences carries a possible or mandatory prison term of up to 5 years, or a fine for the disclosure and possession of classified information, with a permissible penalty linked to the classification level of the information; up to 25 years' imprisonment for the unlawful receipt of state information and for hostile activity offences; and 3 to 25 years' imprisonment for 'espionage and related offences', including a mandatory minimum penalty absent only in 'substantial and compelling circumstances'.

There is still no proper public-interest defence in the Secrecy Bill, which would include protection for journalists, whereas any protection of state information regime should allow 'escape valves' to balance ordinary people's rights of access to information and freedom of expression with the state's national security mandate.

Attacks on journalists and intimidation tactics

Police attacks on journalists appear to be part of a worldwide trend, if one considers research by the CPJ, which in 2018 reported a record number of journalists in jail – 262 in 2018, up from 2017 when there were 259.[33]

The worst countries were Turkey, China and Egypt. The research statement also named its global oppressors of press freedom as Donald Trump; Recep Tayyip Erdoğan, president of Turkey; Abdel Fattah el-Sisi, president of Egypt; Xi

Jinping, president of China and Russian president Vladimir Putin, all of whom use rhetoric, fake news, legal action and censorship to silence their critics.

Journalists in South Africa appear not to be in danger to the same extent. There are no journalists in jail. But worrying trends are developing. In the past decade in South Africa, photojournalists have been targeted by the police, and sometimes by protesters, especially when covering demonstrations. They appear to be targeted because of the power of images – photographs can provide incontrovertible proof of events. Anyone with a camera in their cellphone can be a target of police hostility.

Politics, transformation, regulation and media freedom

Media transformation has always been under discussion. But it means different things to different sectors. In 2012, Iqbal Survé bought Independent Media (the company that owns the most print titles in South Africa) from its former Irish owners who were stashing away profits from the South African newspapers in the UK, to prop up Independent's failing papers there. Transformation was necessary. Survé pronounced that this was the 'transformation deal' enabled by Public Investment Corporation (PIC) and pensioners' funds, but in 2018 Survé was defaulting on repayments and the PIC wrote off R1 billion of the debt. By February 2019 it was revealed that Survé had splashed out on luxury apartments at the V&A Waterfront in Cape Town, just before it emerged that he had defaulted on PIC payments. He is known to tell his editors what to write in response to the exposés about him.

To the South African Broadcasting Corporation (SABC), transformation in the Zuma age meant reporting favourably about him, and when the Zuma cronies, the Guptas, started *The New Age* and the African News Network 7 (ANN7) – propped up with government advertising – no one really bought or watched, and no figures for circulation were available, which says much about certain interpretations of transformation.

The ANC's criticism of the print media is that it is a highly concentrated sector and lacks diversity through the entire value chain, including ownership and control, race, language, gender and content. Black ownership, according to the ANC (using Media Development and Diversity Agency statistics), is minuscule at 14 per cent, and women's representation at board and management level is 4.44 per cent.[34] In a nutshell, there is a lack of transformation in the print sector, the party says. To this end, the ANC would like to see more regulation and 'accountability' via a media charter, for instance, and Parliament's communications portfolio committee reiterated the need for this. Besides a lack of race transformation, according to the parliamentary committee, there were other charges against the print media: it did not reflect a diversity of South African voices; it marginalised the rural and the poor; it was white-dominated not just in ownership but also in issues covered; and there was 'cartel-like behaviour where emergent community and small privately-owned media were smothered through a variety of anti-competitive behaviour'. The ANC subsequently proposed a media charter, which the print industry rejected.

Pressure continued to mount on the media houses following a resolution taken at the ANC's policy conference in Mangaung in December 2012. In its document 'Communication and the Battle of Ideas', the ANC also called for a media appeals tribunal, an inquiry into print regulation, and an investigation by the Competition Commission into anti-competitive behaviour. The media companies, however, felt the industry could be transformed without parliamentary, political or other external intervention. The Print Digital Media Transformation Task Team (PDMTTT) was set up in September 2012, under project director Mathatha Tsedu, to develop a common vision and strategy for transformation and to examine the low levels of black ownership in large media groups; lack of diversity; management; control; employment equity; and skills development. The PDMTTT report noted that women constituted a mere one per cent on boards, and zero per cent at the level of media ownership.[35]

Ownership and the commercial context

South African newsrooms and media are tumultuous places today. The media shifts, slides and resists being pinned down to a fixed landscape. Traditional media continue their decline. According to the researcher Reg Rumney's analysis on ownership and control in his 2017 discussion document 'Towards a Policy on Media Diversity and Development', the 'big four' ownership pattern shows that no company reflects South Africa's demography (table 1.1).[36]

Rumney's most important points were that:
- Caxton is still 'white owned', as Terry Moolman and Noel Coburn hold a 51 per cent stake.
- While some media houses have progressed in terms of broad-based black economic empowerment (B-BBEE) requirements, none yet adequately reflects South Africa's demographics.

Table 1.1:   Media ownership patterns and race demographics

	HDI	Management control	Black ownership* %	Female ownership* %	Total score	B-BBEE status
Media24	22.00	9.47	52.94	24.95	80.44	Level 4
Caxton	14.56	7.74	17.78	6.28	80.04	Level 4
Times Media Group	25.00	11.17	58.47	18.44	91.83	Level 3
Independent Newspapers	18.00	5.83	55.00	25.3	85.87	Level 2
The New Age	18.08	0.00	21.58	0.00	75.16	Level 3
Mail & Guardian	0.00	11.00	0.00	0.00	61.14	Level 5

Source: Courtesy of Reg Rumney (2017)

Note: * Actual ownership percentages – the remaining figures are points calculated in terms of the B-BBEE scorecards.

- The woeful state of black women's ownership requires careful consideration and intervention.
- Naspers owns a great deal through Media24 and MultiChoice – except radio stations. It has book publishing, the DSTV platform, many print publications and the most popular news website.
- Caxton owns much of the 'community' newspaper market and the *Citizen*, as well as Ramsay media. Moolman owns African Media Entertainment (AME) and AME now owns Moneyweb.

And what do these companies above own?
- Tiso Blackstar (now Arena Holdings) owns Business Live and Times Live as well as *Sunday Times, Business Day, Financial Mail, The Herald*, the *Daily Dispatch*, and community newspapers with Independent and Caxton through Capital Media.
- Independent owns *The Argus* and the *Cape Times, The Mercury, Daily News, Mercury, The Star, Sunday Tribune*, and *Sunday Independent*.

Circulation declines

In 2018 there were between 200 and 250 newspapers: 16 dailies, 25 weeklies and more than 200 community newspapers. Then there were 360 radio and 556 television stations – including community broadcasters – and an unknown number

Table 1.2: Newspaper circulation in South Africa, 2018 compared to 2014

	2018	2014	Variance	%
Sunday Times	260 132	405 458	−145 326	−36
Soccer Laduma	252 041	317 013	−64 972	−20
Daily Sun	141 187	283 216	−142 029	−50
Rapport	113 636	177 016	−63 380	−36
Isolezwe	86 342	119 846	−33 504	−28
The Star	75 836	101 711	−25 875	−25
Sowetan	70 120	99 403	−29 283	−29
Isolezwenge Sonto	65 489	93 268	−27 779	−30
IsolezwengoMgqibelo	64 676	no data	no data	no data
Son	62 842	no data	62 842	no data
Sunday Sun	62 674	172 741	−110 067	−64
Die Burger	61 749	no data	no data	no data
City Press	58 566	118 676	−60 110	−51
Ilanga	56 481	100 853	−44 372	−44
The Times	no data	142 603	no data	no data
Sunday World	no data	113 757	no data	no data

Source: Courtesy of the MarkLives' Biggest Circulation Per Issue Newspaper List (2018)[37]

Note: The table provides a snapshot of circulation declines of the biggest circulation newspapers, showing declines of between 20 per cent and 64 per cent.

of online media and digital start-ups. The sector has declined as a result of the downturn in the economy. Independent publishers are the small businesses of the media sector, and it is always the small businesses that feel the bite first. Whereas about ten years ago there were 575 community newspapers, in 2018 there were 275. The mainstream media shows almost as many losses (see table 1.2). In most cases it is less than 50 per cent over four years and yet in three cases it is 50 per cent or more.

The state of South African newsrooms

Besides wide-scale retrenchments, journalists are working twice as hard in newsrooms, and juggling more devices to get more news out on more different platforms than ever before. The newsrooms are highly pressured environments owing to the digital transition and social media. The transition to digital is messy and confusing; the job losses in the newsroom are traumatic; women journalists at the forefront of investigations are harassed and bullied online – and the gender pay gap has increased.

Job losses

Large waves of retrenchments of journalists have occurred every few years in the last decade, as digital news continues to grow, and revenues decline. In just one year, for example, 2014, more than a thousand journalists lost their jobs.[38] In smaller waves, retrenchments took place every year, with 2016 another big year for job losses from already depleted newsrooms. It is estimated that from about 2008 to 2018 the professional journalist workforce halved, from approximately 10 000 to 5 000.[39] According to Tuwani Gumani, general secretary of the Media Workers Association of South Africa (Mwasa), interviewed in 2018, Independent Newspapers employed more than 6 000 media workers ten years ago – in 2018 they employed about 1 400. While newsrooms continue to become more juniorised and depleted of experienced staff and institutional memory, newly trained, tech-savvy content producers, who can also 'do video' and 'mobile journalism', replaced them. Together with these changes, social media has become intrinsic to the newsroom.

The gender pay gap is on the agenda

It is important to re-visit this as we scrutinise the Glass Ceilings findings of 2018.[40] One of the differences between this and previous Glass Ceilings reports is that the world is now operating in a climate of more assertiveness about the gender pay gap.

A report, 'Mind the Gap: Uncovering Pay Disparities in the Newsroom', by student reporters in the Asian American Journalists Association 'Voices' programme in 2017, found that some of the biggest newsrooms in the US were paying women and staffers of ethnic minorities significantly less than their male and white counterparts. That started a larger conversation about pay equity in the industry, and prompted other newsroom unions to publish their own studies about pay gaps. The report also said that diversity in newsrooms had been bad for decades, and would probably not improve.

In South Africa, the pay gap has increased over ten years, from 17 per cent to 23 per cent.

Information disorder

There are over a hundred online news publications in South Africa, and the number is growing all the time. Social media use proliferates. Technology and social media have enabled devastating attacks on credible news media working in the public interest. Propaganda and misinformation aimed at journalists after their exposure of corruption has led to the 'fight back' campaigns of disaffected political factions – for instance, by Zuma supporters. Sometimes readers become confused about what is true and what is untrue. As the media research group Media Monitoring Africa (MMA) has said, one common response by Zuma supporters on social media to #GuptaLeaks was that the leaks were 'fake news'.

Internationally, the media researchers Claire Wardle and Hossein Derakhshan advocate that we stop using the term 'fake news'.[41] In the age of information disorder in the media landscape, fake news glibly glosses over misinformation, disinformation, mal-information (deliberately malicious, intended to harm) and political propaganda, which has been around for as long as politicians. Wardle and Derakhshan are correct to disentangle 'fake news'. However (and unfortunately) the term has gained traction – it is easy and catchy for the public to use.

Political propaganda and misinformation is common, but social media has made it easier (for the creation of robots, and trolls, automated and anonymous accounts created for malicious intent, and fake websites). When consumers of media become confused about what to trust and what not to trust they tend to lose faith in all media, including credible media. In this age, more than ever, we require a culture of transparency. Credible media doing news and investigations in the public interest should be informing the media-consuming audiences about their processes – how they find the news and how they carry out their investigations. They should also be open about who they are, where they get their funding from and what their interests are.

The days are over when journalists and editors simply wrote accounts – they are now under pressure to be cognisant of the business of media, as the Chinese wall (the hard divide whereby managers and owners deal with business, and journalists and editors deal with stories) between editorial and advertising has all but collapsed. Journalists are under the watchful eye of algorithms and analytics, all too aware of the pressures of 'traffic' to the online sites accompanying the traditional product.

The pattern of the past five years, 2013 to 2018, is accelerating in news media, with no viable revenue model or media innovation in sight. Google, Facebook and Twitter have captured huge chunks of the media space, about 50 per cent. News is in huge demand, but consumers of news are now 'platform agnostic', and no longer loyal to brands, getting their news not from traditional sources but from multiple platforms.

The media landscape in South Africa mirrors that of the rest of the world, but it also has its particularities. It has one of the strongest cultures of investigative journalism in the world, but political journalists are often pawns in political factions – as we saw in the *Sunday Times* debacle when it was revealed in 2018 that over 35 stories on SARS were untrue; that stories on Zimbabwe renditions were also false; and the Cato Manor death squad stories – untrue or partially untrue – remained unresolved at the time of writing in early 2019. Traditional media are in rapid, not slow, decline, and newspapers appear to be in decline faster than was expected ten years ago when some analysts speculated that South Africa's print would not decline as fast as that of the developed world, only to find that with the ubiquitous mobile phone generation, and news being passed on Facebook, Instagram and Twitter, young people are in fact unlikely to ever turn to newspapers.

Trust in media is in decline; mistakes in traditional media such as misspellings in headlines and names are increasing, and media watchers know this is due to the death of subs desks and proofreaders. Fake news or lies, political propaganda and trolling, especially of women, is on the rise. Newspapers are getting thinner, with more opinion, syndicated copy and convergence, meaning less diversity and fewer voices.

Social media is intrinsic to newsrooms – the traditional scoop could hardly be owned for more than five minutes these days. Videos are becoming highly popular in the age of multiple platforms, and different platforms require innovative and creative ways of thinking to tell the same story.

The lesson for developing new business models in the digital age is that different publications need different solutions. Journalists are doing more with less and there are stirrings of dissatisfaction; indeed, many say they are just waiting for the next round of retrenchments or redundancies to be announced, so that they can get some 'package' instead of resigning.[42]

2

The Media, the State and Zuma's ANC

Yes to life. Yes to love. Yes to generosity.
Frantz Fanon, *Black Skin, White Masks*

U sing theories of power and democracy, this chapter analyses the tension in the relationship between the (ANC) and the media during former president Jacob Zuma's reign. In the chapter, Fanon is ever present. Fanon slated the new elites, the formerly oppressed, in the post-independence era in Africa as self-interested and greedy vultures – corruption ruling the day, morality in slim evidence. As Dale McKinley has noted:

> Dishonesty and incompetence are either rewarded or simply ignored and replicated,while those who expose and confront the truth, who raise the alarm and who try to uphold collective, social as well as personal account-ability are consistently punished, marginalised, labelled and made to feel like outcast spoilers who do not belong.[1]

The chapter's aim is to show how power works, and how subjects become subjected, for example, in the case of the 'SABC 8', eight journalists who were bullied and ultimately fired by the chief operating officer (COO), Hlaudi Motsoeneng. They turned their backs on his voice, and towards the professional codes of ethics, breaking away to reveal the ugly underbelly of the South African Broadcasting Corporation (SABC) in openly watched, televised parliamentary sessions.

One of the journalists, Suna Venter, died from 'broken-heart syndrome'. Even though this chapter is about the tensions between Zuma and the media, it asks underlying questions that are pertinent today, and will be for the future: about how close journalists should be to political factions and power; whether they should belong to political parties; and why political and investigative journalists so often become pawns of political factions – as we witnessed with the revelations about the *Sunday Times*.[2]

The ethics and diversity subcommittee of the South African National Editors' Forum (Sanef) conducted a survey in 2016, which asked: 'Should journalists belong to political parties? Circle your answer, yes or no, and please give your reason.'[3] The following 12 newsrooms were selected to participate in the one-page survey, to give a broad spread across companies:

- SABC Digital News (public-owned entity)
- Interface (SABC) (public-owned entity)
- *Daily Sun* (Media24)
- *Sunday Times* (Arena Holdings, formerly Tiso Blackstar)
- *Sunday Sun* (Media24)
- *City Press* (Media24)
- *Beeld* (Media24)
- *Rapport* (Media24)
- *Mail & Guardian* (M&G Ltd)
- ANN7 (Gupta-owned television station)
- *The New Age* (Gupta owned)
- *The Star* (Independent Media)
- *Saturday Star* (Independent Media).

The selection was deliberate, to cut across newsrooms whose owners and chief executive officers appeared to be sympathetic to the ANC, and newsrooms that appeared to maintain a distance from political parties. In the end, a quick count shows that about half the newsrooms could be viewed as more politically aligned to the hegemonic project of the ANC – that is to say, attempting to meet the ANC's desire for a more loyal media. The other half would regard themselves as more distant from political alignment.

Of the 102 editorial participants (journalists and editors), 65 said 'no' and 37 said 'yes'. This means that 64 per cent of the journalists/editors said that journalists should not belong to political parties, and 36 per cent said they could. These respondents thought that there was no problem – after all, we are all human, with political views, so let's not pretend otherwise. The most common reason for saying no was to avoid being compromised and unable to serve the public honestly because 'you may have other masters'.

Only a handful of journalists quoted the Press Code of South Africa when they said that journalists should not be members of political parties, which suggests there is insufficient awareness of and education about the code in South African newsrooms. While media companies and commentators engage in feuds and turf wars, professional codes and ethics in journalism – which are probably the most important issue in the age of disinformation – are regarded as Journalism 101 and not 'juicy' enough for some media organisations. The Press Code stipulates in Section 2, 'Independence and Conflicts of Interest', that the media should not allow commercial, political or other non-professional considerations to influence reporting. Conflicts of interest must be avoided, as well as arrangements or practices that could lead audiences to doubt the media's independence and professionalism (see Appendix A for the full Press Code).

The normative idea, that the media should be free from commercial and political influence, is relevant for the next chapter on state capture and media power.

POWER, HAILING AND SHAMING AND LOSS

I use theories of power to understand the attempts to subjugate critical media voices in South Africa through interpellation (hailing, naming, labelling, calling and shaming, as in the Fanonian sense). In addition to interpellation, the concepts of 'master signifier', 'the gaze', 'legitimate adversaries' and 'hysteria' are also deployed to comprehend the relationship. Political power is symbolic in nature, and operates through roles and masks – that is to say, ideological subjectivisation can take place through the performative dimension of interpellations. Quite simply, this means power can work through shaming and calling out. Judith Butler explains how one can turn towards the voice of power, and bow to it, or turn away from the voice of power, exercising one's own agency.[4] For instance, you do not have to accept the terms or conditions for labelling and hailing.

There have been and continue to be attempts to pin down floating signifiers such as 'democracy' into a fixed meaning, tied to transformation and loyalty to the ANC. I examine the empirical findings, through discourse material and newspaper stories, specifically on Zuma's corruption scandals. The conceptual analytical tools enable the drawing together of reflections, and the identification of patterns or attachments, as well as splits and contradictions. In briefly outlining the theory within which the methodology resides I refer in particular to Butler's *The Psychic Life of Power: Theories in Subjection* (1997) and Slavoj Žižek's *The Sublime Object of Ideology* (1989), but other works consulted include Chantal Mouffe's *The Democratic Paradox* (2000), with reference to Fanon's *Black Skin, White Masks* (1952[1967]), and my own *Fight for Democracy: The ANC and the Media in South Africa* (2012).

There is a surplus and excess attached to how the ANC and Zuma viewed the media, but also how single-mindedly the media uncovered Zuma, until more was unravelled during and after the Gupta leaks from 2017 into 2019: the corruption and crooked dealings of private sector companies, consultancies and law firms. For example, KPMG auditors missed the red flags of the Gupta wedding costing R30 million, and missed the money laundering of the Guptas. In 2018 it signed off on the Venda Building Society books, and may as a result be liable for R2 billion. The law firm Hogan Lovells was shown to be the mastermind in shifting power within the criminal justice system to the 'Zupta' cronies. Bain & Company were responsible for changing the operating model at the South African Revenue Service (SARS), which aided the collapse of what was once known to be the most efficient institution in South Africa, and one of the best in the world in terms of tax collection.

McKinsey & Company, and Trillian, ripped off billions from Eskom.[5] Bell Pottinger, whose clients were the Guptas, were responsible for fuelling racial tensions through the social bots (software that creates automated responses on social media to influence opinions and the direction of debates) and social media campaigns on 'white monopoly capital'. The private sector, together with the state, was raiding taxpayers' money, and the investigative media began to widen their scope. The subjected, and those who lost power and money, were everyday South Africans. The interpellated – shamed or called out – were the private sector companies, together with Zuma and the Guptas. Power turned. Zuma is no longer president, the Guptas have fled to Dubai, and some of the private sector companies have left the country. Some have been banned in other countries, and some are limping from crisis to crisis, unable to shake off the lack of morality and ethics (an example is KPMG's role in the 2018 scandal of the Venda Bank Society bank heist).

A concept employed here is 'surplus-attached': what there is in the object that is more than the object itself. Žižek asked what is in Coke more than Coke itself (water, sugar and bubbles) but 'freedom', 'America' and 'fun'?[6] He also asked what if evil resided in the very eyes of those perceiving evil? These three – freedom, America, fun – constitute the surplus. Such theories and concepts are applied here to the ANC's and Zuma's interpellation of the media, when Zuma attached more to the media than the media themselves, until this power was turned around to face him and he became a subject of media power, citizen power, opposition party power and protest. Eventually he lost ground, although the corrupt cronies and loyalists are said to still make up half the ANC structures of 2018.

HOW A SUBJECT BECOMES A SUBJECT AND LOSES POWER

'Hey you,' shouted the policeman and a man turned around, a reflexive turn, as if he was being called, as if he was guilty. Butler uses the Althusserian example of the 'guilty' passer-by, to explain power (the voice of authority, the policeman) and sub-jection.[7] We can apply this example to the media interpellated as 'coconuts,'[8] oppos-itional, CIA agents, enemies of the people or lackeys of white monopoly capital, among other ideological obfuscatory labels. Do journalists turn towards the voice of power in deference when the ANC hails? Perhaps this is exactly what happened at the *Sunday Times*, when some journalists bought and told false stories about SARS.

Althusser's central thesis was that ideology interpellated individuals as subjects; Butler explained that the passer-by, the man in the street, did not know that the policeman was hailing him in particular, but turned towards the voice of authority anyway, as though he was indeed the one being hailed, as though he was guilty. It would appear that subordination takes place through language and through interpellation. The turning around can then be viewed as an act conditioned both by the 'voice' of the law and by the responsiveness of the one hailed by the law. Fanon also theorised this in his explications of colonial racism and dependency theory. 'I am guilty, I don't know of what, but I am guilty,' Fanon wrote while explicating the 'inferiority complex'.[9]

This ties in well with Butler's thesis that subjection is paradoxical. In other words, 'power is both external to the subject and the very venue of the sub-ject'.[10] In this theory of power and subjection, the subject is constantly subjected and constantly emerging. The subjected (to hailing and shaming) journalists can detach from a signifier, in this case the voice of power, and look towards other possibilities; they can look towards professionalism, codes of ethics and inde-pendence from political parties, if they choose. Some did and some did not, illustrating that 'the media' is not one homogeneous community.

THREATS AGAINST MEDIA FREEDOM: ZUMA AND THE MEDIA

When Zuma assumed power in 2009 he was already enmeshed in corruption scandals and had survived rape charges as well as more than 783 charges of fraud, racketeering and corruption. He has since been involved in numerous scandals (for example, Nkandlagate and Guptagate),[11] and during his nine-year rule was subjected to severe scrutiny in the country's newspapers, mainly in the three weekly newspapers *Mail & Guardian*, *City Press* and *Sunday Times*.

But what is this 'South African media', and does it exist as one homogeneous whole? It consists of a diverse ideological spectrum, and is fractured and split, rather than unified, as is evidenced in the views about journalists being members of political parties. The South African media professes to play a vital role in entrenching the articles of the Constitution, ensuring a transparent democracy that holds public officials accountable for their decisions and actions.[12] On the one hand there is a section that exposes the abuse of power and corruption by ruling elites, and within this section there are more splits, for example the *Sunday Times* revelations in 2018 that many stories on the 'SARS rogue unit' were false. On the other hand, there are those such as the Independent Media, owned by Iqbal Survé, with close alignments to the ANC, as well as African News Network 7 (ANN7) and *The New Age*, both owned by the Guptas (and which by 2018 ceased to exist after a corrupt relationship with Zuma was exposed – they then sold their media, renamed Afro Voice, to Mzwanele Manyi). The SABC, under Hlaudi Motsoeneng, held that media should be more patriotic, do more sunshine journalism, and handle the ruling faction softly, and was thus involved in propagandist news in factional politics.

The media freedom activist and veteran journalist Raymond Louw wrote that issues related to threats of access to information include the stalling of the set-top boxes roll-out, the corporate behaviour of MultiChoice (the main subscription television provider), the Cybercrimes and Cyber Security Bill, which is written in such vague language that it could be interpreted as repressive, enhancing powers of surveillance by security agents.[13] Louw also drew attention to another bill, the Prevention and Combating of Hate Crimes and Speech Bill, which would criminalise 'bringing contempt and ridicule to figures of authority'.

In the 2018 book *So This is Democracy?* Louw tracks incidents of violations and victories:

10 January 2017: Killed or missing
South African photojournalist Shiraz Mohamed, was kidnapped in northern Syria by unidentified armed men as he tried to leave the country in the company of members of the South African charity Gift of the Givers. Amid fears for his safety, attempts are still being made to have him freed [he was freed in 2020].

23 February 2017: Threatened
Two members of the SA Police visited the offices of the *Mail & Guardian* newspaper in Johannesburg regarding what they described as an investigation of a complaint by the Public Protector. They requested a statement from journalist Philip de Wet on the source of a 'leaked' draft report by the Public Protector on a questionable apartheid-era state financial bailout, that has become known as the Absa-Bankcorp matter. Sanef protested, reiterating that the confidentiality of sources was not only sacrosanct but the cornerstone of the ability of whistleblowers to expose corruption and other malfeasance in the public interest.

24 February 2017: Assaulted
SABC journalists reported attacks by demonstrators taking part in protests in Pretoria. They were robbed of their mobile phones and equipment.

8 April 2017: Censored
Freelance photojournalist Jacob Mawela complained of intimidation attempts by security officials of the Gauteng member of Executive Council, Lebogang Maile. Mawela was covering the Township Entrepreneurship Awards at Carnival City when he was accosted by the security officials for having focused his camera on the MEC. He was ordered to either pack up his photographic equipment and leave, or be physically removed from the venue.

7 May 2017: Assaulted
SABC journalists covering public protests in Vuwani, Limpopo were physically attacked. One cameraperson was assaulted and three vehicles belonging to the public broadcaster were damaged.

Continued

8 May 2017: Assaulted
Protesters and farmers in Coligny attacked and chased away journalists who were covering the violence that erupted in the aftermath of a court decision. Photographic equipment belonging to journalists from various media houses was also damaged. The minister of police, Fikile Mbalula, condemned the attacks.

3 October 2017: Threatened
SABC correspondent in Lesotho, Nthakoana Ngatane, had to flee the country following numerous threats on her life. This was the latest in a series of incidents of violence and intimidation against journalists in the landlocked country. Due to the deteriorating security situation in Lesotho, the safety of journalists in the country is under threat, and therefore imperils press freedom. Sanef offered its support to Ngatane and issued a protest to the Lesotho government.

19 October 2017: Noteworthy development (commemoration)
Sanef commemorated the 40th anniversary of Black Wednesday, the day, October 19, in 1977, when the apartheid government in an attempt to gag the media banned scores of newspapers aligned with the Black Consciousness Movement, along with 19 pro-democracy organisations, and arrested a number of prominent journalists. Black Wednesday triggered years of resistance to the government on the issue of media freedom and stoked Sanef's fight for media freedom in South Africa and across the continent. Sanef commemorated Black Wednesday by launching its new identity and a Media Freedom Campaign.

14 November 2017: Censored
Journalists in KwaZulu-Natal expressed concern about plans by the eThekwini (formerly Durban) Municipal Council to introduce new Rules of Order which would deny access by reporters to some meetings; and/or restrict the use of electronic equipment in filing stories. Sanef called on the council to drop the plan because the contemplated restrictions would be an unconstitutional infringement of media freedom, thus illegal, and would restrict the public's right to know about developments that affect their lives. The issue has been deferred to the next council meeting.[14]

The box shows assaults, threats and acts of censorship during Zuma's rule. The main policy interventions by the ANC during Zuma's regime include the proposal for a Media Appeals Tribunal (MAT), and the passing of the Protection of State Information Bill in Parliament. These proposed closures of access to information for the public, censorship of the media, and threats to democracy broadly, will be discussed briefly below, but the main focus here will be the interpellations (or hailing, naming and shaming) of media by Zuma, after his own shaming in the newspapers, and then the 'SABC 8' case, in which theories of power are deployed to make sense of the tension between the ANC and the media.

The first direct threat to the independence of the press emerged at the ANC's national policy conference in Polokwane in 2007, when a resolution to investigate a MAT was adopted. The aim of such a tribunal would be to abandon self-regulation in favour of Parliament as the ultimate arbiter of whether or not a story was fair. It would be a post-publication punishment, which would create a climate of self-censorship among journalists. It would also include the registration or licensing of journalists. This resolution has been affirmed at every subsequent ANC policy conference. The ANC appears committed to its demand for an investigation into a statutory media appeals tribunal, because it finds the self-regulatory system, which has now changed to co-regulation,[15] has 'no teeth'. The tribunal, according to its supporters in the ANC, will aim to make the media more 'accountable' by making it pay for 'mistakes and sensational reporting'.[16]

At present, the print medium employs a self-regulation mechanism consisting of a Press Council, press ombud and the Press Appeals Panel. When the ombud rules that a publication has erred it orders an apology. But the ANC believes the apologies printed are not commensurate in size and placement with the mistakes made. The Press Council has now changed the system so that apologies are on the front page, and commensurate in size with the offending article, but this has not softened the stance of the ANC.

The Protection of State Information Bill (dubbed the 'Secrecy Bill') was introduced to replace the apartheid-era Protection of Information Act of 1982 – ostensibly to align it with the new Constitution. But the Bill fails that very test. Advocacy groups such as Right2Know (R2K) say that problems include a 'cloak of secrecy',[17] and that it will cover up many of the state's workings, because more than a thousand state bodies will be allowed to classify their documents. In addition, there is no provision for a public-interest defence to be used by whistleblowers, journalists and members of civil society, who could be jailed for up to 25 years for handling classified documents. The Bill was passed in

Parliament in November 2011, but by 2018 still awaited the signature of the president before becoming law. All the new president Cyril Ramaphosa has said is that he knows it is still in his in-tray.

What are we, theoretically, to make of the MAT and the Secrecy Bill proposals of Zuma? In Žižek's chapter 'Che Vuoi',[18] translated not so much as 'what do you want?' but rather as 'what's really bugging you?', we can try to apply this concept to what was really bugging Zuma vis-à-vis the media. It appears as though a series of floating signifiers were quilted into the one master signifier, 'ruling party', which in the quilting signification meant loyalty to the ruling party – and, as head of the party and the country, loyalty to Zuma. But more than this, he needed to cover up his crimes against humanity and South Africa; this corrupt relationship with the Guptas. I suggest here, especially when highlighting some of the headlines in the investigative units, that Zuma did not understand the role of the media in a democracy, and also that it did not suit him to understand. He expected democracy and its legitimacy to be consigned only to the signifiers 'ANC' and 'Zuma' in the media's reporting, irrespective of the corruption uncovered by the media. This could be what was really 'bugging' Zuma.

HOW THE MEDIA INTERPELLATED ZUMA IN 2016

While Zuma threatened with two interventions, the Secrecy Bill and the MAT proposal, like swords dangling over the heads of the media, investigative journalism still did not turn towards or succumb to the voice of power. On the contrary, the country's three investigative units from the weeklies, *City Press*, *Mail & Guardian* and *Sunday Times*, were remorseless in uncovering corruption scandals that have surfaced since Zuma assumed power. My aim is to elucidate the direct interpellations on Zuma, via front-page headlines in 2016 deliberately selected from the country's three weeklies with investigative units. This is by no means an exhaustive list, and indeed this chapter's aim is not to show in detail what the media uncovered about the president's corruption but merely to highlight the kinds of interpellations made, which cast light on the master signifier in the investigative media discourse, through highlighting the headlines used over the specific time frame. In *City Press* they were:

- State capture investigation: Kill Zuma's deal (13 November 2016)
- Zuma's ANC leadership left hanging by a thread (27 November 2016)

- Zuma tells MPs to vote against motion or else (12 November 2016)
- Calls for Zuma to resign increase (3 September 2016).

All these stories interpellated Zuma as an inept and corrupt president, of both the ANC and the country. They projected all the ANC's problems onto him, then projected all the country's problems on to the ANC. The stories revealed details about him and state capture related to the Gupta family, and the nexus of politics and business. The stories anchored themselves to the watchdog role of the media in a democracy, holding power to account – and, importantly, exposing corruption. The *Mail & Guardian* front-page lead stories reveal similar interpellations, with corruption emerging as the master signifier:

- Zuma at the precipice (4–10 November 2016)
- Zuma pals score first nuke deal (16–22 September 2016)
- Zuma's hit list (26 August – 1 September 2016)
- Concourt klap: What next for JZ? (1–7 April 2016).

As in the *City Press*, Zuma was interpellated as a corrupt president deeply involved with a shady business family. The *Sunday Times* headlines overlapped with the same theme as the discourse of the *Mail & Guardian* and the *City Press*'s signifiers of exposure of corruption:

- For the sake of your country, Mr President, GO NOW! (3 April 2016)
- Operation Exit Zuma (17 April 2016)
- Nkandla fall guy hits out at Zuma (27 March 2016).

Some of the issues emerging from the *Sunday Times* included calls for the president's impeachment, as reports painted pictures of plunder, patronage and rot. 'Damning reports', 'gross misconduct', 'deceit' and 'outright unlawfulness at the highest level of government' were among the words and phrases used to describe the conduct of the president. In the 'Nkandla fall guy hits out at Zuma' story, the president was revealed to be a liar about the upgrades to his personal homestead. The words 'GO NOW!' in capitals in a headline, and using an exclamation mark, reveal a certain hysteria – ironically, the same kind that Jackson Mthembu from the ANC used against the media when he talked about imprisoning journalists.

This list of front-page story headlines is not an exhaustive one, and the chapter's aim is not to delve deeply into precisely what the investigative news media uncovered, but merely to show that they turned Zuma into a subjected object, and interpellated him as corrupt. They named and shamed. The normative role of the media was in action: the gaze of being a watchdog and holding power to account, the master signifier being exposure of corruption at all costs, and sometimes there was hysteria attached. In turn, Zuma interpellated the media in a few ways via discourse, and beyond the interventions of the proposed MAT and the Protection of State Information Bill.

ZUMA'S INTERPELLATION: HAILING AND SHAMING OF MEDIA

The following is an extract from a long letter from Zuma titled 'The Voice of the ANC Must be Heard' and published on the ANC's website, *ANC Today*, in January 2008:

> Every day brings fresh instances of a media that, in general terms, is politically and ideologically out of sync with the society in which it exists … The media, viewed in its totality, should be as diverse as the society which it serves and reflects. This is clearly not the case in South Africa today. At times, the media functions as if they are an opposition party … The freedom of the South African media is today undermined not by the state, but by various tendencies that arise from the commercial imperatives that drive the media.

Zuma dreamed of unity or reconciliation with the media as though it were possible, but he shows a complete misunderstanding and does not accept that the media is a legitimate adversary in a democracy. How could the media be 'ideologically out of sync with a society', as if society and media were one, whereas there can be no unified society as such because of society's fractured, plural and diverse nature? In normative theories of the role of the media in a democracy, you can have media that reflects diverse voices, and this is what the media should be striving towards. But in the letter Zuma seemed to be arguing for media ideologically in sync with the ANC, because the ANC was the true representative of 'the people' – as if the ANC is the true and only representative of 'the people', and 'the people' support the ANC. Therefore, if the media are critical of the ANC, the media are out of sync with 'the people'. It is a social fantasy.

'At times, the media functions as if they are an opposition party.' Here, Zuma was referring to the media as a totality. In effect, this inaccuracy did not reflect the social fantasy in operation, as neither the media 'as a whole' nor society 'as a whole' exists. Both are diverse, fluid and unfixed, with shifting floating signifiers. His discourse is an example of how attempts are made to stabilise the ruling party's identity by creating 'the other' – the media as outsiders in a democracy, and as antagonists rather than legitimate adversaries. Zuma was the first ANC president to call for a media appeals tribunal. Such a measure would signify the most repressive measure ever taken against the media, either during apartheid or in the democratic era in South Africa.

In 2010, speaking in response to the debate on regulating the media, Zuma said 'the implementation of the MAT was not to control the media, and reports of it doing so were misleading', and reiterated that the Act's role was to regulate the media. 'Can a guardian be a proper guardian when it does not reflect the society it claims to protect?'[19] In a very clear further misunderstanding of the role of the media in a constitutional democracy, Zuma stated in 2013 that the South African media claimed to act as the society's watchdog, but 'they were never elected ... I've argued with them that they were never elected, we were elected and we can claim that we represent the people'.[20]

Zuma's 'logics', out of sync with the role of the media in a democracy, were further expounded in a reply to questions in Parliament. Here, he opined that the call for more 'patriotic' coverage of news was a general call to all media, not just the SABC. The media must 'put the country first' when reporting in a 'balanced and fair' manner. He expressed his frustration even further, also in 2013, when he addressed journalism students from Tshwane University of Technology: 'When I'm in South Africa, every morning you feel like you must leave this country because the reporting concentrates on the opposite of the positive.'

In another negative interpellation of the media, Zuma said: 'When I was still MEC in KZN, there was a lot of violence, people were dying. My view was the media perpetuates the violence, without realising it, in the manner with which they report. Why when someone is killed, do you take a very horrible photo and you show it?'[21]

In turning the gaze around to being a victim, Zuma blamed the media in 2015 at a breakfast briefing in Cape Town: 'I have a problem with that type of reporting. It is not balanced. Now some people who are far away ... not in South Africa, still believe that the president is very corrupt.'[22] Zuma was saying that he was not corrupt; it was the media that said he was. In 2015 at a presidential lunch in Pretoria to mark Black Wednesday/Media Freedom Day, Zuma addressed members of Sanef: 'I am the victim of unregulated media, which have failed to apologise for incorrect headlines that have damaged my reputation by associating me with corruption. While I am fully committed to media freedom to uphold democracy, the media must be regulated, and there is a need for a tribunal.'[23]

Zuma's discourse was embedded in victimhood – it was disingenuous, hinging on hysteria. He deliberately did not understand many issues: the watchdog role of the media; why the media plays the role that it does to uncover corruption; why its role is not to be 'patriotic'. He felt all would be well in society if there was more unity with the media. The only solution he could see was for more control of the media, as there would then be no stories about corruption. The media was a 'Big Other' for Zuma. It had taken on an almost obsessive significance in his life, because it was through the gaze of the media that he could see himself, and he did not like what the mirror was showing.

THE 'SABC 8' TURNED THEIR BACKS ON THE RULING POWER

Zuma and the then COO of the SABC, Hlaudi Motsoeneng, had a close relationship, and Motsoeneng called Zuma 'uBaba', father. During Motsoeneng's rule (he referred to himself in the third person), there was a culture of fear. 'The culture of censorship at the SABC continues, the culture of fear in the newsroom persists,' the 'SABC 8' said in an affidavit.[24]

In 2016 Motsoeneng declared, against the existing editorial policies of the SABC, that protests in the townships should not be covered. After all, he claimed, it only led to more violence – as soon as people saw the cameras they started acting up.[25] Eight SABC journalists – Suna Venter, Foeta Krige, Krivani Pillay, Thandeka Gqubule, Busisiwe Ntuli, Lukhanyo Calata, Vuyo Mvoko and Jacques Steenkamp – were dismissed by the public broadcaster in July 2016 for speaking out against Motsoeneng's policy of banning the airing of violent protest footage. He did not consult with anyone in the journalistic world before he made his decision, or consult the public broadcaster's own editorial policies, but the minister of communications, Faith Muthambi, a Zuma fan, supported him.

The Independent Communications Authority of South Africa (Icasa) met in July 2016 and asked the SABC to withdraw its decision not to broadcast violent protest footage, pointing out that the SABC ban was not in line with its licensing requirements, or the Bill of Rights, which stipulated freedom of expression.

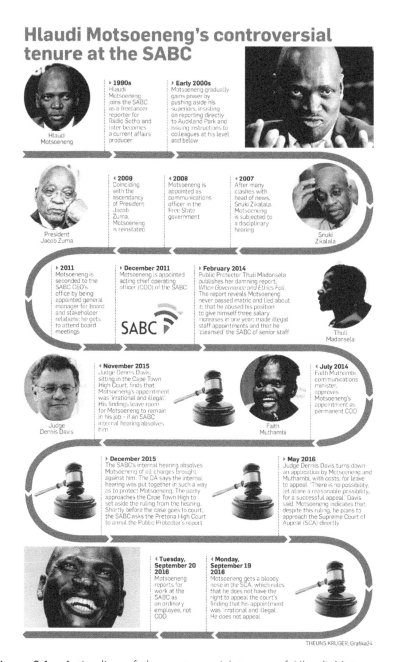

Figure 2.1: A timeline of the controversial tenure of Hlaudi Motsoeneng, acting chief operating officer of the SABC from 2011 to 2013

Source: Graphic courtesy of Theuns Kruger, Grafika24

But Motsoeneng dug in his heels. He was not going to be subjected to broadcasting policies, editorial independence or any such thing. He said the SABC would not apologise for refusing to promote irresponsible journalism. Instead he would take the matter to the highest court if need be. 'If we need to go to the Constitutional Court, that is where the matter will end. We are not going to change anything. People can forget [about that happening].'[26] He would not allow anyone to dictate how to run the public broadcaster. 'We are going to run the SABC professionally, the way it needs to be run, and we are not going to be influenced by anyone.' An R2K campaign activist was ordered to leave an SABC briefing after shouting 'Hlaudi must go' and 'away with censorship'.[27]

The SABC subsequently lost all its legal cases in trying to defend its censorship policies, and was told to reinstate the journalists. Meanwhile, journalists at the SABC anonymously told of the culture of fear and intimidation. They were petrified to speak, so they whispered. They said their phones were tapped, some were followed home, some had their tyres slashed, and some were threatened with murder if they did not toe the line.[28]

In July 2016, the eight journalists were presented with the Nat Nakasa award for bravery. In December 2016, the 'SABC 8' appeared before the ad hoc committee in Parliament which was inquiring into the SABC board's fitness to do its work. A journalist from EyeWitness News (EWN), Gaye Davis, commended the SABC staffers for their courage in giving their bold testimonies and explained that only four of the eight agreed to appear before the committee, yet they represented hundreds of SABC employees who felt as strongly as they did about what they described as 'bearing painful witness to the demise of public service journalism'.[29]

The SABC and Motsoeneng lost their case in the Labour Court against the journalists, and were ordered to pay a portion of the costs to the unions representing them. They were also ordered to reinstate the eight. This was a tremendous victory for the eight, reaffirming the power of the Constitution's guarantee of freedom of expression, the SABC's policies of editorial independence and, most of all, for the public broadcaster's mandate: the public's right to know. But there was also a cost.

Loss: Suna Venter died on 29 June 2017

'Broken Heart Syndrome Kills "SABC 8" Journalist Suna Venter,' wrote Jenna Etheridge in News24 on 29 June 2017.[30]

Figure 2.2:   SABC journalist Suna Venter, one of the 'SABC 8'

Source: Photograph courtesy of Deon Raath, *Rapport*

The body of senior radio producer Suna Venter, one of the 'SABC 8' journalists, was discovered at her flat in Fairland, Johannesburg, on Thursday morning, her family confirmed.

Venter, 32, had recently been diagnosed with a cardiac condition known as stress cardiomyopathy, or 'Broken Heart Syndrome', which could cause rapid and severe heart muscle weakness.

The family believed this had been caused by trauma and prolonged periods of unnatural stress.

Venter was shot in the face with an air pistol at the beginning of the year, after coming out of a restaurant in Linden, Johannesburg, while buying take-away food.

She received surgery to remove two metal pellets from her face. Over the past year, she also received threatening messages on her phone.

Venter joined the SABC as a producer at *RSG Current Affairs* eight years ago. The show's executive producer Foeta Krige said she had been passionate about international news and current affairs from the start.

She was involved with Gift of the Givers in various humanitarian missions in Libya, Gaza, Egypt and Syria.

'She cared so much about the situation in Syria that she took leave right after the war began to report for RSG from the frontlines,' said Krige. 'She remained passionate about the welfare of the children she encountered on these assignments up until her death.'

Continued

> It was revealed that Venter's main aim had been to establish an independent newsroom, free from editorial interference, within the embattled public broadcaster.
>
> Krige said Venter had been one of the most dedicated and passionate journalists.
>
> Doctors had advised her to leave her stressful working environment, but she apparently replied that she 'could not go before the battle was won'.

Venter was bullied by power but she stood up to it and against it. There was an excess and hysteria in how she was intimidated. From what her colleagues, for example, Krige in the above excerpt, says, this was a huge loss for journalism.

CONCLUSIONS

The gap, or missing signifier or misunderstanding (whether deliberate or real) is that the media have to exist in unity, 'ideologically in sync' or in tandem with the ruling party. The unconscious fantasy at play is that if only the media would be more patriotic there would be fewer problems in South Africa. In the cases of the SABC 8 and the stories about corruption the media was labelled as unpatriotic and negative (and many other adjectives); investigative journalists were subjected to the voice of power in the president's direct shaming of them, but they did not bend to the ruling faction of the ANC – in the sense that the investigations into the nexus between power and business corruption continued.

For his part, Zuma also did not bend to the hailing of investigative journalism. He neither apologised for nor denounced corruption, nor did he begin to act within the framework of the Constitution. Zuma's threats to the media through the Protection of State Information Bill, and the proposal for a MAT, as well as his discourse, showed his ideological interpellations and gazes as somewhat hysterical. This again raises the Žižekean question: what if evil resides in the very eyes of those perceiving evil?[31] The example Žižek provided was how children were portrayed in the films of Charlie Chaplin – teased, mocked and laughed at for their failures. The question to ask, then, is from which point or gaze should we look at children so that they appear to us not as objects of bullying and teasing, but rather, as creatures in need of protection – and the answer is, of course, from the viewpoint of children themselves. Zuma gazed upon the media as something that was negative, and destroying the image of the country. Was it not Zuma himself who was destroying the image of the country?

The ANC's discourse, and in particular Zuma's,[32] elucidated a need for more unity in the social sphere, without acknowledging that society is fractured, open-ended and diverse. A symptom of the ills of society was Zuma himself, not the media that exposed him. There is excess and a surplus attached to 'the media'. In an analogous way, Jews were made the social symptom for the racists in Europe at a particular time, and in 2017 Donald Trump made the figure of 'the Muslim' negative. Today in South Africa many 'big others' are found, to blame for problems: the public protector's office (when headed by Thuli Madonsela), the opposition parties and the media.[33] The flawed logic is that if they stopped carping there would be more unity in society. It is an attempt to stitch over the fractions and social antagonisms such as poverty, the slow or lack of economic growth, unemployment, crime and corruption. But the antagonisms are constitutive, and intrinsic to a democracy.

The master signifier in Zuma's discourse was unity with the ruling party, rigidly designated and fixed to loyalty to the ANC. The media, particularly the investigative media, has positioned itself as a friendly adversary, wanting to play a role in a democracy by stamping out corruption, yet this was not acknowledged in Zuma's or the ANC's discourse. The media was interpellated as the enemy, but it has not turned around in deference or 'guilt', as in the Fanon and Butler theorising. There was a refusal to accept the terms of subservience and no evidence of turning towards the voice of power when interpellated. The missing signifier in the ANC's discourse on the media was indeed the role of the media in a democracy, and how this role can be fulfilled only if it maintains a critical gaze on political power, if it keeps a distance from political parties. The ANC did not accept that journalists who uncovered corruption were legitimate adversaries in a democracy, antagonists but not enemies. If the ANC instituted a MAT, and the Secrecy Bill in its current form became legislation, the freedom and independence of the press would suffer. Journalists would probably be required to register and acquire 'licences' to publish, and if they published information the authorities deemed 'classified', they would be jailed. These interventions signify closures, and also constitute a 'surplus attached' – in other words, more is attached to the media than the media itself.

The implications are serious. Who would then decide whether a journalist could practise? Journalists would probably self-censor for fear of being hauled in front of Parliament for stories that could be considered embarrassing for the government, the president or the ANC. Zuma's words showed a pattern of pursuing his desire to create a society with more consensus, rather than an understanding of the media's role in a society that is fractured and split, full of fights and contestations, and where his corruption scandals were laid bare on the front pages of the newspapers. These interventions signify closures in the present democratic space, and they miss and misunderstand the signifier in the media's role in a democracy: to censure and to hold power to account. The words used (discourse) and the interventions such as shaming suggest that for the ANC and Zuma as its president, the master signifier was loyalty to the party which perceived the media as 'big other' and saw outsiders as creating ills in society, rather than as legitimate adversaries sharing a common symbolic space.

One of the most important conclusions in this chapter is that through hailing and shaming Zuma failed to subject the media. The media, the investigative media, in particular, turned their back on the subjecting voice of power, to continue instead with the investigations into corruption.

The SABC 8 stood up to the ultimate bully in the media, the man who called Zuma *uBaba*. In ruling that protests about service delivery must not be covered, Motsoeneng laid down the law against the public broadcaster's own editorial policies. The majority of journalists agreed that he was wrong, but the SABC 8 were subdued in the atmosphere of fear, intimidation and censorship. Nevertheless, they decided to challenge and turn against the voice of power. They won the fight, and seven of the eight are still employed at the public broadcaster. Venter suffered and died. The story of Venter ties in appositely with the theme of power and loss in chapter 6: the anti-feminist backlash and the attacks against women in the newsroom and in the media, including the new threat of cyber misogyny.

3

'Zupta': Power and Loss in Investigative Journalism

> *Humanity is waiting for something other from us than such an imitation,*
> *which would be an almost obscene caricature.*
> Frantz Fanon, *The Wretched of the Earth*

Fanon slated African leaders for imitating the West with their colonial greed, the formerly oppressed imitating their oppressors. He argued that we must not desire to 'catch up with Europe' but, rather, that we strive to find a different path to advance humanity. The Zuma era showed the imitation of apartheid's corruption. In this chapter I show the excesses of Zuma's corrupt leadership, a stolen decade from the country's democracy, if you like, and a huge loss for the country. The chapter covers the contribution investigative journalism has made to exposing corruption – but also the crisis that journalism faces. The last part of the chapter gives voice to journalists themselves.

Sometimes journalists are named and shamed, and sometimes they turn their backs, in misrecognition. Following theories of Fanon, and borrowing and simplifying concepts of naming and shaming from Louis Althusser, Michel Foucault and Judith Butler, in the second part of this chapter I focus on what was referred to as 'media capture' after the *Sunday Times*, in 2018, retracted many of its investigative pieces, for example, the South African Revenue Service (SARS) 'rogue unit' stories, the 'illegal Zimbabwe renditions' and the 'Cato Manor death squad' stories. The newspaper was called out and shamed in the public sphere. South African National Editors' Forum (Sanef) launched an inquiry into 'media capture', which would include the failings of the *Sunday Times* as the impetus for such an inquiry. But the gaze in this chapter is not on the details of what investigative journalism found about Zuma and his Indian businessmen cronies, the Guptas, as all of that is already out in the public domain.

The Althusserian notion of interpellation, where the subject is constituted through hailing, naming, shaming, and Fanonian misrecognition is used here to apply to investigative journalism. It recalls the attempted shaming by the Zuma government: hey you, investigators (mainly white),[1] why do you focus only on corruption in the public sector (mainly black, therefore you are racist)? The *Sunday Times* was hailed and shamed and the terms of the interpellation appeared to be accepted. The editor apologised on behalf of his predecessors and for the fact that the investigative journalists (both black and white) had not done the proper checks on their sources but had used one set of sources, ignored the other side's story and, in the process, furthered the agendas of corrupt politicians attempting to weaken key state institutions.

The policeman on the street (the voice of power) shouts: 'Hey, you there!' and the person turns around guiltily as though he or she has committed a crime. This is the performativity of naming,[2] and is an attempt to bring the subject into line – but there can always be misrecognition. The one who is hailed may fail to hear, misread the call, turn the other way, answer to another name, or insist on not being addressed in that way. For Foucault, disciplinary words, injunctions, or calling out, are not automatic and linear, to constitute obedience and subjection but can also, or even simultaneously, constitute the conditions for de-constitution, re-constitution and resignifications.

Resignations can happen if norms are unsettled, through debate or by turning away from the voice of authority. These theoretical reflections are used to scrutinise investigative journalism in the country and the role it has played in deepening democracy. In the *Media Online*, Herman Wasserman wrote that South African journalism faces a crisis of conscience.[3] He cited *The New Age* newspaper and its sister television channel African News Network 7 (ANN7), which were widely viewed as attempts by the Gupta family to extend their state capture agenda to the media sphere. The close relationship between the executive chair of Independent Media, Iqbal Survé, and members of the ANC have repeatedly raised serious concerns about editorial independence at the group's publications. Wasserman, Niren Tolsi,[4] and Steven Friedman[5] have censured

South Africa's mainstream media for not listening to and reflecting closely enough the voices of the marginalised and the poor, as evidenced during the coverage of the fires in Knysna (an Eastern Cape holiday area) where forest fires spread and burned down lovely holiday homes. (About 80 people died; the media were able to name the pets of the white people, but not the names of the black people.) When miners at Marikana went on strike and were gunned down by police, killing 34, there was huge coverage but the voices of the miners were not heard – the focus was on the mining companies, the union officials, the government, the police and the ruling party.

The backdrop to media coverage and journalism is the era of disinformation, misinformation and propaganda in the world, where politicians have used the public's distrust in the media to serve their own agendas, as Wasserman further wrote in his *Media Online* article. In this context, accountability and transparency are crucial, and it is apposite to say that 'if journalists demand accountability from the state and politicians, they too should be accountable to the public'.

THE POWER: GUPTA LEAKS AND INVESTIGATIVE JOURNALISM

The Gupta leaks, over 250 000 emails, exposed rampant corruption between the private and public sector and specifically how the business family from India, the Guptas, friends of the president had captured the state's decision making. The scandal reverberated around the world and fingered the international companies Bell Pottinger (public relations), KPMG (auditing) and McKinsey (consulting) and the local Gupta company Trillian, which stole millions of rands' worth of tenders from Eskom, through collusion.

South African investigative teams – amaBhungane, *Daily Maverick*'s Scorpio unit and Media24 – collaborated and used the #GuptaLeaks to expose how the Guptas captured political decision making as well as which tenders were won without due process, and money laundering. They did this in over 70 articles, during a watershed year for investigative journalism and democracy in South Africa: 2017–2018.

The story of state capture and the Gupta leaks was as eye-popping as a thriller novel. The difference is that it happened in reality, over the nearly ten years of the Zuma presidency, and the media played the largest role in exposing massive corruption at the nexus between the public and private sector, with the president right at the centre of the scandals. The investigative media exposed these in bits and pieces and the leaks confirmed it via the emails between the corrupt players.

The Zuma scandal itself goes back more than ten years. In a series of articles about Zuma and his excesses with public funds (R250 million of public money spent on upgrades to his Nkandla homestead from 2007) and his closeness to the Guptas, the South African public was thrown the whole gamut of evidence. Investigative journalism contributed to ousting a corrupt president in February 2018. The Guptas fled the country, variously to Dubai and India, to avoid prosecution.

In June 2018, at the Sanef Nat Nakasa awards for bravery in journalism, the Gupta leaks' dissemination and redaction were the most obvious choice for mention. The editor of the *Daily Maverick*, Branko Brkic, was the overall winner because, as the then Press Council director and judge of the award, Joe Thloloe, said,

> A cache of emails – a cache that defined the South African story in the last year – landed on his lap. If he were just another ordinary journalist, he would have heard the words 'scoop!' and 'exclusive!' dancing in his head. But he was extraordinary and thus did two remarkable things: one, he realised this was not a story his publication could hoard – it belonged to South Africa; and two, he had to protect his sources. He arranged for the safety of the sources and he put together a team from his own publication, some journalists from the unique South African investigative journalism centre amaBhungane, and from his rivals, Media24, to give us #GuptaLeaks, the journalism that brought down the Gupta family and their mentor, ex-president Jacob Zuma.[6]

The reason this is quoted at length here is not only to describe the impact of the contribution but also to show how journalism has changed. Collaborations now work, unlike in the past, when the focus was on competition and beating your opponents to produce a scoop. The award is named after and in honour of the South African journalist Nat Nakasa, who died in exile in 1965 at the age of 28. 'This year we had the largest number of nominations ever and the quality of the entries was outstanding, and it was out of this cream of South African journalism that we selected the winner of the Nat Nakasa Award 2018,' Thloloe explained.

'Gupta Mine Grab: How Brown Misled Parliament' is one of the many headlines that spelled out the Gupta story as amaBhungane revealed it in 2018. Appendix B of this book lists more, as well as headlines from other investigations into state capture going back to 2011. There are investigative stories from more than a decade ago which placed Zuma at the centre, broken by Mandy Rossouw in the *Mail & Guardian* in 2007–2008 when she spotted Zuma's Nkandla homestead on a casual drive to KwaZulu-Natal and investigated further to find out that the personal homestead was being built with taxpayers' money. To consider the many headlines, however, is to be reminded of the sheer number of investigations, to highlight the issues – how many there were, what they uncovered – and then to reflect on the concepts of power related to journalism and allow us to philosophise about the mission of journalism. What is it for?

I would like to take a small tangent back to the theory before reflecting on present investigative journalists, what they do and what they think their contributions to democracies are, and on former journalists – how they turn around and look back. One of the big criticisms of investigative media is that it singles out certain people to expose ('why is it called "collusion" when about the private sector but "corruption" when about the public sector?' as one member of the public complained). Is it a fact that investigative media attaches a surplus to 'corruption' which could also be the last support of ideology, an over-investment, if you like? The investigative media misrecognised the hailing – that they were (mostly) white, and therefore biased against public officials (mainly) black, but lenient on private sector corruption. According to Althusser, we are all subjects of interpellation: we get named and shamed, we can turn towards the voice of power interpellating us, calling us to order, or we can ignore it, misrecognise it and carry on.

This is exactly what happened with investigative journalism over the two decades during which they persisted with investigations. In the process of investigating 'Zupta', the media exposed private sector corruption which were indeed private sector and white – Bell Pottinger, KPMG and McKinsey. By 2018, more private sector corruption was exposed through the Steinhoff saga, termed the biggest case of corporate fraud in South African history.

Then, in January 2019, more corruption was exposed at the nexus between the private and public sectors during the Zondo Commission of Inquiry into state capture, and Zuma was again at the centre when it was revealed that over the past decade the securities firm Bosasa had bribed state-owned enterprises officials for government contracts worth millions.

SELF-REFLEXIVITY: THE CRISIS IN JOURNALISM AND JOURNALISTS' GAZE ON THEMSELVES

One of the questions I raise in this chapter is whether journalism is a public good and should be protected as a public good. Some say journalism is dead, long live the internet, where social media thrive, news is often for free, and the big companies rake in enormous profits from ads and analytics. For others, journalism has never been more important in the age of technology, populism and fake news. 'Without journalism, accountability is dead,' mused amaBhungane's partner Sam Sole in a keynote address, 'Journalism in the age of Zupta', to Rhodes University's 21st Highway Africa journalism conference on 31 August 2017, on what the full frontal attacks on journalism are today, and some possible strategies for survival. He referred to observations by Nic Dawes,[7] that press freedom was about accountability systems and about everyone's rights. I agree with both Sole and Dawes that media need to convince the public that they were on their side (people's side, readers' side, audiences' side) and not on the side of the elites, private capital, governments and ruling parties – in other words, all those who already have power.

Indeed, as Sole opined, the standards of journalism as craft were there to support the mission of democracy; enable accountability; afflict the comfortable and comfort the afflicted. His words relate to power and subjection – where there is transparency there is more accountability. The media's accountability, in the meantime, lies with the public. It has power, but how it exercises that power, and with whom in mind, is the question.

Sole articulated the purpose of journalism by sketching the confluence between technology, commerce, political partisanship and ideology, which has led to fake news in the current bewildering landscape. Some of the crucial points he raised – with which I agree and which have resonances in this book – include that there is a crisis in journalism, locally and internationally, because of unregulated capitalism and unregulated technology. This is in parallel with the crisis in democracy. It appears as though the power of the nation state, and trust in politicians, are over. Sole was correct when he stated that the loss of trust extends also to the mainstream media.

This book deals with some of the issues raised in Sole's address: that advertising in mainstream media has plummeted and the beneficiaries have been digital non-news media tech companies such as Google, Facebook and Twitter. These giant corporations have eaten into advertising spend to mainstream media and analytics. Algorithms, clickbaits and ratings are the order of the day. The implications are that professional journalism has been struggling in this morass of social media, and its concomitant fake news (misinformation, disinformation, mal-information and propaganda) is part of the media ecosystem and is used to distort reality and undermine accountability. For journalism to survive in future, Sole said, journalists should shun clickbaits, which enable fake news, and should not become politically partisan – even when the task is political – and build trust in the news business by being correct and factual. The media industry should support institutions of solidarity; should build relationships with donors; should consider building a media union (refer to chapter 4 on job losses for how unionism disappeared in journalism); should build a public understanding of what journalists do and how they do it; and should build alliances. At the time of writing there were no coordinated efforts to protect journalism.

The bottom line is that journalism must be protected as a public good. At the time of writing, in 2018 to 2019, unions that once bustled with activity, for example, the Association for Democratic Journalists (ADJ) and the South African Union of Journalists (SAUJ), were dead, and the Media Workers Association of South Africa (Mwasa) and the Communication Workers Union (CWU) told how media companies were shutting them out and how difficult it was to organise journalists, who were a 'difficult bunch'.

In the New Beats survey 2018, of 158 journalists who had left the newsroom, over 70 per cent had no union support when negotiating redundancy, dismissal, being laid off, retrenchment packages, dealing with the loss of a job and the emotional issues that arose from this – and other traumas related to loss of identity and income (this is elucidated fully in the next chapter). It is clear that the sector had no cohesion and was losing power as a whole. And yet, when investigative journalists descended on Wits University for the Global Investigative conference in November 2017, the sector exemplified significant power, particularly in investigative journalism. The conference was hailed as the biggest of all ten global investigative journalism conferences to date (also called the biggest muckrakers' gathering in the world).[8]

JOURNALISM IS DEAD, LONG LIVE INVESTIGATIVE JOURNALISM: THE TENTH GLOBAL INVESTIGATIVE JOURNALISM CONFERENCE

Wits Journalism hosted about 1 200 delegates, mainly investigative journalists who shared the trends in their craft and what they thought the future held. One of the participants, at the session on the future of journalism, set an interesting tone when she said: 'Journalism is dead, long live investigative journalism.' It was a rather self-important declaration, given that she was herself an investigative journalist.

However, others in attendance were not all investigative journalists when they observed that there will be artificial intelligence doing the job of journalists; that news organisations were consolidating and diversity was being lost; that news was turning into entertainment information (or infotainment); that misinformation and propaganda was increasing; that marketing and public relations were mixed up with news; that opinion was sold as comment and analysis; that content was now news; and that the new medium would be visual and audio.

News24 editor, Adriaan Basson, was enthused that, in tandem with investigative journalism, there was what he called 'a new spirit of activism that is fantastic' and a fight back by civil society. Basson was correct. South Africa is indeed a society with robust civil society organisations, including about 20 associated with media, but the activism has not appeared to reach out to, or deal with, job losses in the sector, and unionism had indeed died. Jacques Pauw, author of the bestselling book, *The President's Keepers: Those Keeping Zuma in Power and Out of Prison*, made a prescient point, that we have to be careful in thinking that if Zuma goes everything is going to be all right. The capacities of the state agencies SARS, Hawks, crime intelligence, South African Broadcasting Corporation (SABC) and National Prosecuting Authority (NPA) all have to be built up again – 'it's going to take years'.

Basson spoke about the role of journalism. 'Our role is to uncover stories and put them in the public domain, so that no one can say they didn't know.' Indeed, this is what journalism, and particularly investigative journalism, did, yet it took a long slow build-up to the revelations in the Gupta leaks till the country finally took note. One of the most frequently asked questions during the session on state capture was 'so now what, you uncover all this, but what's the impact?'

Addressing 'fake news', Basson added: 'Old journalist principles in the age of fake news will continue to apply. Check your facts, verify your info, and don't just publish. Triple check your sources … Corruption is corruption – private and public.'

An investigator from amaBhungane, Susan Comrie, did not answer the question directly but she did explain what state capture was. 'It was a systemic form of corruption – it is complex, where huge chunks of the state are involved in looking after particular groups. People are placed in positions to carry out the mandate of who has captured them. The state collapses quickly.' She said that the Gupta emails 'took us to another level'.

According to Basson, journalists were aware that the South African public was as capable of corruption exposure as the journalists were themselves. 'People get fatigued by corruption. State capture helped me connect the dots between politicians and business. State capture is far from one-on-one tender corruption. It is also about when policy is affected to favour certain groups, for example, nuclear policy shows the nexus between politics and business, tenders and corruption.'

Thanduxolo Jika, then at the *Sunday Times* (in 2020, an investigative journalist at the *Mail & Guardian*), said:

> We connect the dots. It is about seeing that a combination of events is taking place, for example, a turning point was the firing of Nhlanhla Nene. No explanation was given for why he was fired. The Guptas needed certain positions, they needed treasury. From then onwards there were trips to Dubai. A set of events took place. They got reckless and we connected the dots. For state capture you need enablers and protectors in official positions, for example, Berning Ntlemeza, acting head of the Hawks, who turned a blind eye. The Guptas were giving instructions to senior government officials. Themba Maseko (formerly the head of Government Communication Information System) spoke about how he received a call from the Guptas, but as long as law enforcement agencies do nothing, nothing will happen.

Jika continued:

> Many of us had bits and pieces of information and the Gupta leaks connected the dots. Good government officials lost their jobs because of the Guptas. Nhlanhla Nene was about to be fired. We had to go through a lengthy process to verify. We knew but we had to be one hundred per cent sure. We put the story out – Jonas Mcebisi [former deputy minister of finance] was offered R600 000 in cash. That Sunday we were told by Zizi Kodwa that we were gossip masquerading as news.

Whether investigative journalism in South Africa focuses on public sector corruption, to the exclusion of the private sector, was naturally also a topic at this session. Jika admitted, 'Yes, we had too much faith in the private sector but now look at what's been exposed – Trillian and McKinsey. They are driven by profit and they don't care how it comes to them. It's now been exposed.'

These words of investigative journalists show faith, idealism and the belief that they were fighting the good fight. These journalists prodded, poked and prised open to the public the kernels of information that some institutions were not fulfilling their institutional mandate – for example, the president's office, the new public protector, the NPA, the Hawks and SARS – although it had to be noted that, as pointed out by Pauw in *The President's Keepers,* some journalists were complicit in the destruction of SARS and were used to achieve the ends of the president.

A year after the words of the investigative journalists Basson, Jika, Pauw and Comrie, investigative journalism suffered a blow when the *Sunday Times* apologised for false stories that resulted in the destruction of key institutions.

LOSS: WHEN INVESTIGATIVE JOURNALISM 'GOT IT WRONG'

The *Sunday Times* editor Bongani Siqoko apologised in his paper's issue of 14 October 2018: 'We got it wrong and for that we apologise.' He took responsibility for stories under the previous two editors and, in particular, for the misdemeanours – some call them mistakes, some call them deliberate collusion with a certain political faction – of the investigative unit.

Lacan's jouissance – the ideology is in the excess

About five years ago, in 2014, the *Sunday Times* began leading with front-page 'investigations' about a 'rogue unit' at SARS. The revenue-collecting institution, which was presumably investigating people's tax affairs, was apparently using illegal means.

The stories began with an affair, on a front-page spread, between Johann van Loggerenberg – a senior SARS official and head of investigations, who was wrongly reported to be an apartheid spy – and a Pretoria lawyer, Belinda Walters, who was acting for someone Van Loggerenberg was investigating. The stories coincided with Van Loggerenberg and his unit probing the affairs of former president Jacob Zuma, his son, his nephew and the Guptas. The story about the affair was apparently true, but in the end Walters turned out to be an agent who was triple-crossing people. The stories read like a thriller. Then, the *Sunday Times* reported that SARS was running a brothel. This did not exist. The newspaper ran a total of 35 stories that damaged the reputations of individuals and of the institution itself. But in the end the reputation of the *Sunday Times* was damaged. The Press Council found in a series of judgements during

December 2015 and January 2016 that these stories were 'inaccurate, misleading and unfair' and a 'serious breach' of the Code of Conduct. The *Sunday Times* was ordered to retract and apologise.

With the passing of time, the muddy waters became less so. It became 'clear' that journalists had been used either unwittingly or deliberately when they chose one set of sources, because they were part of the Zupta political faction themselves. Pauw, in an article in the *Daily Maverick* on why *Sunday Times* journalists should be testifying at the commissions of inquiries in 2018 – the Zondo commission into state capture and the Nugent commission into SARS capture – wrote:

> Good individuals were replaced by Zuma lackeys and investigations into the corrupt stopped. It tarnished the name of journalism; what journalism is for ... It was journalism at its worst. In most cases, their subjects weren't asked for comment or not given enough time to respond. They stated everything as fact and the word 'alleged' or the phrase 'we were made to believe' disappeared from their vocabulary. This was not 'normal' journalism. This was contrived, manufactured, engineered and machinated by a 'higher hand' to serve a 'higher end'.[9]

Not every investigative journalist at the *Sunday Times* embarrassed the industry. In January 2015, the senior *Sunday Times* journalist Pearlie Joubert resigned and said in an affidavit afterwards that she was not 'willing to be party to practices at the *Sunday Times* which [she] verily believed to have been unethical and immoral'. The following is a series of extracts from an interview she gave.[10]

It wasn't [only] one event. You must remember that the investigative unit at the Sunday Times *was involved in many stories that shaped our history. Many of the stories happened before my time. I arrived there, and didn't choose to be in the investigative unit; as a woman you often gag on the testosterone. The investigative unit was quite macho ...*

Not really toxic, but very kind of macho. Stories turned out to be rubbish. I was working on the Mark Lifman [underworld tobacco dealer with a huge income tax bill] investigation that SARS did. Then a bizarre set of incidences happened when my colleagues stopped having morning meetings with me, and then I was excluded from the weekly news diary. I was kind of iced out ...

They were speaking to double agent spy Belinda Walters and to a rhino poacher and they published. I was screaming and shouting about the evidence: where is the evidence? There was no evidence of the brothel ...

The illegal renditions of Zimbabweans was rubbish. I resigned because I couldn't breathe at night any more. Then I got a series of emails saying "I am a whistle-blower at SARS", but I couldn't share with my colleagues because I couldn't trust them. So I resigned. I was unemployed for a long time ...

I have a job now. But then, I applied everywhere to get a job, but journalism is like: You don't piss on your own front stoep.

The men (four male investigators) who wrote the stories were all allowed to reinvent themselves, all in the same media camp. None of them has taken the public into their confidence about who fed them the stories.

Pearlie Joubert felt shamed by being ignored, and 'iced out' but did not toe the line. She turned her back against the voices of authority and turned towards her conscience instead. She was subjected to their power, but refused to succumb, and in the end she felt she had to resign. She practised the Fanonian misrecognition by refusing to be called into line by her peers in the investigative unit.

Were these stories about structural problems at the *Sunday Times*, as some believed, or was there something more sinister at play? It is a question that cannot be answered immediately. In his personal WordPress blog, 'The Harbinger', Harber wrote that just over ten years ago 'we interviewed most of the staff and wrote a long report which revealed the structural problems in the *Sunday Times* newsroom that led to these mistakes. Some of them still seem pertinent.'[11]

Too many people were interceding between the reporters and the end product to rewrite and 'sex up' stories. Reporters lost control of their stories, and the search for racy introductions and headlines sometimes distorted facts. Fact-checking had become a formality, rather than an embedded culture. The investigations team operated in secrecy, as an untouchable elite. Insufficient planning meant that there was too much pressure on a Saturday afternoon to find an impressive front page, and caution was sometimes thrown to the wind. Many have been damaged by these practices, including journalists, and journalism as a whole is under scrutiny.

REFLECTIONS ON JOURNALISM TODAY

Investigative journalism has made a huge contribution to exposing corruption and thereby playing its role in democracy, but there have been problems, as in the *Sunday Times* saga. In the next section I bring in voices from the journalist community itself. Seldom has there been an opportunity for journalists to talk about journalism. They offer voice for others (and are vilified), but they have not used their own mediums to talk of the meaning of their craft.

The following section comprises a series of interviews reflecting on journalism today from those who have recently left the newsroom. They were asked only: 'What are your thoughts on journalism today?'

Charlie Mathews, writer and former advertising agency owner; interviewed on 25 July 2018

I'd like to quote Dan Tynan who wrote this on Quora *in response to the same question: 'On a respirator – and the prognosis isn't good.'*

Listen, there is more media today than ever in our history – there's probably two or three times as much media now as a year ago, and probably ten times as much as three years ago. We are swimming in it. But journalism? Actual fact-based, multiple-sourced, authority-questioning journalism? It's on the endangered species list.

Mass media is corporate owned, thus the narrative is extremely narrow. With the exception of sudden horrific events, which seem to be happening on a continual basis these days, it's pretty much scripted and numbers driven, especially on 24/7 cable. Which is why The Donald is still with us today, threatening us all with the rise of new American fascism. He's ratings gold.

On the flip side, now anyone with a smartphone is a journalist waiting to happen. The ability to film anyone doing anything (and, all too often, a cop shooting some unarmed teenager) gives us all direct access to events as they actually happened, not a rehashed second- or third-hand account. This is a good thing.

What isn't happening is the deep reporting around that story. Why do these things keep happening? What are the forces in society that prevent us from changing this? Who are the people who decided that a black man whose spine was separated in the back of a police van was somehow not murdered by anyone? Who is the judge? What is his background? Who are his friends? Who appointed him? What political pressure was exerted? Who is really calling the shots there, and who is trying to change this?

Obviously there are exceptions. Some publications, like the New York Times, Washington Post and the New Yorker, still dig deeper. The reason we don't get answers to these things? Because almost nobody is willing to pay for reporters to dig into it. Watch the movie Spotlight. It wasn't that long ago that major city newspapers had the resources to devote a team of four reporters to a single story for months on end. Not because the story would help them snag big advertisers or increase their circulation base or just sell papers (though I'm sure it did the latter); they did it because it was a story that had to be told. It was important. It was part of the paper's mission. This is the reason why newspapers were created. That kind of journalism hasn't disappeared entirely. But it's more and more rare, and one day it very well might. And no one will be left to report that story. Back home, newsroom owners are still sipping self-congratulatory champagne for having ousted Zuma. But the same issues that dog journalism remain. It is untransformed. It doesn't represent the majority of South Africa. The business model is flawed. Zuma might be gone – but journalism is still in big trouble locally. Really big trouble.

Themba Sepotokele, former senior journalist at the *Sowetan*; interviewed on 5 July 2018

As much as the media is doing well as the fourth estate by shining the spotlight on corruption, the media needs to focus on development journalism. The training of journalists should also change, as media in general, and newspapers in particular, are competing with social media.

Secondly, journalists are and should not just be the transmitters of infor-mation. Journalists are activists and should form or belong to organised bodies and unions, and not expect Sanef to deal with issues facing working journalists.

There is lack if not failure of mentoring and training young journalists. Most are thrown into the deep end and expected to swim and survive. Not investing in training for journalists is but suicidal to reporters themselves, respective media houses and the death of journalism as a career and a craft.

Moshoeshoe Monare, former editor of the *Sunday Independent* and deputy editor at the *Mail & Guardian* and, in 2018, deputy managing editor of Tiso Blackstar (now Arena Holdings) media division; interviewed on 27 July 2018

Despite the decline and tough trading conditions, journalism – in whatever form – must survive. Whatever happens, we need to understand that jour-nalism is not an ordinary commercial transaction but a constitutionally, socially and morally essential service with a beneficial value for the whole society. Freedom of expression and of the media are not confined to the protection of the profession but to the extent that they give platform and space to the aspirations of all people to freely express themselves and hold the powerful to account. We need to differentiate these principles and phil-osophies from the business and politics of media institutions. Journalism, seen from this perspective, should transcend institutional rivalries.

I think journalism is at risk from financial pressures faced by media companies. I think there is a need for a new ownership model that's in pursuit of fulfilling the constitutional duty of the press and not distracted by the need for profits. There is a fundamental philosophical contradic-tion between the constitutional requirement and the imperative to make money. The contradiction is sharper and more evident among those media companies that are struggling to adjust to the digital revolution as well as the slowdown in the economy. Traditional media companies are under pressure and are unable to sustain large and skilled newsrooms which our constitutional democracy desperately needs.

Louise Flanagan, former editor at Independent Media and, in 2018, freelancer; interviewed on 24 July 2018

There's some great journalism out there still (who could have invented the treasure trove of the #GuptaLeaks and the astonishing stories it produced?) but there's also a swamp of rubbish. In the months after I left journalism, I would occasionally throw down newspapers with despair at drivel presented as news (but I did that while working as a journalist too). I worked briefly for another news organisation (a nice team of smart people) and learnt more online media skills in three months than I had in nearly a decade at my last employer. That was great, but I realised I had become bored with the sort of news which our media outlets obsess over nowadays. There is too much gossip presented as 'news'; and this is also the fault of the readers who endlessly lap up such drivel and expect all news to be free.

Then I stopped reading news almost entirely for months. What a relief. I realised news had become a boring drudgery, an endless feeling of home-work that Must Be Done. There's a sense of loss about no longer being inside a busy newsroom focused on hard news, but there's also the won-derful novelty of reading for pleasure not work, the release of ignoring the badly written in favour of interesting, inspiring writing.

I worry about the younger generation of journalists, who will likely get starter jobs reasonably easily due to their youth (cheapness to employers) and digital skills. But they may find after a few years that they are stuck, unable to progress unless they leave journalism for media management or even other careers. It is harder and harder for those with experience to make a living as actual reporters, which is what I had tried to hold on to. It's a pity that the industry seems to value good journalism so little.

Reliable, informative, well-written news is not free. It's not easy to collect, to write or to sell. South Africans should support the good media left, or one day we'll find it's disappeared and we'll have nobody but our-selves to blame.

Crystal Orderson, southern Africa editor of the *Africa Report* and 702 Talk Radio; interviewed on 16 July 2018

I still love being a journalist, but [I hear] from colleagues working full time – whether at the SABC or elsewhere – they are really feeling the pinch: politics; no money; tough environment. They seem rather unhappy. And while I may not have a regular big salary every month, I am happy and my bills are paid. I love what I do, am open to new ideas and think with the industry changing so much I made the right move at the right time.

Heather Robertson, former editor of *The Herald* and *Weekend Post*, and deputy editor of the *Sunday Times*, in 2018, owner and director of Change Routes Development Communication; interviewed on 13 July 2018

I think the reputation of journalism in South Africa has been tainted, weakened and sullied by: 1) The SARS rogue unit planted stories in the Sunday Times *and the obvious factional ANC biases in* The New Age *(which became Afro Voice, and closed down in July 2018) and ANN7 (which became Afroworld View and also closed down July 2018), the SABC and Independent Newspapers, which has raised huge question marks about editors and journalists' biases and motives, leading to public distrust; 2) The juniorisation of newsrooms and the culling of more expensive senior journalists leaving juniors with little to no mentorship; 3) The use of weaponised social media by factions of the ANC, Black First Land First, Afriforum, various marginal right-wing racist groupings, the Guptas and the so-called journalists they pay to share their views; 4) The public war between Tiso Blackstar [now Arena Holdings] and Independent with stories and adverts published in attacks and counter attacks; 5) The use of junior journalists by Iqbal Survé to supposedly investigate journalists who he sees as his detractors, amongst various other dubious self-serving, self-congratulatory publishing in his newspapers; 6) The clickbait and churnalism online with an endless repetition of the same stories, which largely appeal to the same elite biases and largely neoliberal agenda.*

I think there are glimmers of good journalism happening in SABC radio debates that engage the public. I think the integrity, courage and determination shown by the SABC 8 journalists in fulfilling the true public broadcast mandate to serve the national audience with quality journalism, and the rigour and their involvement in turning around the SABC, is starting to bear fruit and should be guarded zealously by all who understand the mandate of a public broadcaster. The investigative work by amaBhungane, a sponsor and crowd-funded journalism organisation, has done more than larger mainstream media houses to uncover stories about state capture, but I wonder how long it can survive on exposes alone as an independent outfit.

I think the Daily Maverick *has managed to carve a space for quality analysis and long-form journalism, through investing in senior experienced journalists, and organisations such as New Frame, GroundUp and Amandla. Mobi are filling the gap in coverage of non-middle class issues that mainstream media ignores. I like the collaborative work between academics and journalists in* The Conversation Africa, *which does lead to new ideas and voices reaching the public domain. Apart from the examples mentioned, I think there is not enough innovation in South Africa to utilise the collaborative engagement affordances of digital media, to work with audiences as partners in news. Most mainstream media houses– the SABC, News24, TimesLive and Independent Media – have chosen to shut down the possibility of a richer discourse with their readers, through limiting comments and user-generated content. Livelier debates now happen on social media and radio rather than on news websites.*

Globally, I am inspired by the Filipino digital news start-up Rappler, *who don't position themselves as a news provider but as a social news network which provides perspective, community engagement, smart conversations and action for social change. And I like the way the US digital start-up Axios breaks down the fundamentals of a story for mobile news readers into sections, saying what happened, why you should know about it and what the writer's or an expert's opinion on the matter is. I am also greatly inspired by the Dutch member-based news site De Correspondent, which works with its paid-up reader base to help guide them on sourcing and suggesting stories. I believe somewhere in all of these new digital news sites lies a promising new future for journalism in which journalists work with members of the public to keep the powerful in check.*

CONCLUSIONS: POWER AND LOSS

The main themes emerging from the above commentary are that unless something radical is done journalism risks being extinguished. There is more media but less journalism that is fact based. As Mathews observed, 'Journalism is an endangered species'. The theme of superficiality runs throughout the words of the journalists – for example, Flanagan talking about reading 'drivel' and 'gossip' which is passed off as news. For Sepotokele, the issue of training for the social media age was important. He pointed to the lack of mentorships today, which is a problem for the development of journalists. Monare insisted that journalism must survive as it is a public good, but must be separated from commercialism. Orderson expressed fears that corruption would thrive without senior and investigative journalists. The issue of credibility was raised when Robertson stated that journalism was now tainted by political interference.

Journalism gained power through the fall of 'Zupta'; it lost credibility through the revelations of the *Sunday Times* false stories, or one-source stories, or captured stories. It was difficult, at the end of 2018, with the inquiry not yet started, to uncover the whole truth about what happened, who fed the stories, and how were they let through – this will emerge in the years to come. In November 2018, Sanef was debating terms of reference for the inquiry: should it be restricted to the *Sunday Times* and the SARS rogue unit stories; should it include those journalists who once supported Zuma and then pretended afterwards to be independent reporters and analysts? Then, what about Independent Newspapers which, some say, is captured by the Chinese who part-funded the sale from the Irish to Dr Iqbal Survé (who uses his newspapers to promote himself and his political agenda). And what about MultiChoice's dances with 'Gupta TV' (that is, ANN7), and what about the SABC being used as a propaganda tool by the ruling party? How wide should one go to look into what has happened and is happening in the media world?

The disillusioned journalists who had left the newsroom expressed the view that profit-driven journalism cannot be sustained and a radical overhaul was needed. Most of the interviews showed that they felt journalism was losing its purpose, driven as it was by media companies which were cutting costs, retrenching, not training and getting younger journalists to do more with less – and this showed in the superficiality of news.

This chapter started off about the power of journalism residing in investigative journalism, but as the data unfolded in the case of the *Sunday Times*, as well as the interviews from former journalists, it has ended up as a chapter about the sense of both power *and* loss. As for good investigative journalism, it turned around to the subjecting voices of criticism, unconsciously or consciously, from 2008 to 2018, and uncovered the corruption of the private sector: Bain, McKinsey, KPMG, Steinhoff, Bell Pottinger. But it could also be that the investigations uncovered the transgressions of the private sector in the process of uncovering public sector corruption. So, fortuitously, rather than deliberately, investigative journalism uncovered a festering network of private and public corruption. The hailing and shaming of investigative journalism consisted of the accusation: you are only interested in uncovering public sector corruption, therefore you are racist. This bark appeared to have abated somewhat by the end of 2018, when the private sector was shown to be at the centre of the corruption, feeding as greedily at the trough.

There were other trends, and some were positive, in investigative journalism: collaboration among the teams of amaBhungane, *News24*, and *Daily Maverick*'s Scorpio in the Gupta leaks. They supported each other rather than competed, then jointly won the Nat Nakasa award for bravery in 2018. The new trend will be cross-border collaborations, as the companies that were exposed – for example, KPMG, McKinsey and Bell Pottinger – were international. The global investigative conference showed that journalists were sharing information on how to catch the crooks, and making them accountable to the public. A significant trend is that this journalism was not driven by commercial profits but was paid for through philanthropy and crowd sourcing, so it was not beholden to companies seeking profits, nor to politicians holding back the exposés.

Theoretically, most investigative journalists misrecognised the bark of power. Within one investigative unit, Joubert resigned because she didn't toe the line with the rest of the team. Investigative journalism did not, in its entirety, become a subject of political power, but some sectors did, when they allowed themselves to be used deliberately or accidently by the forces of corruption. The issues that I have raised in this chapter include that if we ourselves are sites of liberation, what kinds of self-reflexivity, if any, did journalists exercise when they threw themselves into partnership with the corrupt? As for investigative journalism, there could be some self-reflexivity in the sense of listening and hearing the publics asking them to tackle private sector, and white, corruption. The usual answering refrain is that 'we are investigating those who steal taxpayers' money and are investigating the nexus between public and private sector'. Perhaps it needs to be made more obvious. Indeed, a radical questioning is required all round.

4

The Job Loss Tsunami

It is not only a theoretical question but a part of our experience.
Michel Foucault, 'The Subject and Power'

Like an unkindness of ravens, traditional media companies slashed journalist jobs in chunks over the past decade. The professional journalist workforce,[1] according to a number of calculations,[2] could be half of what it was ten years ago. The slashing took place in waves, some small, others gigantic – and unexpected. There were about 10 000 journalists in South Africa a decade ago but by 2018 there were approximately 5 000 – however, it is estimated that there are many more 'media professionals' (who freelance, produce content and work in public relations in the private and public sectors) than 5 000.

The halcyon days of bustling newsrooms in traditional media are gone, forever. Digital disruption is characterised by the 24-hour cycle of news, algorithms and social media often filled with the unverified information and disinformation characteristic of growing political populism. Digital disruption has replaced the tobacco fumes of the old newsroom in fundamental ways. The legacy newsrooms in South Africa today are like leaky ships owing to the tsunamis of retrenchments resulting from declining circulations, with no revenue model that works. About a thousand journalists were shed in the year 2012–2013, one of the big years for job losses.[3] Times Media Group, which became Tiso Blackstar (now Arena Holdings), retrenched, as did eTV, and Media24 in the following years. In 2018, the American *Huffington Post* shut down *Huffington Post SA*, DSTV shut down Afroworld View television channel, and Afro Voice (*The New Age*) was liquidated, with hundreds of job losses.

Then the unexpected monster job-loss wave occurred on 29 October 2018 when the public broadcaster, the South African Broadcasting Corporation (SABC), which journalists in the past had experienced as a safe haven from job losses, if nothing else, announced that it would shed about a third of its 3 376-strong staff, including journalists. It declared through a press release on 30 October that 981 permanent jobs would be made redundant, and of the 2 400 freelancers 1 200 would be cut. The process was to be finalised by February 2019 – but it was not.

I use a variety of methods to reflect on job losses and loss of power in journalism: information-gathering journalist techniques to find figures on job losses; in-depth interviews with senior journalists and editors who left the newsroom; the New Beats survey results 2018;[4] interviews with unionists and, finally, some theoretical concepts pertaining to power and loss. In the New Beats survey, 158 journalists who had left the newsroom over the past decade participated in a questionnaire in July/August 2018. On the record, the interviews highlighted the experiences of former professional journalists and editors, who reflected on their treatment by media companies, their experience of losing their jobs and professional identities – and on journalism today.

Over the six years since the first *State of the Newsroom South Africa* research,[5] consolidation of titles took place and the same news was syndicated widely. The 2018 research showed that subs' desks were emptied out, beats had by and large disappeared and generalist 'content producers' were working long hours handling reporting, blogging, Facebooking, tweeting and uploading videos. Journalists had to do more with less, and many, especially the experienced layer (in the age bracket of 40 to 60), were retrenched through voluntary and involuntary processes.

The underlying question of this chapter is: Why is journalism necessary and what have job losses got to do with it? My argument here is that democracies could die as – with shrill stridency – disinformation, hate speech, misogyny, populism and right-wing xenophobia rises. This is why journalism that does more than chase social media in the digital age ought to survive. The interviews with former journalists in this chapter show quite a strong perception, gained from experience, that journalism is being led by social media and technology, while many are thankful for investigative journalism which has made an enormous contribution to exposing the corrupt powerful of the Zuma era. Many reflect that initially, in the transition to digital, everyone knew they had to be faster, and deliver on whatever platform people wanted, but there was a cost: a downgrade of skills, context and ethics. It appears as though content producers who are technologically proficient and have replaced journalists are not taught the basics, Journalism 101, especially fact checking and double checking. The competition to be first with the news has also tripped up some traditional print media, as witnessed in the *Sunday Times* debacle in the previous chapter.

According to radical democracy theory, which aims for a deeper and more expansive democracy than what is current in the Western world, the more voices and the more diverse the voices, the better for the deepening of the democratic project. Journalism, in particular, is meant to be a pluralistic space where different views can be expressed and dynamic deliberations and contestations can and do take place. Why use a 'radical democracy' framework rather than the more mainstream liberal democracy, or merely democracy? Because a radical democratic framework demands acknowledging difference: the particular, the multiple, the heterogeneous, and everything that has been excluded. The various media are spaces for, or platforms for, a diversity of views but, even more importantly, a medium for the contestation of meaning in politics. In addition to radical democracy theories, I deploy in this chapter the concepts of power, loss, passionate attachment (to identity), rage, relief and ambivalence (at having left the newsroom), subjection to power, digital and commercial, pressing down upon journalists to make sense of massive change from their point of view.

In a re-reading of Hegel's *Unhappy Consciousness*,[6] Judith Butler, theorising about power and subjection, states: '… we are given to understand an attachment to subjection is formative of the reflexive structure of subjection itself'.[7] She continues: '… wretchedness, agony and pain are sites or modes of stubbornness, ways of attaching to oneself, negatively articulated modes of reflexivity … because they are given regulatory regimes as the sites available for attachment, and a subject will attach to pain rather than not attach at all'.[8]

In this chapter there is evidence of how journalists attached and detached from the pain of losing their jobs. Most feel deep ambivalence about their professional identities and journalism today.

Power operates in different ways: pressing upon one from the outside (as with the journalism industry); one's own turn towards the voice of power, accepting terms and conditions – or away from, in defiance or fighting back. And, so, subjection is paradoxical.

One of the problems with getting exact numbers of job losses is that the definition of what a journalist is, and who is a journalist, has become fluid in the digital age of social media – citizen journalism, blogging, Facebooking, tweeting and opinion making (including disinformation, misinformation and propaganda, often referred to as 'fake news'). The definition of what a journalist is, and how many journalists have been retrenched, is further complicated because some were calling themselves employed journalists when they were working casually in the newsroom for two days a week, earning hourly rates, after having been retrenched, sometimes by the same company.

The issue is even further compounded by the fact that the main union looking after the interests of journalists specifically, the South African Union of Journalists (SAUJ), folded in 2009, at the time when redundancies were just about to take off. However, there are a few unions servicing 'media workers' in general, for example, the Media Workers Association of South Africa (Mwasa), the Communication Workers Union (CWU) and the Broadcast, Electronic and Media Allied Workers Union (Bemawu). One unionist felt that the figure of the media worker force (which includes journalists) being reduced by half was conservative: ten years ago, Independent Media (formerly the Argus Group) had employed 6 400 workers, but this figure was now around 1 200. In addition, the estimate was before the next wave of retrenchments was announced in October 2018. After a crashing wave of retrenchments in 2016, and two years later in October 2018, Independent Media announced that another Section 189 notice was imminent before the year ended, which would further decrease the figure of 1 200. Section 189 of the Labour Relations Act (LRA) 66 of 1995 as amended permits an employer to dismiss employees for operational requirements or reasons. The phrase 'operational requirements' is a broad term referring to the economic, technical, structural or similar needs of an employer. Before effecting such dismissals, however, the LRA places an obligation on employers to engage in a meaningful joint consensus-seeking process in an attempt to reach agreement, inter alia, on appropriate measures to avoid and/or minimise the number of dismissals. An employer could, as part of the Section 189 process, advise employees that in order for it to remain viable and operative, employees would have to agree to a reduction in their remuneration or other terms and conditions of employment.[9]

WHAT THE NEW BEATS SOUTH AFRICA SURVEY REVEALED

The survey was conducted in July/August 2018 and consisted of 25 questions. There were 158 respondents. The biggest group in terms of age (at 54 per cent) fell into the bracket of 40 to 60, but the age range spread from 20 to 70.

The average number of years' experience was 18. Those who responded to the survey included a wide range of positions: editor, journalist, photo-editor, sub, head of news, reporter, lifestyle editor, managing editor, news editor, arts editor, feature writer, senior journalist, bureau chief, associate editor, senior specialised journalist, production editor, executive producer, assistant editor, chief copy editor, sub editor, executive editor, deputy chief sub editor, senior specialist journalist, provincial political editor, executive producer, and group editor in chief. However, 'editor' followed by 'journalist' were the highest categories.

The vast majority of respondents, 82 per cent, had lost full-time jobs. In a surprise finding, nearly 50 per cent of the respondents were earning more than when they were in the newsroom in full-time jobs. However, this still means that by a small lead the majority were earning less than they did in full-time jobs. The numbers of respondents' job losses were in this order:

- Independent Newspaper Group
- Tiso Blackstar/Arena Holdings (in 2019)
- Naspers/Media24
- SABC
- The community sector/local newspapers
- eTV
- *Mail & Guardian*
- Primedia
- The commercial radio sector.

One of the more important findings is that the former newsroom occupants were keen on digital training (88 per cent) but 70 per cent said they did not receive any training or re-training for the digital age. The majority (72 per cent) said that they had no union or journalist association support during their retrenchment process and over 90 per cent said that there was no employer-funded career support. Not all the survey data and graphs have been used in this chapter, but a few which have relevance – journalists' experience of support or lack thereof, and where they are today – are outlined and discussed. In terms of where they are today, the research showed that they were part of the 'gig' economy, freelancing, doing a bit here and a bit there, with a mix of journalism (68 per cent) and public relations, and with a small percentage having moved out of journalism completely.

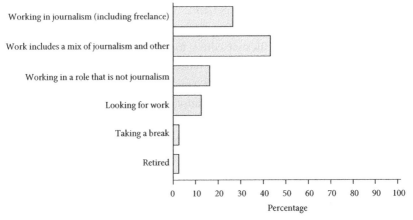

ANSWER CHOICES	RESPONSES	
Working in journalism (including freelance)	26.11%	41
Work includes a mix of journalism and other	42.04%	66
Working in a role that is not journalism	15.92%	25
Looking for work	10.83%	17
Taking a break	2.55%	4
Retired	2.55%	4
TOTAL		**157**

Figure 4.1: The work status of the journalists who participated in the survey

Note: Answered: 157; skipped: 1
Source: Author

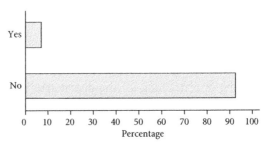

ANSWER CHOICES	RESPONSES	
Yes	7.09%	10
No	92.91%	131
TOTAL		**141**

Figure 4.2: Was there employer-funded career support as part of the redundancy package?

Note: Answered: 141; skipped: 17
Source: Author

The next section of this chapter goes on to highlight the experience of leaving the newsroom; treatment by the media company they left; feelings about losing identity; and reflections on journalism today. In the online survey, asked to choose between 'relief or sadness', most respondents said 'both'. This attests to the ambivalence experienced in the majority of cases. Other experiences that emerged frequently included 'trauma', 'post-traumatic stress disorder', 'shock', 'great sense of loss', 'painful', 'feeling jaded now', 'disorientating', 'I lost my identity', 'I feel sorry for those left behind', 'I feel emotionally numb', 'it was surreal', 'I experienced feelings of failure' and 'I am angry'.

The following ten interviews were done one-on-one in July/August 2018, with permission from the interviewees for their names to be used. Some responded via email. The questions were: When and why did you leave the newsroom? How are you feeling about leaving? Is there relief or sadness? What are your thoughts/ reflections on journalism today?

TRAUMA, LOSS AND AMBIVALENCE

There was also some joy at having left the profession. Some of the ten interviewed were freelancing and part of the gig economy of casual work, some have moved completely out of journalism, some to public relations. More than one began a 'start-up' or enrolled in postgraduate studies. One was recently retired but would never touch journalism work again. The pattern of the pain, loss, sadness, relief and ambivalence was the same throughout.

Those interviewed were: Heather Robertson (former editor who began a start-up and was completing an MA), Paddi Clay (recently retired), Charlie Mathews (senior journalist who started a growth marketing company), Mpumelelo Mkhabela (former editor who moved to research and academia, doing a PhD), Moshoeshoe Monare (former editor who moved to management in another media company), Themba Sepotokele (former senior journalist who began a communications/public relations company), Crystal Orderson (former SABC journalist who moved to *The Africa Report*), Yunus Kemp (former senior journalist who developed a PR company), Seamus Reynolds (senior journalist/ trainer who started a small business completely unrelated to journalism), Barbara Ludman (copy editor and now part of the gig economy) and Louise Flanagan (senior journalist who went freelance).

Heather Robertson, former editor of *The Herald* and *Weekend Post*, former deputy editor of the *Sunday Times*, now at Change Routes Development Communications; interviewed on 13 July 2018

I left my job as editor in chief of The Herald *and* Weekend Post *in December 2015. I had worked in this position in Port Elizabeth since August 2010. This ended a long career in full-time journalism, which started as a cub reporter at* South *newspaper in 1987 and included working as a journalist at the* Sunday Times, *a features editor at* Tribute *magazine and* Sunday World *newspaper, a deputy editor at* Elle *magazine and ten years in various senior editorial roles up to deputy editor at the* Sunday Times.

I had become increasingly frustrated with the heavy burden faced by publishers, editors, journalists and advertising sales teams to maintain and grow profit levels from the pre-digital past, while audiences were moving en masse to free digital news sites. I was burnt out and stressed after working twelve to fourteen hours, for fifteen solid years, fighting the windmills of declining circulation and advertising, transforming newsrooms to become digital first and more gender and racially representative of our country's demographics, while trying to motivate staff to produce beautifully designed, well-written and researched stories in print and online, ensuring that our readers could be served without fear or favour. I had lost my mother in a tragic car accident a year before, in 2014, and this led me to reflect deeply on the inordinate amount of time I was spending at work, fighting fires and windmills, while neglecting my own family, in particular my two children and my partner. As a woman editor among mostly male colleagues, I realised I was constantly trying to prove my worth and always felt that I had to do more, and this was to my own and family's detriment. I started feeling that the reasons I became a journalist (exposing injustice, deepening democracy, making sense of the society and culture we were and are becoming, educating and informing the public and working in partnership with readers to come up with constructive solutions to some of our many social problems) were lost in the news media's institutional struggles for survival. These internal and external power struggles often led to journalists, editors and publications owned by the same company, in addition to competitors, being pitted against each other, in a way which I felt was not conducive to good journalism or good mental health.

How did you feel about that?
I initially felt guilty and anxious about throwing away secure employment and jeopardising my children's future, but that feeling has passed. Yes, I am not earning as much as I did as an editor, but I am earning enough and I am a happier, more fulfilled human being, living a much more balanced life. I may not be able to buy my sons expensive gaming consoles, but I am able to spend time going to their soccer matches and piano recitals, and help them with schoolwork, so the guilt of changing their material circumstances has been supplanted by a greater sense of well-being and connectedness. I have also been intellectually stretched through doing my Master's.

I still connect and engage with friends and members of the journalism fraternity, and as my former editor at the Sunday Times *and friend, Mondli Makhanya, always said, journalists are a 'tribe'. Wherever we find ourselves in the world, whether we are in the mainstream or out, in employment or freelancing, there is a camaraderie that stems from being in the trenches. Obviously, we are all not like-minded, so I have on occasion come across the obsequious behaviour of some members of our tribe towards the leadership of the institutions in which they work. This behaviour is often accompanied by a sometimes smug, and sometimes exclusionary attitude towards any outsiders, including ones who have left the institution's fold for whatever reason. I find this disappointing and it saddens me, because it indicates a lack of mutual support and independent mindedness in some of the remaining institutional journalist core. These feelings of guilt, anxiety, sadness and disappointment do not consume me and have overwhelmingly been supplanted by a sense of relief, and freedom to be true to my own values and explore partnerships with like-minded people.*

Relief or sadness?

I was relieved of the burden of fighting windmills and fires with no end in sight for a purpose which did not feel like the original purpose I had signed up to when I became a journalist. Stepping off the treadmill gave me space to rediscover my own values and purpose. I was also able to interrogate and understand, in a global context, what I had experienced in my working life as a journalist, through my readings and research for a part-time Master's in digital journalism studies which I registered for at Rhodes University in 2016. I was also able to rethink the values and roles of journalism in not just political but everyday life, and think of what journalism could become in a digital age dominated by mobile devices. Through my Master's studies, attending both global and local journalism conferences and workshops, and setting up my own communications consultancy, I have been able to re-establish friendships with former colleagues and make new friendships with younger digitally savvy colleagues who share a similar passion for journalism to become more than a profit-making, career ladder climbing or politically partisan endeavour. I am really excited by the affordances of digital media and don't see it as the death knell of good journalism, but if worked on wisely and creatively, could do what my soon to be new employer Amandla.mobi is attempting to do, that is, 'turn every cell phone into a democracy building tool'.

Crystal Orderson, former SABC foreign correspondent, now southern African editor of the *Africa Report*; interviewed on 16 July 2018

The last year at SABC was miserable, being caught up in internal politics. I applied for another job and it was blocked by Jimi Matthews. No reason given. He just didn't like me and made my life hell. The internal politics were just too much and I resigned without another job.

At first, I was just depressed about the situation at the SABC. It felt like a living hell after leaving a job I loved, but after I made decision and took some time out, I was very happy and relieved about leaving a toxic environment. I felt I was being tortured for being assertive and having an opinion.

Themba Sepotokele, former senior journalist at *The Star* and *Sowetan*, now heading TS Headlines Consultancy, a media and communications consultancy; interviewed on 5 August 2018

I left the newsroom in 2004 after realising the prospects of growth and promotion were getting thinner and slimmer by the day. I was overlooked for promotion, despite having 13 years of experience and journalism as well as communications qualifications. Despite the prospects of growth, I was saddened by failure to invest in tools of trade like laptops and cellphones. Worse was lack of trust towards journalists, including experienced and senior reporters. I was demoralised. I was paralysed. Not only was I overlooked for promotion, I was also denied opportunities. For instance, for the nine years I spent at The Star *newspaper (1 July 1997 to 30 January 2005), I was not considered for any international trip to either study or cover a story. In 1999 I applied for the International Journalism Programme in Germany and the company refused to pay my salary for the three-month duration. I fought to the bitter end and they conceded.*

Relief or sadness?
Although I was saddened because I was suffocating in the then newsrooms, I felt relief because I was leaving a place where I was suffocating as a professional, committed to the journalism craft.

Charlie Mathews, former senior journalist known as Mandy De Waal, now freelancing and heading a marketing consultancy; interviewed on 25 July 2018

I exited permanent employment in journalism in 2013. I quit journalism entirely in 2017. I did so because of a loss of faith in the management of most of the media I worked with/for. I had moral conflicts with some of the management. I found it unacceptable that some of the media I worked with acquired funds from donors and/or private investors and that there was no transparency about this (and no transparency about the influence

73

*these parties had on that media, and the lack of oversight in this regard).
I was disheartened by the management of the media where I worked in
terms of their inability to meaningfully transform from a gender perspective, and from an empowerment perspective, as well as their failure to satis-
factorily address transformation issues that have dogged the industry since
democracy. I was disappointed in management's inability to create sustainable business models and subsequently provide a meaningful, sustainable
career for journalists that would enable them to adequately provide for their
families in turn. I was disappointed by newsroom ethics in general. This is
more related to worker/management relationships than actual news ethics.
I am happy that I have taken a decision that is in my best interest, and to
move to a sector where I have greater participation, opportunity, and economic reward. I feel I have achieved greater self-determination outside of
journalism.*

Relief or sadness?
*Relief and sadness. Relief at having left and being able to create my own
opportunities and improve my life. Sadness at the fact that journalism is
in such a sorry state.*

**Louise Flanagan, retrenched by Independent Media,
November 2016, now freelance; interviewed on 24 July 2018**

*I'm angry at the way it happened, as I believe the company cheated us, so
it was a bad way to leave. I miss my former colleagues but I do not regret
leaving and have found better challenges.*

Relief or sadness?
*I feel an enormous sense of relief about not having to walk into that
building again but great sadness at the loss of a fabulous team of colleagues.
I haven't even been able to face going back to visit former colleagues and
friends because I don't want to go into that building. I also feel a sense of
adventure, that there's a world of new challenges and new experiences out
there to play in.*

Moshoeshoe Monare, former editor of the *Sunday Independent* and deputy editor of the *Mail & Guardian*, now deputy MD of Media Division at Tiso Blackstar (now Arena Holdings); interviewed on 27 July 2018

I left the newsroom in March 2015 following my stint as managing editor of The Times *and* Sunday Times. *I was appointed deputy managing director: media division of the Tiso Blackstar Group. I didn't see this as a radical departure, as I was still responsible for the editorial operations of the group. But it was a wider responsibility that included taking business and financial decisions, so I am still contributing, albeit from a different office/position. I had been in editorial for two decades and I felt it was time for change, but I still contribute to the media industry. At the time I felt that I had betrayed the profession that I spent my entire professional life believing in. And I also felt like an industry sell-out when I was forced to take business decisions that are interpreted as not in the best interest of editorial. However, in general I am happy that I am still in the industry and having been on the other side, I am sensitive to the needs and values of editorial staff in general, and I still believe in good, quality journalism.*

Relief or sadness?
Both. It was not easy to leave after 20 years, having built relationships with colleagues in the industry. Relief, because it was time for a new challenge and learning. Sadness, because of the inability to effect changes and make a difference and improve the circumstances in the newsroom. Relief, because I don't have to be that guy who is expected to perform miracles without any resources.

Paddi Clay, former head of training at Tiso Blackstar (now Arena Holdings), now retired; interviewed on 31 July 2018

I left when I turned 62 (January 2017) as per my contract (65 was originally retirement age at Johnnic as it then was, but that was brought down to 62 by the time I signed my permanent contract with the company).

How did you feel about that?

I was quite happy to go. I had not had an internship programme to manage for the past two years (the shrinking industry did not really justify it), nor was there any money available for such training from the trust that had previously funded the graduate training programme because it had diverted the money to the digital change project. I was managing only a few interns, and many of those I had trained were moving on or taking retrenchment packages. There was not much money left over for the digital skills training that was needed. I was also tired of corporate life, and the stress and strain of the digital revolution of journalism.

Relief or sadness?

I was relieved and sad – relieved because it is frustrating to see need and have no way of addressing it, and to feel my contribution to management circumscribed because I was regarded as a 'training expert' rather than the experienced journalist and manager of journalists I am, as well as knowledgeable in change management – having done a Master's (paid for by the company) focused on managing digital change, with some of the foremost thinkers in this area globally (probably because we had new owner/management). I was also sad because it was the end of an era both for me and for the training programme that had been started (in somewhat different form) in 1998, and had turned out around 200 young journalists.

Thoughts/reflections on journalism today?

I have no desire to go back to journalism or to writing columns or interviewing people. I suppose that may be because I do not have much respect for many of our publications and platforms, or many of the editors in the business locally (this is perhaps a factor of age).

I am disappointed in journalism today. I think it is being led too much by technology. I know it is in a desperate pickle, trying to get paying audiences/customers to sustain it, and the search for sufficient critical mass is urgent, but it is still making mistakes such as failing to ensure that it adds value to the information it is passing on. I do thank the heavens for our brave band of investigative journalists, though.

In the first stage of transition to digital we could be said to have added value by being quicker, then we realised we also had to deliver in the format or platform people wanted – but in doing so it seemed we abandoned some of the basics – in skills and in ethics and taste. Being faster at getting the news out or processing it, or more attention grabbing or being more opinionated (from an uninformed or non-specialist base) is not what journalism should be doing (especially in developing countries) and I do not believe it is what people both want and need. Essentially 'responsibility' has dropped out of the old saying with regard to the press: 'no power without responsibility'.

I think journalists today have a tendency to exist in a bubble and to practice 'me' journalism (I think the US media demonstrates this), and this is exacerbated by reduced budgets and resources for newsrooms which keep them trapped inside and also unable to specialise or deepen their skills.

In South Africa there is also a tendency to produce what I'd call 'the voice of power' journalism – we mainly hear from those in power or in official authority. I prefer journalism that strives to be as fair as possible to all parties, and is not trapped in a binary paradigm.

I am quite enthusiastic about solutions, or constructive journalism, and tried to interest the company in looking into it as an approach that would better serve South Africa and appeal more to our loyal consumers. I believe there is both scope and a need for this type of journalism, but is there any platform that will practice it here and also be able to make a living – and of course a profit – enough to sustain it?

I do not think our mainstream news media are neutral when it comes to politics. But they do not admit their biases. Ideally I would like mainstream media to openly declare their political beliefs or leanings while at the same time provide quality journalism – fair, original, factual, creative, stylish, appealing, well researched and well argued.

Mpumelelo Mkhabela, former editor of the *Sowetan*, now lecturer at University of Pretoria and doing a PhD; interviewed on 3 August 2018

I wanted to pursue other interests – albeit a year earlier than I had planned. I think it was a good decision as I was able to pursue my other interests. I have done extremely well since. My departure also allowed space for other journalists to be considered for the editorship of Sowetan.

Relief or sadness?
I wrote a valedictory when I left. I was sad then, because I wasn't sure if I'd find fulfilment in whatever I had planned to do. I was also not sure if I'd have a platform outside the newspaper to express my opinions on current political affairs. But I have a platform now through News24 and I am happy.

Thoughts/reflections on journalism today?
I think journalism is at risk from financial pressures faced by media companies. I think there is a need for a new ownership model that's in pursuit of fulfilling the constitutional duty of the press and not distracted by the need for profits. There is a fundamental philosophical contradiction between the constitutional requirement and the imperative to make money. The contradiction is sharper and more evident among those media companies that are struggling to adjust to the digital revolution as well as the slowdown in the economy. Traditional media companies are under pressure and are unable to sustain large and skilled newsrooms which our constitutional democracy desperately needs.

Seamus Reynolds, former eNCA trainer, now director of Africanborn Investments; interviewed on 24 July 2018

I was head of training, running a boot camp for TV reporters at eNCA eAcademy, and now I am director of Africanborn Investments. I was retrenched in 2017.

How did you feel about that?
I had a breakdown. I feel relief now, as I am charting a new course for myself. I'm not tormented by a very fast and vicious news cycle. It's very shallow. The biggest frustration was social media and inexperienced juniors as editors. I am trying to query a story but everyone wants to react because of something on social media, and I would say 'hold, let's check, let's verify'. Winnie Mandela said something about Nelson Mandela and they wanted to run with it and I said let's check. It wasn't true. We are here to ask if things are true or largely true.

I miss the camaraderie when I joined eNCA in 2008. I wanted the buzz of the big newsroom, the intensity and the competition. 'The Marikana Massacre' was in our term. Regardless of the footage, we were rolling with it ... reality coverage.

Hard news journalism is over for me, and I am now applying these skills in different ways – doing some TV work, but I'm not doing training, as although organisations need training they won't pay for it. Some people have transitioned but are not happy. I may not be earning yet, but I am coping and lucky to have the support of my wife.

Africanborn Properties (under Africanborn Investments) is all about buying and selling. I also source below market properties for other investors. I meet new people, and I have a positive outlook. In journalism your head is perpetually buried in the negative. Something positive happens and we look for the other side, the negative, digging for dirt. I'm also involved in Bitcoin and cryptocurrency block chain technology – I used some of my pension to invest. I've got an entrepreneurial mindset. I like building. I built a newsroom. I am happier than I've been in many years. If I was given a sabbatical I would still be in journalism.

Thoughts/reflections on journalism today?
You can see the under-investment in the training of journalists today. They have canned training schools, and cut budgets. We now suffer the consequences of under-investment. I could see that journalism was losing its purpose. But this, by no means, is disrespect for the good crop out there today, the investigative journalism we have. They have

tenacity and perseverance. But the reality is social media has eroded the quality of journalism. I remember once wanting to wait before breaking news; I wanted to query a particular story. Everyone else wanted to react straightaway because other media were reacting to something Winnie Mandela apparently said about Nelson Mandela. She didn't say it.

Is journalism over because of social media?
Yes and no. Hard news is over. Journalism is more important than it's ever been, precisely because of the proliferation of social media. But the investment in journalism is dying. It's a double-edged sword.

Barbara Ludman, former sub-editor at the _Daily Sun_, now free-lancer; interviewed on 22 July 2018

My last job was three days a week as a sub at the Daily Sun. *I was training, subbing and proofing. I get bored easily so whenever the editor needed anything I did it. I was happy to work on Sundays so that other subs could get time off. In January 2018 they decided that on the basis of race and age, I had to go. It would be OK if they had replaced me. But they didn't. They saved my salary, which was higher than other subs. I understand black economic empowerment and Africanisation but then they must replace me. Training is crucial, and now it's not done at all. I've been thinking about why I was let go at* Daily Sun *after four years, and I don't think age had anything to do with it, because they knew from the beginning that I wasn't 21, and that didn't seem to bother them. In fact, they were very happy with my years of experience.*

However, they had been ridding themselves of whites for about a year and a half, maybe two, before I got the chop. First to go was the publisher, then guys in sport, then we were warned that the white subs were surplus to requirements. They were quite clear on that. I had regularly turned down the offer of a contract because it would bind me, so I was easy to get rid of. If it was my whiteness, that's OK, but it would have been useful to have been replaced. Now nobody's doing training. The news desk hasn't the time or the inclination, the subs are overworked, and I have no idea who's proofreading. Anyway, they're saving money.

There is one white sub who has survived so far – young and inexpensive – and two white rewriters, one as a three-day-a-week freelancer. In the paper's hierarchy, there are two or three heads of department who are white males and they have survived. I suppose, although our experiences across the globe are pretty similar, maybe the racial aspect is a special South African sidebar.

How did you feel about that?
I am devastated. I love newsrooms – open plan where the ideas flow. I don't like silos. I spent my life, 50 years, in newsrooms.

Relief or sadness?
No relief at all. I miss all of that. The people around me, the better ideas, seeing people grow, especially someone whose first language is not English. Now I watch to see what they are producing. I was a mentor from 1976 when I came to South Africa from the US. I won best feature of the month within one month of being here, and from then on copy got sent to me. I'm not ambitious. I was good at being number two.

Thoughts/reflections on journalism today?
It seems like the reader does not want to know anything. My impression is that journalists are not being trained. On radio you get a long sentence and the verb at the end. No one is teaching them how to write for radio.

I'm in love with print and can't stand electronics. However, I have had to learn to write for electronics; 75 per cent of News24 is digital. Daily Sun is print and it's cheap. The point of communication is to communicate. They are not communicating. Soon people won't know anything. Journalism can be saved if people are taught how to write properly, whether it's digital or print. And they are not being taught.

Yunus Kemp, former editor at Independent Media, now director at HWB Communications; interviewed on 12 July 2018

I left Independent Media at the end of April 2018. I landed another job and started in May 2018.

How did you feel about that?
It was bittersweet leaving Independent after working there for around 18 years collectively. The first few weeks of the new job, as expected, was an adjustment and I initially questioned my decision to leave Independent. PR presents a different challenge. Content pipeline is different and because you work for clients the focus for each is obviously tailor-made to whatever message/story projection they want to have distributed to media. It's been an interesting learning curve. PR, like most other industries, has its own coded language which has been at times amusing to engage with.

Relief or sadness?
A bit of both. Years of work relationships forged (although many colleagues had left previously, landing another job, retrenchment, retirement), a reputation forged at Independent, growing a newspaper, and the newsroom's skills, made leaving sad, but I knew that this opportunity with my new employers was a chance to learn new skills in a different environment. I also felt relief, because many at Independent fear for their jobs and many are unhappy about the company's (Sekunjalo) running of Independent.

Thoughts/reflections on journalism today?
I fear that corruption – state and in the private sector – will thrive (even more) as there are not enough senior/investigative journalists around. Journalism's ethos and values are being sacrificed at the altar of corporate creep and greed. Newsrooms used to be great learning environments and while pockets of this still exist, it is not unusual to find the 'senior' reporter at a daily publication with only a few years' experience. I think with online (and the speed thereof), journalism schools should teach the

why more than any other aspect. We get the snapshots/headlines, but to a large extent, media engages in soundbites without having a deeper understanding of the issues. I do hope that someday soon, we will have journalism collectives like Mother Jones, which is independently/crowd funded.

CONCLUSIONS

Ambivalence

The most glaring conclusion to draw from these interviews is the ambivalence in everyone's story: relief, but also sadness. In all cases, journalists and editors expressed that they had once loved what they were doing, and then, when the pressure of digital started to occur, the newsroom became a changed environment – for example, juniors became editors, lacking the experience to do the job, as Seamus Reynolds observed. Reynolds had a breakdown, but a year later felt that he was free from the 'negativity' of the newsroom. Others pointed to other opportunities, albeit still in the media, where they were making a difference after the frustrations of being an editor and not having the resources to fulfil one's mandate (Monare), of uncertainty of future fulfilment (Mkhabela), and of feeling rejection because of being white (Ludman).

Over and over again, journalists said they felt both sadness and relief. Robertson initially felt guilt and anxiety, and even though she is earning less now, she is relieved of the burden of 'fighting fires'. Orderson also felt 'depressed' at first, but is relieved be out of a 'toxic' environment. Sepotokele also felt sadness, but was then relieved to end the feeling of 'being suffocated'. Mathews felt 'relief and sadness'. Flanagan was 'angry', but then experienced relief when she realised that she 'never had to walk into that building ever again'. Kemp expressed ambivalence as well, saying it was a 'bittersweet experience' leaving the newsroom. The trauma is apparent in all the stories.

According to journalists who told their stories in the New Beats job losses survey, beat reporters and specialisations have all but disappeared, clear distinctions between reporting and opinion are blurred, the hard 'Chinese wall' between advertorial and editorial is blurred, mentorships are a distant dream, and shift work has become one long, never-ending cycle, with no year-end bonuses, and no farewell parties for long service either.

Loss

As jobs were lost in journalism, diversity, skills and training, mentorships and specialised beats were also lost, and this affected the quality of democracy, especially in the political era of populism, propaganda, disinformation and misinformation.

The words of the journalists highlighted their loss and what they felt about it and the profession they left, or were forced to leave. They also showed that identity was by no means fixed and settled, and that in losing your job, you could easily take on another identity (for example, Reynolds going into business), but there was still attachment to the identity of 'journalist'. There was some evidence of relief, although for Ludman, there was 'no relief at all'. In many cases, the journalists felt subjected in the newsroom to commercial pressures and the new world of social media (for example, Clay pointing to technology leading news). They formed attachments to the identity of being a journalist but had to extract themselves from it, as in Robertson's transition.

Let us return to Butler's theories of power and subjection. In a re-reading of Hegel's *Unhappy Consciousness,* she stated: '… we are given to understand an attachment to subjection is formative of the reflexive structure of subjection itself'.[10] She continued that 'wretchedness, agony and pain are sites or modes of stubbornness, ways of attaching to oneself, negatively articulated modes of reflexivity … because they are given regulatory regimes as the sites available for attachment, and a subject will attach to pain rather than not attach at all'.

As retrenched journalists and editors, as well as those who left because the environment had changed so much, their identities had to float rather than be fixed to one thing. There were emerging re-significations: journalism now floated as an identity, it was one of many signifiers, of many different identities. But there was ambivalence. Foucault theorised that there are two meanings of the word 'subject': 'subject to someone else by control and dependence, and tied to his own identity by a conscience or self-knowledge'.[11] In the case of the job loss tsunami in journalism, we witnessed all of this as power of commercial companies, which did not offer care, empathy or digital training, pressed down upon the newsroom. The journalists who participated in the research showed self-knowledge as they talked about their feelings of pain, trauma, sadness and relief. One said, 'Thank you, this was cathartic, like the exit interview I never had.'

As Foucault theorised in the opening quote to this chapter, power is not only a theoretical question but a part of our experience. I have demonstrated in this chapter how power worked, how it was lost through job loss experiences, but how many managed to exercise an internal power against their loss. They turned their backs against the forces of subjection but also felt that journalism today was not what they had signed up for. The fact checking was gone and ethics was rare too.

The next chapter, on community media and going online, further develops this theme about democracy, diversity and loss of voice, as well as power and loss at the hyper local level. The next chapter also has an underlying base question: what is journalism for, who should it serve, how and why?

5

Going Online When You're Offline: The Case of Community Media

Who we are, and from where we speak.
Paula Moya, 'Who We Are, and from Where We Speak'

More than half of all South Africa's community newspapers have closed, without any mention in the mainstream media or any other form of acknowledgement. It seems like no one knew and no one cared, and it was a case of 'you don't know what you have until it's gone'. The constant closures of community newspapers did not happen in one gigantic tsunami wave, but in incremental choppy ones. The newspapers have been going online but not in a way that advances the interests of communities. The loss of community media speaks directly to the marginalisation of the poor, which is central to decolonial theory.

The Media Development and Diversity Agency (MDDA)defines community media as any media project that is owned and controlled by a community where any financial surplus generated is reinvested in the media project.[1] 'Community' means a geographically founded community or any group of persons or sector of the public having a specific ascertainable common interest. This definition, together with that of the Association of Independent Publishers (AIP) that identifies community media as 'publications that are locally owned in publication and distribution' is used here. Geographically, the newspapers are spread across the country. Most of the community newspapers are published in the big cities – Johannesburg, Pretoria, Durban and Cape Town. The community newspapers in this research do not include knock-and-drops (with more advertising than editorial pages) owned by corporates,[2] and dominated by Caxton, but are the 'real independents' as described by the AIP.

In her seminal work of 1988, *Can the Subaltern Speak?*, the postcolonial theorist Gayatri Spivak asked whether intellectuals and ruling elites were going to continually speak for the subaltern,[3] without acknowledging that knowledge is never completely known or complete. In the same politico-philosophical borrowing, my research examines the demise of print community media and the shift to online from what is left of the sector.

We cannot completely escape our location in power structures (for example, racial hierarchies) and our knowledges, too, are situated. Hence the importance of the decolonial turn, a term we owe to Frantz Fanon and Aimé Césaire that refers to a shift in knowledge production, but is also more than this: it is an attitude that demands responsibility and willingness to take on the injustice of the hierarchies. Globally and nationally, journalism is in a quandary because of commercial, digital and social media pressures, and community media does not have the same high-profile, glossy status as mainstream media; thus it is at the bottom of the hierarchy in terms of visibility and has even fewer resources to sustain itself. This is part of the injustice it suffers. From this decolonial turn perspective, which consists of acknowledging diversities and multiplicities of methods of knowledge, there can never be one universal truth and knowledge that is privileged above all else; that is centred, with everything else – the black, the poor, the women, the transgendered – hanging on to the periphery.

In South Africa there are huge particularisms. Even neighbouring informal settlements such as Khayelitsha and Gugulethu in Cape Town have differences, due to competition over resources.[4]

Decoloniality demands new ways of approaching knowledge, and so, when we apply this gaze to South Africa's community newspaper sector, it becomes an important part of the analysis of power and loss in journalism. For example, more than half the community newspapers were, or are, in indigenous languages. One of coloniality's marking points is the survival of English as a language, and the culture that goes with that endures. And so, coloniality survives colonialism. As modern subjects 'we breathe coloniality all the time and everyday,' Nelson Maldonado-Torres famously observed.[5]

Some of the important characterisations of the decolonial turn, which can be called democracy of a decolonial type, include these points, which have a direct bearing on community media: breaking the racist but also victimhood stereotypes; including decolonial love; giving voice and visibility to the marginalised; *with* not *about* the subaltern; acknowledging diversity as well as local contexts and struggles; recognising that one size does not fit all; and shifting the geography of reason. These seven underpinnings of decolonial thought are pertinent to community media's value, power and loss, in this chapter's discussions.

So here the main question is: What would happen if all community media went online? The assumption is that digitisation and online media enable democracy, and level the playing fields so that all can have access to information. But about 50 per cent of the population does not have access to smartphones. It is well known that the cost of data in South Africa is one of the highest in the world.

GLOBALLY IT MAY BE EVEN WORSE

Internationally, many countries are finding that regional and local publications are dying and this directly affects how the concerns of poor communities, indigenous and first peoples are given voice, or not covered.

In the US, trust in media is at an all-time low, with nearly one-third of Americans agreeing that 'the media is the enemy'. The Poynter's Media Trust Survey 2018 found that trust in local media is considerably higher than for national media.[6] By blending watchdog reporting with community engagement, newsrooms can build on this foundation. But what happens when local media disappears? It appears that our trust in democracy is lost and divisive national politics rules the day. This loss is especially true for local news at grassroots level.

In Australia, the New Beats research has found that 'boots on the ground' coverage, reports by beat reporters covering court cases, rural issues and indigenous people's concerns, is disappearing from media coverage according to Matthew Ricketson, speaking at a seminar at the New Beats symposium in Melbourne, in 2018. In Australia, news about indigenous groups comes for the most part from activists' tweets or from research conducted by academics, rather than from the mainstream media. In November 2018, the philanthropist Judith Neilson pledged a $100-million fund for a new institute for journalism in Sydney, in recognition of the need for fact-based journalism in Australia.[7] Also, in November 2018, Facebook gave £4.5 million to fund 80 local newspaper jobs in the UK. Then, in Canada, the country's federal government introduced a tax package of CA$595 to bolster the country's journalism market.[8] These efforts will all boost local journalism. Meanwhile, the South African community media sector is shrinking quietly, with no plan in action.

In South Africa, the community print media sector has been slashed by more than half since its heyday a decade ago, and the beneficiary of both advertising and community appears to be Facebook. The state pulled out of its plan to roll out set-top boxes in October 2018, further isolating the marginalised, rural and poor from access to information and services they could have received through their televisions. There has been a delay in the migration to digital, and yet if community media do digitise there needs to be more internet spectrum, the lifeblood of the wireless industry. The print sector cannot be separated from broadcast, and one of the ways to provide accessible information to all would be to switch from analogue to digital, given the access a large section of the majority has to television sets, as opposed to smartphones.

The next section focuses on interviews with community media people, asking how they view the demise of community media, what they think the value of their community newspapers were or still are, what they think the reasons are for the demise of the sector, and what if anything could be done. The questions to the interviewees were:

- What would happen if community media went online?
- What changes have you observed in print community media over the past five years?
- As mainstream newspapers decline in circulation and slowly go online, will community media follow suit? How does this affect diversity and democracy, and the function that community is meant to play in society, providing citizen information?
- Sustainability issues have always been present in this sector. Does it get worse now with the rise of technology?
- The model for community media in South Africa seems to be outdated and ineffective – what are your ideas to make things better for the sector?

THEMBI MOYO, EDITOR OF THE *INNER CITY GAZETTE*

This nine-year-old Johannesburg weekly paper is distributed free, and services Bellevue, Berea, Bertrams, Braamfontein, Johannesburg Inner City, Crown Gardens, Doornfontein, Fairview, Fordsburg, Hillbrow, Jeppestown,

Jules, Kensington, Lorentzville, Malvern, Marshalltown, New Doornfontein, Newtown, Park Meadows, Rosettenville, Selby, Troyeville, Turffontein, Village Main and Yeoville.

Thembi Moyo was co-editor with her husband, Moses Moyo, until he died suddenly in October 2018. She then assumed the full editorship with the help of her university student daughter and, in an interview on 11 December 2018, she revealed that she would go online in 2019 'because it's not the eighties after all', although she would attempt to keep the hard copies going. *Inner City Gazette*, which has a circulation of 5 000 copies a week, was already giving its news away for free on Facebook, however. 'We can't pay journalists and we often use interns from Damelin.' Most of the news comes from the City of Johannesburg and provides a service – accommodation adverts and jobs.

The positive aspects of going online, for Moyo, include that 'it boosts the overall image of the publication; it caters for an online audience'. She elaborates that it would mean broader reach to followers outside their immediate circulation channels and would provide interactive feedback with followers in real time ('we are able to talk to users instantly'). It would give advertisers an added advantage in gaining an online presence, would enable community activities or problems to be within easy reach of policy makers, and would bridge the gap between community members and local government.

There were, however, serious problems with going online, Moyo reflected. 'We would also lose some readers at some point, as people don't have data and it's expensive.' Even though these readers would still have access to the hard copy, they would miss out on the interaction in real time, and any robust discussion about any local government plan, for example.

Moyo, addressing some of the other challenges she foresaw for 2019, said the publication needed funds to run the online department, and at present (in 2018) the newspaper made no profit. Staff training was required to facilitate adaptation to digital. There was also a need to redefine clients to generate more traffic, with targeting a crucial element in developing Google analytical profiles. 'Gaining more clicks and likes is a challenge for a community publication as we cater for a smaller, defined audience rather than bigger, funded media sources which provide investigative journalism compared to our reliance on press releases, conferences and speculation,' Moyo said.

Data costs also made it difficult for the readers of *Inner City Gazette* to become regulars on its platforms, thus inhibiting online traffic; and advertising, due to traffic demands for generation revenue through Google AdSense and pay per click, made it difficult to realise revenue on the website. 'Free advertising platforms pose an even greater threat to advertising revenue – OLX even advertised on eTV for a long period to gain traffic to its website, thus making it difficult to realise revenue from newspaper classifieds online,' said Moyo. Online consumers also wanted frequent news updates, and weekly community newspapers could not compete. 'We need more journalists on the ground.'

Online media has its advantages, however, and community newspapers should be facilitated to realise its full benefits in the long run. 'We need staff to adapt to digital migration – training, funding, technology advancements and support from sympathetic organisations, to take advantage of all online platform opportunities,' said Moyo.

CHRIS LOUW, CAXTON DIGITAL EDITOR

Many community newspapers have already gone online, usually in the form of Facebook pages, Twitter accounts or WhatsApp distribution groups, according to Louw, who felt that a campaign should be started, urgently, to tax the behemoth, Facebook.

'The barriers to entry are extremely high, however. Many community organisations do not have the funds, the resources and most importantly the knowledge of how to run a fully integrated online business. From a hard cost perspective, equipment is a big issue,' he said.

Connectivity and access to information, and particularly access to information in areas that are not metropolitan, were still a huge concern, and this was inevitably why smaller community organisations would always struggle to be digital, he said. 'Because of lack of access to internet spectrum, cost of data is an inhibiting factor. Younger black people are looking to the internet to find information, but they struggle to find information that speaks to their community.'

There had been huge changes in the community media industry. 'There is a lot of consolidation in the print market and a loss of titles – for example, *The Louvelder,* one of our flagship products in the Caxton stable, and many others, like *White River Post, Hazy View Herald* and *Nelspruit Post*, which are struggling in the smaller communities. There is a long-term vision to consolidate these titles, so you see fewer titles.'

These events at Caxton, the biggest printing, distribution and publishing company in the country, have led to a growing disparity between large and small community organisations. It meant there were fewer voices in the community media space, and that Facebook was becoming more important in that space than many titles. 'Often, the most important community matters are being discussed on Facebook. This is great in one sense – community members have a voice that is heard by a wider audience, but at the same time it's given rise to misinformation and subsequent false beliefs.'

Within Caxton, there were about 150 community newspapers, and the Association of Independent Publishers (AIP) had about 200 members, said Louw. 'Many titles have closed. Since the economic recession in 2008, printing newspapers has become increasingly expensive. At the last MDDA conference, many smaller community organisations had to use the larger organisations to print their newspapers. This often results in huge sums of money in printing costs alone, never mind to pay staff – and for offices,' he said.

'The market is under serious pressure from an advertising perspective. It's very hard to attract small local advertisers. There isn't a strategic approach on a local level and this has resulted in Facebook adverts. Remember cars being advertised in hard copy, classified advertising? All gone to Facebook. There is a lack of control and oversight, and this revenue is leaving the market never to be seen again. For a small title based in the Eastern Cape, that money has gone and often the publisher doesn't even know where. Added to this, what a lot of small organisations do is run to Facebook on behalf of their businesses. So, Facebook is taking that money again.'

That the diversity of voice is in decline and has been for some time is due to many factors such as the consolidation of printed media and the lack of funding for community media from the private and government sectors.

Information about communities is making its way to Facebook and this inevitably excludes most people in rural areas. There is a real danger that mainstream narratives will become the norm around the country, rather than smaller narratives. Municipal office bearers, for example, are not held accountable to the degree they used to be. The reason is that community media is very thinly spread. As Louw said, 'We rely on press releases being sent to us. Everything starts at local level and if public officials could be held accountable at this level, then they would never get to national and high-ranking level. National/mainstream media have neglected community media and local issues. Without community media, the job of mainstream is a lot harder.'

Worsened by the recession, already strained community organisations must now conjure up money from other sources. 'I've heard stories where guys have pawned their cars to get a newspaper out on the street, and this was happening well before the recession,' said Louise Vale, the chief executive of AIP, in an interview in 2018. 'The unfortunate reality is that in many cases no one will even know when these community titles close. There will be no fanfare, no press release. They will just disappear.' Vale also said that although the government should make a concerted effort to assist community media, financially and by providing training, equipment, internet access and resources, there was also an onus on the private sector to spend money on issues that would make a real impact on society – and that included enabling community media.

Both Vale and Louw spoke of community media playing a core role in South Africa's democracy in that it could hold office bearers to account at much lower levels than the mainstream media, which meant that corruption and irregular expenditure is exposed sooner than at a national level where the impact is far bigger.

They also felt that the MDDA should standardise compliance application forms, making them simpler, and should appoint someone to train community media staff to fill in these forms. 'Training is happening for this, but we are not getting close to doing what we should be doing, taxing Google and Facebook,' according to Louw. He felt that one of the critical ways of helping community media survive would be to 'tax the big companies who are gobbling up the market share of advertising'.

In the interview below, the community media expert Louise Vale expressed the irony of going online, and outlined the struggle of the sector, the progressive role it played in local communities (for example, its anti-xenophobia stories) and how the sector has been decimated.

LOUISE VALE, ASSOCIATION OF INDEPENDENT PUBLISHERS

About a decade ago, the AIP's membership for community newspapers was 575. It is now down to about 200. There were once about 4 000 jobs in the sector and today the number is less than half. 'The sector never recovered from the economic downturn in 2008,' explained Louise Vale. 'We had a nice time in 2006 as the economy was OK. Black-owned newspapers started. There was a lot of excitement. But all this has changed a great deal. If you are an SME [small or medium enterprise] you are the first to be hit in an economic recession. They are so much on the borderline, anyway. We are seeing community papers closing, 50 per cent of those in the Eastern Cape closed. Some of them were 150 years old, not black owned only but also white owned. Two of the oldest newspapers were the *Craddock Koerant* and the *Somerset Budget*. One was 124 years ... all gone. They were run by a family the Van der Walt family ....'

Vale then recounted that Anton van Zyl, the owner of two papers in Louis Trichardt, told her that 2018 had been the worst year ever for advertising. 'He said he couldn't actually believe it ... in the economic downturn, there is a complete lack of the implementation the government has been talking about in terms of funding support, and it gets lower and lower every single year. He said the few millions from the MDDA was not enough.' Vale explained that the business model for maintsream was dead. 'The SASSA advertising was inserted in the *Sunday Times* and it should have been in community media.[9] Government is not attempting to assist community radio either,' she said.

'There is a movement to online. All our papers have Facebook websites and there is social media training at AIP. We also teach skills on how to interview on the phone. No one has found a way on how to earn money. Community media is as ignorant of this as mainstream and everyone else,' said Vale. 'But you can't go online if community is offline,' she said. 'We see some making adverts in the local spaza shop, and developing adverts for NGOs [non-governmental organisations] in Xhosa and English. Not everyone has a cellphone which is a smartphone.'

THE STATE OF ICT IN SOUTH AFRICA – A SERIOUS INDICTMENT

Half of the South African population remains offline, according to the latest report (2018) conducted by Research ICT Africa. In addition, the cost of data is a significant problem and the lack of internet-enabled devices and digital literacy remain the key challenges to accessing the internet. Despite greater access to smartphones, including in rural areas, there remains a significant digital divide. Highlights from the Research ICT Africa study included that although South Africa has far more internet users than other African countries, 47 per cent of the population does not use the internet. Data prices remain unaffordable to the majority, and despite numerous public hearings on the cost of data, the new regulations announced by the Independent Communications Authority of South Africa (Icasa) do not address this significant problem. The lack of internet-enabled devices and digital literacy, both of which are associated with poverty, are the main barriers to getting online.

Mobile phone penetration among owners of informal and small businesses is very high at 93 per cent, yet few use mobile phones for business purposes, no doubt because of its cost.

Interesting international research published by NiemanLab, a journalist research institute based at Harvard University, claims that shutting down print doesn't drive those readers to print-like consumption habits on digital devices.[10] Instead, they become much like other digital readers – easily distracted, flitting from link to link. The research examined the case of the *Independent*, the national British daily that, in 2016 and after 30 years in print, became online only. What happened to its reach and influence? Not much, it seems. Joshua Benton, who wrote the article on the research explained that the study compared the number of the total audience of each national newspaper, in the periods before and a year after the *Independent*'s end of print. Benton wrote that 'if you're a half-glass-full type, the good news is that *The Independent*'s total audience was basically flat, despite killing off print. The number of print readers it lost and the number of digital readers it gained basically cancel one another out.'[11]

But, what of South Africa?

SOUTH AFRICA'S NATIONAL VERSUS LOCAL VOICES

There are a few key words and phrases to explain the rationale for the existence of community or local newspapers that are free of charge: voice to the voiceless; servicing rural, poor and marginalised communities; supporting diversity; and, most importantly, providing information to publics so that they can make informed decisions about their lives and their futures.

Does the community media print sector do all this? Is it able to, given its meagre resources? What is the content of its local voices compared with that of its national voices? Has this improved from five years ago, as recorded in *State of the Newsroom, South Africa, 2013: Disruptions and Transitions*? I am unable here to comprehensively explore every aspect of the community newspaper sector in South Africa, but will pick a few important slices to examine. First, in broad terms, I list the challenges, then scrutinise the sector's contribution to diversity, for instance, by looking at the diversity of voices in stories and quantifying them. Are they local (citizen voices emanating from the community) rather than national voices? Are the newspapers mere imitations of the mainstream papers or are they firmly rooted in their communities? I consider gender diversity, as well as citizen participation (but not race, as all the newspapers chosen were black owned and edited).

For my research, I attempted to find 30 print community newspapers, but they could not be found easily in hard copy. Two postgraduate researchers, Fiona Chawana and Mbuyisi Mgibisa, helped me find them online, as they appeared not to exist in print any longer. An August 2018 assessment showed that local newspapers still have their place in South Africa as a resource for communities to be informed of news and affairs that affect them directly (table 5.1).

Table 5.1: Record of news stories appearing on the first two to three pages of community newspapers, August 2018

Publication	Stories	Date
Zululand Observer	City of uMhlathuze Mayor outlines development progress	24 August 2018
	Protesters block entry into Mkhuze	20 August 2018
Chatsworth Tabloid	23 injured in multi-vehicle collision	1 August 2018
	Chatsworth great-great gran turns 100	1 August 2018
Grocott's Mail	The Wife, with Glenn Close, opens in cinemas this weekend	23 August 2018
	Karate women promote confidence	31 August 2018
Alex News	Father and daughter get reunited	28 August 2018
	Joburg eHealth system reaches half a million patients	29 August 2018
Excelsior News	Service delivery is our priority	31 August 2018
	Public meeting on land expropriation without compensation	31 August 2018
Pinetown and Hammersdale Izindaba Online	Baphume besuthi yizeluleko kowembokodo Bagqugquzelwe ukuthanda izibalo abafundi	21 August 2018
	Kwenzenjani? Bafuna kwehle intengo kaphethiloli abakukeli	10 August 2018
Cosmo City Chronicle	Boys and Girls Youth Africa embraces National Science Week	23 August 2018
	Power shortages spark anger among Cosmo City residents	
Cosmo City Chronicle	Local authorities vow to permanently end Cosmo City's sewage crisis	14 August 2018
	Women's day in Cosmo	
Durban North News	Women expedition for conservation	1 August 2018
	Board workers embark on a strike	
	Tee off for a good cause	15 August 2018
	Two killed in R102 carnage	

Continued

Publication	Stories	Date
Umlazi Times Online	Ubashiwe obanjwe eshushumbisa insangu	30 August 2018
	Balwa nokuhlu kunyezwa kwabesifazane	
	Baqwashiwe ngobungozi bokusebenzisa izidakamizwa	9 August 2018
	Babambe imashi elwa nokuhlukunyezwa	
Southern Star Online	Police women lead the way	14 August 2018
	Youth has a blast at Folweni SAPS	
	Silvergul Drive residents feel powerless against illegal connections	21 August 2018
	Off-duty Bluff cop shoots armed robber	

Source: Author

At 77 per cent, local voices were in the majority (table 5.2). A local voice is one that is embedded in that community and it emanates from that community – from the butcher, for example, or the community worker, or the unemployed. A voice that is not local would be that of a national politician.

Table 5.2: Local voices in community newspapers, 2018

Publication	Local voices	Non-local voices
Chatsworth Tabloid	3	0
Excelsior News	1	1
Grocott's Mail	1	2
Zululand Observer	3	0
Alex News	3	0
Pinetown and Hammersdale Izindaba Online	4	5
Cosmo City Chronicle	6	5
Southern Star	11	0
Durban North News	5	1
Umlazi Times	10	0
Total	**47**	**14**
Percentages	**77.05**	**22.95**

Source: Author

As for diversity of gender, the voices of men were in the majority, in approximately the ratio of 56 per cent to 44 per cent (table 5.3).

Table 5.3: Voices in community newspapers, by gender, 2018

Publication	Female	Male
Chatsworth Tabloid	1	2
Excelsior News	0	2
Grocott's Mail	2	1
Zululand Observer	1	2
Alex News	0	3
Pinetown and Hammersdale Izindaba Online	5	4
Cosmo City Chronicle	6	5
Southern Star	4	7
Durban North News	3	3
Umlazi Times	5	5
Total	**27**	**34**
Percentages	**44.26**	**55.74**

Source: Author

Criticisms of community media are that they are often press releases replicated, with national voices dominating. I found this not to be the case, which attests to the community media space as an important one which could hold the key to the transformation of media.

The 2013 *Report on Transformation of Print and Digital Media* noted that community and small commercial publishers are key to the transformation of the print and digital media space,[12] and made recommendations such as possible partnerships with major commercial media groups, where facilities could be shared and issues of mistrust such as alleged anti-competitive behaviour could be dealt with. (The report did, however, explicitly state that its focus was not community media but transformation of the mainstream media from the Big Four conglomerates.)

But community media was a 'hand-to-mouth', or precarious existence, even in its heyday. Vale, at one of the AIP's biggest conferences to date, held in September 2013 in Kempton Park, said then that the sector generated an annual profit in the region of R250 to R350 million, and was responsible for between 4 000 and 5 000 jobs. Out of more than 250 publications in August 2013, 97 (42.9 per cent) were published in indigenous languages.

It is worth listing some of the challenges in the sector that emerged from the AIP's Kempton Park conference, 'The future starts now: Role of the independent media in the current South African context'. Panellists and members from the floor raised the following points, in summary:

- The sector urgently needs expert knowledge about financial models for economic sustainability. Skills are lacking in financial management, technical systems, management and adequate knowledge about distribution systems.
- Rampant poaching of journalists by mainstream media is taking place and hampering progress.
- Language issues abound in that mother tongue or indigenous languages are insufficiently utilised, whereas indigenous languages should be developed to capture the nuances of issues in the contemporary world.
- Barriers to enter the sector include competition from the mainstream media.
- Competition by big companies persists, particularly regarding the monopoly of distribution networks, routes and advertising market share, putting community media at a disadvantage.
- The sector needs more funding from the MDDA, and partnerships with the mainstream commercial print companies.
- Community media needs stronger support from advertisers, both commercial and government, at different levels of local, provincial and national advertising.
- Community media needs to be able to access cost-effective, original, relevant content and images, training in design skills, and ongoing journalism training. The sector also needs access to up-to-date market research and access to lucrative urban markets.

FIVE YEARS AGO

In 2013, the *State of the Newsroom: Disruptions and Transitions* report included a study of 14 community newspapers, but at that time there were all in hard copy. The 14 were purposively selected, chosen to represent a cross-section of geographical areas and languages. The research was conducted by deploying the content analysis method using a coding technique. Three researchers conducted a content analysis of two copies each of the 14 different titles (equalling 28 editions), with an average of about five news stories per edition, producing a total sample size of about 140 stories.

The research project took place during the month of August, coinciding with 'women's month', when awareness about gender issues, including violence against women, is traditionally highlighted in South Africa. The main areas of research into diversity included local versus national voices in stories; local issues versus national issues; and gender and race representation.

The newspapers selected cut across several languages and regions, for example, besides English, the sample contained stories in other official languages: Tshivenda, Afrikaans, isiXhosa and isiZulu and regions covered included Gauteng, KwaZulu-Natal, Eastern Cape, Limpopo, Western Cape and Northern Cape. The newspapers were small and independent. Some were given away for free and some were sold for a small cover price, but the most important determinant was they were not linked to the big conglomerates in ownership or distribution networks. The majority were published every two weeks, but some published once a month and some weekly.

The list of the newspapers, the language in which they publish, geographic location, and publishing frequency, is:

Zithethele: isiXhosa and English, Port Elizabeth, Eastern Cape. Published fortnightly.

Grocott's Mail: English, Grahamstown (Makhanda), Eastern Cape. Published weekly.

Inner City Gazette: English, Johannesburg. Published fortnightly.

Alex Pioneer: English, Alexandra, Johannesburg. Published fortnightly.

Kwela Xpress: English, Braamfontein, Johannesburg. Published fortnightly.

Galaxy: English, Pietermaritzburg, KwaZulu-Natal. Published monthly.

Skawara News: isiXhosa, Cofimvaba, Eastern Cape. Published fortnightly.

Muslim Views: English, Athlone, Cape Town. Published monthly.

KZN Community Newspaper: isiZulu/some English, Durban. Published fortnightly.

Ngoho News: Tshivenda, Thohoyandou, Limpopo. Published fortnightly.

Intuthukoyase Mbumbulu: isiZulu, Durban. Published fortnightly.

Ikamva Lase Gcuwa: isiXhosa and English, Butterworth, Eastern Cape. Published monthly.

Die Horison: Predominantly Afrikaans, Siyanda, Northern Cape. Published monthly.

Cosmo City Chronicle: English, Johannesburg. Published fortnightly.

Local voices and local content

Local voices quoted directly and indirectly in the newspapers' stories were categorised as all those that were not official, not those of authorities such as police or municipalities or political parties, nationally prominent and well-known individuals and celebrity voices. In this way, the aim was to establish what kind of channel for expression a local community in South Africa has and, thus, what measure of diversity community papers bring to media in this country. 'Voices' that appeared in the stories were 'counted' to make findings about the origin of stories.

The study used a coding structure and took 'local' to mean all those voices of people from within the community the newspaper serviced. For instance, *Galaxy* services South African Indians in Allandale, Northdale, Bombay Heights, Orient Heights, and Raisethorpe in Pietermaritzburg, KwaZulu-Natal. We understood local voices to mean people who are a part of the community – a shop-owner, housewife, hairdresser, street sweeper, community worker, a child at a local school and a church volunteer involved in feeding schemes – and who did not represent the authorities. Therefore, if, for example, a police officer or a mayor from Allandale was quoted in a news story, their voices were not counted as 'local'.

We defined 'local content' for the purposes of this research to simply mean all the content that appeared in the newspaper which originated from the community the newspaper served. For example, if the content came from a press release from the South African Press Association (Sapa) press agency, or from the Congress of South African Trade Unions (Cosatu), or from the national office of political parties, or if it was a story lifted from a commercial 'mainstream' newspaper, it was not regarded as local content.

The count of local voices versus non-local voices across the 14 newspapers is shown in table 5.4.

Table 5.4:   Local voices in community newspapers, 2013

Publication	Local voices	Non-local voices
Grocott's Mail	73	9
Inner City Gazette	15	25
Galaxy	9	9
Skawara News	19	1
Ikamva Lase Gcuwa	20	13
Cosmo City Chronicle	2	11

Publication	Local voices	Non-local voices
Muslim Views	15	23
KZN Community Newspaper	3	11
Die Horison	7	8
Ngoho News	13	3
Intuthukoyase Mbumbulu	8	12
Alex Pioneer	36	1
Zithethele	29	3
Kwela Xpress	17	42
Total	**266**	**171**
Percentages	**61**	**39**

Source: Author

The majority of voices, at 61 per cent, were local. Even though local newspapers were hitting even harder times, the voices were not replicated via national press releases to fill pages, but by 2018, the local voice component had in fact increased from 61 per cent to 77 per cent.

Citizen participation, difficulties and struggles

All the newspapers selected for this study asserted that citizens participated in generating news, in feeding news to their papers and in giving feedback to editors. Both editors and journalists said that the issues covered in their newspapers were local issues that directly affected their communities. The data analysis showed that in most instances this was the case (but sometimes it was not).

Use of social media by newspaper staff to engage with readers was clearly increasing despite a lack of technology resources. But no research has yet been done on how many were left out of this social media equation as community and local newspapers made slow moves to digital. This is an area for further research.

Most editors and journalists in 2013 cited, as major obstacles in the community media sector, financial constraints; low pay (the doubling up of roles such as publisher, editor and sub-editor, and in some cases distributor too); delivery issues and competition with the powerful commercial press; losing good journalists to the mainstream media; and inadequate resources for basic expenses and equipment like transport and computers.

The representative of *Kwela Xpress* said the paper really struggled with inadequate resources and had to turn away some stories because reporters did not have the money to pay for the transport to get the scene of the story. A spokesperson for the *KZN Community Newspaper* said one of the major challenges was the reluctance of businesses to advertise in the smaller community newspaper, and highlighted lack of resources such as computers, cameras and vehicles for reporters, who had to use public transport to cover stories. *Inner City Gazette* is a paper that gave Johannesburg's inner-city residents information on the big issues in their community, politics and the world. The primary target audiences were the residents and business community. Local black males were quoted in some stories, but female voices made up only a small percentage even though the editions selected for this study were printed during 'women's month'. The representative of *Muslim Views* said he could not employ any more journalists because of financial constraints. He also complained about limited access to corporate and government advertising. 'We generate enough advertising to break even,' he said. 'There are two bumper editions per annum, which make up for the months when revenue falls below the break-even margin.' *Skawara News* also highlighted difficulties with transport as a challenge for reporters. Because many journalists did not own their own vehicles, they had to walk or use taxis to get around. Competing with the major newspapers for government advertising was very difficult and there was a tendency among officials to close all the advertising doors of local government if they were not happy with what the paper was writing about. The spokesperson for *Intuthukoyase Mbumbulu* said there was a downside to getting MDDA funding, which was paid to the newspaper on a quarterly basis, but sometimes delayed. 'The big challenge at times has been printing on time, because funds from the MDDA are sometimes not sustainable ... We have a cordial relationship with local government. Generally, the newspaper has good relations with the office of the premier in KwaZulu-Natal in matters, including getting government advertising spend for the newspaper.'

For *Ngoho News*, skills were a major issue. Its spokesperson believed that regular training would improve the standard of journalism in the newsroom and enhance reporters' understanding of their role as community journalists. Some local government officials viewed *Ngoho News* as 'anti-African National Congress ... the government figures think you are against them when you ask questions, and at times you get taken off the emailing list and do not get invited to some events. But we are journalists. The good thing is that there is no interference with us doing our duties, and this does not lead to us being intimidated in our editorial content.'

The editor of *Ikamva Lase Gcuwa* said intimidation of journalists by authority figures was a problem, with one of the paper's reporters being threatened by a police station commander after an article about the poor treatment of persons filing reports at the station. 'But we were merely doing our job,' he said. 'That particular case has died down, but it's one of many when we have to deal with government figures, who think that we are against them when we ask critical questions concerning people's grievances.' A reporter noted the challenges of being a female journalist. She had tried to cover a meeting about the high rate of initiate deaths.[13] 'Because I'm a female, and this is a male traditional issue, I was asked to excuse myself and not be present when the matter was being discussed at the gathering. There are other situations where some male figures, for instance, local chiefs, may not respect you or want to discuss certain issues with you simply because you are female.'

This chapter has highlighted the digital divide in urban areas, where some of the local newspapers are located. In rural areas, it is even more pronounced. The shift to digital appears to mean that readers of print get cut off from information about their local community. This is the conundrum for community publications, as government drags its feet on its own commitments to providing broadband across all communities, especially for the urban poor and rural communities.

CONCLUSIONS: DEATH AND LOSS FROM THE DARK SIDE OF MODERNITY

Modernity insists that media goes online but this comes with a dark side – the newspapers are going online, but not in the way one would imagine, with improved access and democracy for all. By going online, they are not necessarily providing more access to information for more people but are enhancing the profits of big companies (Facebook is not paying for advertising that comes from the *Inner City Gazette*). The local communities are gathering on Facebook pages, but those who cannot afford data are unlikely to access and engage in their discussions. They are left behind. Those who are getting their local news on Facebook are also likely to wonder if the news is true or false, given the social media's propensity for gossip and rumour, and users have to wade through junk before they find the facts. The poorest of the poor are marginalised even further because of high data costs.

Some key trends and changes between 2013 and 2018 include that in 2013 community newspapers were readily available, so the data was easily collected, collated and assessed. By 2018, doing a sizeable assessment meant finding online versions of the community newspapers. Modernity insists that we go online. Yet without broadband and internet spectrum, compounded by sky-high data costs, poor communities are further marginalised. Community newspapers were 'going online' – most gravitating to Facebook where the adverts were going as well – even though the communities were mainly offline.

Most voices and content in community newspapers were, and remain, local. In 2013, the figure was over 60 per cent and in 2018 it was over 70 per cent. Community newspapers were making a significant contribution to diversity of South African news coverage in terms of content, plurality of voices and serving their communities' interests.

In the month of the research, August, 'women's month', women's voices were in the minority. One must then question how much of a loss community media is to women specifically. There was decolonial love in community media, giving voice and visibility to the marginalised, but black women were not at the centre – the sector was dominated by black men. The loss is huge for communities, of which women are part. The loss vis-à-vis democracy of a decolonial type (referred to at the beginning of this chapter) is also clear. Those points included breaking the racist but also the victimhood stereotypes, which communities were doing for themselves via providing local news to local people.

In this chapter I have acknowledged the decolonial theoretical point about diversity as well as local contexts and struggles, showing and recognising that one size does not fit all. There are calls in South Africa for the international giants, Facebook and Google, to be taxed and regulated, so that the commercial and the community sectors can survive, but this is not yet a coordinated campaign that has gained much traction. Internationally, such calls are more strident, while the two massive companies are hiding under the guise of being 'tech companies', and not media companies.

In the meantime, some of the important contributions that community media makes to democracy can get lost. For example, local communities are thought of as deeply xenophobic and yet a cursory examination of the news stories covered during the sporadic xenophobic attacks points to the opposite. The fact is that most voices were local, as seen in both quantitative studies, 2013 and 2018, showing that voice was given to the marginalised, with the exception of women. Decolonial love for women is at the heart of decolonial theory, which is the story of the next chapter: the anti-feminist backlash and the glass ceiling for women in the newsroom and media.

6

The Anti-Feminist Backlash, the Glass Ceiling and Online Trolls

The anti-feminism backlash has been set off not by women's achievement of full equality but by the increased possibility that they might win it.

Susan Faludi, *Backlash*

Women in the media are experiencing a harsh anti-feminist backlash via social media, (but they have also brainstormed strategies to fight back).[1] The example of the backlash shows how women in the media in South Africa veer between power and loss.

The anti-feminist backlash in South Africa is in line with international trends, if one considers the Troll Patrol,[2] a study released in January 2019 which monitored the abuse of women online. Amnesty International and Elemental AI analysed 300 000 tweets aimed at women politicians and journalists – labelling abuse targeting gender, race and sexuality – to find that approximately 1.1 million abusive tweets were sent to women politicians and journalists, or one every 30 seconds on average. The list comprised all female members of Parliament in the UK, female members of Congress in the US, and a selection of journalists working across a range of titles in a broad political spectrum. 'Troll Patrol means we have the data to back up what women have long been telling us, that Twitter is a place where racism, misogyny and homophobia are allowed to flourish basically unchecked,' remarked Milena Marin, senior advisor for tactical research at Amnesty International. The study found that black women were the most targeted, and were found to be 84 per cent more likely than white women to be mentioned in abusive or problematic tweets.

In South Africa, one of the most significant findings in the report of the largest research project to date on this topic, *Glass Ceilings: Women in South African Media Houses 2018*,[3] was that trolling journalists, or online abuse using Twitter, was on the increase, and the biggest sufferers were women journalists. There were other backlashes: the number of women media leaders such as editors is declining, as documented in *State of the Newsroom South Africa: Disruptions Accelerated 2014*.[4] This was once one area in which women, in particular black women, had made progress since democracy. However, in 2018–2019, as owners, board members and as editors, women were in the minority, and black women the smallest minority. Even though in numbers female employees outstrip their male counterparts (55 per cent to 45 per cent) they are mostly in the lower rungs of media houses, as a *Mail & Guardian* data desk study found in January 2019.[5]

Of the top 100 companies in the world, women in top management comprise 17 per cent according to the World Association of Newspapers and News Publishers (WAN-IFRA) Women in the News (WIN) conference, which took place in South Africa in 2018. The WIN conference also revealed that only 25 per cent of women featured in news content (internationally and including South Africa, as seen in various studies by Media Monitoring Africa), a number that hasn't changed in more than 20 years.

It is against this background that Gender Links and the South African National Editors' Forum (Sanef), in partnership with the Media Development and Diversity Agency (MDDA), which sponsored the research, undertook the Glass Ceilings 2018 research project. The research took nearly a year and consisted of an online survey, interviews and analysis. Before a discussion of the results and an analysis in terms of the anti-feminist backlash, it is valuable to ask why we need women in the newsroom, and in media leadership. Why is diversity important, and what does decolonial theory say about women's place in the world at large?

Women's voices deepen democracy, adding the diversity needed for inclusivity and plurality and, as Julie Reid wrote: 'The value of a diverse spectrum of media, particularly news media content, is widely recognised as integral and at times regarded as synonymous with a well-functioning democracy in which an informed citizenry is actively able to participate.'[6] Otherwise, it is the same old elites talking the same language to each other, with male and liberal white narratives dominating. And, as Michele Weldon, assistant professor emerita of

Medill and director of Medill Public Thought Leaders also observed, 'If you have a newsroom that's predominantly male, then the story ideas, source choices and way a story is presented will reflect that point of view. When that happens, you get a skewed view of the world and that's not what the world is like.'[7]

WHAT IS A GLASS CEILING, WHAT IS AN ANTI-FEMINIST BACKLASH AND WHY DECOLONIAL THEORY?

A glass ceiling is an invisible but real barrier to the advancement of women in the workplace, where they can be blocked by sexism, sexist practices, sexual harassment, pregnancy, patriarchal views and prejudices, in hiring and promotions as well as salary disparities with men, according to the International Women's Media Foundation.[8] There can also be gains for women when they break through the glass ceiling, and then a 'backlash' against this triumph. The research in this chapter points to exactly this: struggling to break through, sometimes breaking through, and then the backlash – hence the experience of power and loss.

The feminist theorist Susan Faludi described a backlash as a historical trend, generally recurring when it appears that women have made substantial gains in their efforts to obtain equal rights.[9] It is a counter-assault to halt or reverse the hard-won gains. The British cultural theorist and feminist, Angela McRobbie, explained the Faludi backlash as a 'concerted, conservative response to the achievements of feminism'.[10] In an interview on eNCA, 8 September 2017, Amanda Gouws, professor of political science and gender researcher at Stellenbosch University, argued that women have been experiencing a backlash in all three continents of the global South in the last three years because of neoliberal capitalism – the overarching global political framework which has not created justice and equality for those on the margins of mainstream politics and economics. This is how decolonial theory fits in here.

At the heart of decolonial theory is the love for women. Nelson Maldonado-Torres wrote in 'On the Coloniality of Being' that colonialism posits its targets as racialised and sexualised subjects which become mere bodies, part of the economy of sexual abuse and control.[11] Maldonado-Torres pointed out that Walter Mignolo, a key decolonial thinker, was one of the strategic actors in decolonial turn theorising – as an unfinished project which continues to unfold. Women, I argue in this chapter, are at the centre of this unfinished project. Maldonado-Torres also acknowledged that the more substantial decolonial turn emanated from W.E.B. Du Bois in the early twentieth century, and Aimé Césaire and Frantz Fanon in the mid-century, to Sylvia Wynter, Enrique Dussel, Gloria Anzaldúa, Lewis Gordon, Chela Sandoval and Linda Tuhiwai Smith, among others, throughout the second half of the twentieth to the beginning of the twenty-first century. These thinkers, along with black consciousness ideology in South Africa, are gaining traction among the youth, marginalised, unemployed people and women because of the unfinished democratic project.

Decolonial love, which is anti-war and would therefore also be anti-rape, abuse (physical and emotional) and online trolling, is not romantic love but 'invented love, love as a political technology', as Sandoval expressed.[12] She reflected that 'it is a body of knowledges, arts, practices and procedures for re-forming the self and the world.' Decolonial love is political struggle against structures of dehumanisation and self-hate. Black women suffer the most, and as Maldonado-Torres theorised, black women are at the centre of the unfinished project of decolonisation as the *damnés*, or the wretched or condemned of the earth.

Women journalists are not the invisible needing to be made visible. Indeed, they are visible and the hegemonic structures of power seem not to like this. Women in media are not the poorest and the most marginalised in the world that Maldonado-Torres is speaking about in 'On the Coloniality of Being' – but there is an overlap: 'The black woman is seen as a highly erotic being whose primary function is fulfilling sexual desire and reproduction.'[13] The abuse online is often of a sexual nature, as in trolling, and cyber misogyny. The attempt is to silence women journalists for speaking out about corruption, patriarchy and sexism, as well as simply exercising their freedom of expression. For this, they are pushed back upon, and they experience emotional violence on social media, particularly Twitter.

The Glass Ceilings 2018 research showed that there was a severe backlash against women working in media in South Africa as revealed in patriarchal attitudes and bullying, sexist jokes, lack of promotions, the old boys' networks where decisions are often made, an increased salary gap between women and men, 'paying the family penalty' (having children) and the latest trend of trolling and bullying women in newsrooms and the media at large. However, there were some changes since the Glass Ceilings research from a decade ago – for example, the numbers of women and men in the newsroom, equalled out for the first time in 2018 (although at the top rungs of power males still dominate). Also, for the first time, there was a percentage of people who identified themselves as gender non-conforming, and there is a chapter on cyber misogyny in the 2018 study.

In the countrywide research, 203 journalists/editors filled out the perceptions survey; 41 companies collaborated with human resources information in the institutional survey and 18 more on perception questionnaires, providing data for over 10 054 staff, while 10 senior women journalists told their stories about their particular experiences of sexism in the newsroom in the book: *Glass Ceilings: Women in South African Media Houses, 2018.*

The findings show that the challenge today is not about the numbers game, but about sexism, which is alive and well, and taking ugly forms in the digital era. Although there have been dramatic shifts in the race and gender composition of the media since the first Glass Ceilings study, more than a decade ago, black women are still not fairly represented in media decision making; the pay gap is widening, especially in the age of digitisation.

The zeitgeist of the time is the #MeToo and #TotalShutDown era, where the conversation is moving to the underlying patriarchal norms that fuel sexist attitudes, harassment and its newest ugly form – cyber misogyny. The key messages are #TimeisUp for the South African media, and #TimeisNow to walk the talk of gender equality.

Black men now comprise half of top media managers. The proportion of black women in top media management has increased five-fold but is still 20 percentage points lower than that of black men – but black women, 46 per cent of the population, constitute 40 per cent of senior managers in the media, suggesting that change is on the way. The findings come at a turbulent time, with new media forms sweeping across the landscape, and South Africa fits the global media pattern of traumatic job losses, messy digitisation processes, a huge downturn in advertising revenue and a decline in sales and circulation.

While only 3 out of the 59 media houses that participated in the study gave data on wages, general perceptions suggest a growing gender wage gap, compounded by there being fewer women in senior and top management positions, and a growing throng of junior women cadets running the social media platforms of media houses. Many women in the survey said, 'We know we earn less than men with the same experience.'

A new threat is cyber misogyny (which includes some of the ugliest forms of sexism) to try and silence media women. But the media is also operating in a climate of the #MeToo movement globally and the #TotalShutDown movement nationally, which has seen an increased assertiveness from women about sexism and patriarchal domination.

WHAT THE WOMEN SAY: PERCEPTIONS AND COMPARISONS OVER TEN YEARS

Patriarchal systems

The old boys' network was alive and well, with men in senior positions making editorial decisions, including in social circles that exclude women, and often blocking the rise of capable women. Patriarchy, as reflected in society at large, was mirrored in the media, with gender stereotyping, and women being assigned to soft beats. In 2018 there were more women in media houses, but mostly in junior positions.

> *'The inherent patriarchal structure that's practised in society is just replicating itself in media houses.'*
>
> *'The Zuma rape trial alone highlighted, through reactions to what was being carried, the complexity of power relationships between men and women. It highlighted the dominant perception of what women are and their place in society.'*

Sexism

Although there was more awareness of sexist language, jokes, innuendo and sexual harassment in newsrooms, it still existed and was tolerated in 2018, almost as much as it was a decade ago. In 2006, women in the newsroom had said they experienced prejudice and being 'patronised'. Much the same commentary persisted in 2018.

> *'Women are patronised and their opinions do not appear to be taken as seriously as those of men. This can be subtle, like jokes made at their expense when they give their opinions, or teasing. It seems friendly and even affectionate, but it is actually demeaning.'*

Salary disparities

There was more assertiveness in calling out salary disparities between women and men with the same experience. Of 202 respondents, 157, or nearly 80 per cent, said they knew that they were paid less than men with the same experience.

Women more assertive

Women were speaking out more, it appeared, assisted by the #MeToo and the #TotalShutDown movements. As for men, they were more aware of sexism today than they were a decade ago, even though sexist attitudes persisted.

Cyber bullying

Whereas this was not the case ten years ago, women journalists in 2018 were contending with trolling and cyber bullying. There were extra dangers for female journalists who had to tackle not only physical danger but the prevalence of online trolls, and attacks – real and threatened – of a sexual nature.

Gender policies

There was still little clarity on gender policies in newsrooms compared to ten years ago, women with children still paying the 'motherhood penalty',[14] and missing out on good assignments and senior level jobs as a result. The situation had improved slightly at some companies, however, where flexible working arrangements are offered, and paternity leave introduced.

Promotion

As was the case ten years ago, most respondents in 2018 felt that men are still taken more seriously for promotion. Women were also seen to fail in demanding recognition and pushing for promotion. However, in 2018, only 24 per cent of women said that women are their own worst enemies.

Race priorities

Race inequality still trumped gender discrimination as an issue that media houses must deal with, although disability and HIV/Aids were also still on the agenda.

Quotas

In 2018, the issue of quotas was met with mixed feelings, as it had been ten years ago, with opponents still concerned about being a 'quota appointment'. Many respondents favoured quotas to undo historical bias and to create entry for skilled women.

PERCEPTIONS – LITTLE HAS CHANGED

Little has changed the overwhelming perception that women are kept back from top positions in newsrooms, and that men who have achieved high office have sewn up that territory for themselves. Most respondents in all three surveys said that ambitious women are denigrated and blocked, or take themselves out of competition. There are exceptions, however, particularly in broadcast journalism, where there are more women than men in studios and female respondents feel they stand a better chance of rising to decision-making positions.

> 'There are a lot of women at the SABC as reporters, managers and produ-cers. But they rarely fill senior roles, which are mostly occupied by black and white men.'

Remuneration is still low. In ten years, there has been very little movement in equalising salary discrepancies. Women still feel they are unfairly remunerated, and this remains a key issue in 2018. Entry-level salaries in most media houses are not in line with the R17 400 per month suggested by the Department of Labour.

Old boys' networks are alive and well. Every year that the industry has been surveyed, women have called out the 'old boys' network'. In the first survey, in 2006, it was the old white boys' network, but by 2018 in many newsrooms it had been replaced by a new network of black men. For women, however, black or white, the effect was the same – and in 2018, women were still being blocked by the 'old boys' club' which works in subtle ways, embedded in patriarchal culture. As one respondent put it, 'Women are excluded from the informal discussions which precipitate many of the decisions taken by senior editorial management in bars and after-work drinking sessions. Even though women do most of the work in the newsroom, they are overlooked for top positions because the men do far less work and have time for self-promotion and networking, which facilitates their entry into the top tier.'

> 'When we look at South African society and the myriad capable women and statistics indicating the lack of women in management positions, one can conclude that women are under-represented because of the patriarchal system where men remain preferred candidates for leadership positions.'

The situation may have improved when it comes to sexist attitudes. In 2018, respondents agreed by overwhelming margins that sexist language is not tolerated in newsrooms and that the level of sexual harassment is not high (in 2006, men weren't even aware that their attitudes towards women in the newsroom were sexist). In 2018, men were more aware – but often their attitudes remained, and they still didn't know how and when they were being sexist, causing frustration. As an example, here is the 2018 evaluation of a cadet: 'X is surprisingly reticent for such an attractive young woman.' It went a great deal further in 2006:

> 'I regularly see relatively junior women staffers asked (half-jokingly, maybe?) to get tea, referred to as "girls" and if not exactly sexually harassed, then certainly expected to participate in banter that many might find undermining. Some senior editors still automatically try to date attractive younger female colleagues, but that's thankfully getting rarer.'

> 'I think senior men think they are gender sensitive when in fact they are not. And the fact that they don't know that they don't know is even worse than to argue/debate with those who are outright discriminating.'

> 'There are some men in the work environment who still make sexist remarks disguised as "jokes" which we often just ignore instead of calling out the person.'

In one company, mentioned in all surveys, although sexism was not overt, some comments and behaviour by managers suggest that men are not aware that they are sexist and how that affects their engagement with women as well as decisions they make about work-related matters. One company holds workshops on sexual harassment at the workplace – in case potential harassers don't know what's wrong with this behaviour.

> 'We have found in our internal processes that female staff are harassed. Junior male staff are mostly responsible. Our company policies around this are clear and communicated via email, available on our internal intranet and reinforced at department and staff meetings.'

A Media24 respondent noted that 'under the leadership of our [woman] CEO, incidents of sexual harassment declined rapidly and are now almost unheard of in our business'. However, another respondent was out of patience with the manifestation of sexist attitudes that were still widespread. 'Can someone offer a course on why "mansplaining" is a bad thing, please? I have a few candidates to suggest.'[15]

'Family penalty' still a reality

Is a woman's place in the home? Must family come first for women, but not for men? In 2006, one senior journalist said, 'Journalism is 24/7 work and workplaces do not take account of the impact on family responsibility. I don't know, for example, if I could do this work if I had children. There is a lot of external work: interviews, functions, travel, et cetera, that are intrinsic.'

Having a family need not limit a woman's rise in the news environment if there are structures in place to support her. But once a woman becomes a mother there is very little done to accommodate her. 'There is no accommodation of a woman who needs a flexible working day – not a shorter day, just a more flexible one,' said one respondent.

> 'Many women are single parents and have to take care of a full life at home with children, while the majority of men do not have those obligations.'

It has been described as the 'family penalty', and respondents said it was one of the biggest issues that women face. Women who fall pregnant, or have a number of responsibilities outside the workplace, raising children, often suffer professionally and are less likely to be employed or promoted than men who are not expected to carry the same burden in their personal lives.

> 'We have capable women who can occupy top positions but they are bypassed. There is still a problem of perception – women take maternity leave, women have emotional issues, women can't/won't work long hours because of family responsibilities, women should be at home looking after children.'

The situation in some media houses has improved since the first survey in 2006. In one, unnamed, the work environment was described as sensitive to the needs of women, with flexible working arrangements to support a work-life balance – time for family commitments, gym or study. In one company, Media24, paternity leave has been initiated. At an unnamed community radio station, all employees have a standard number of 'family responsibility days'. But there is still a way to go. A Caxton respondent noted that the company does not make allowances for family responsibility issues that women face, such as suddenly being dropped by a babysitter, while 'family responsibilities for men have never seemed like a concern'.

It is perhaps linked to the age-old perception that – as a male respondent noted in 2006 – 'men are more deserving because they have families to support'. Many women also have huge financial commitments such as ageing parents to support, or children or relatives to educate, yet this is not seen in the context of the traditional view of men as breadwinners.

Women still seen as 'soft'

Are women more emotional than men? Should they be relegated to the 'softer' side of journalism, the features and magazines, leaving hard news and investigations to the men? Are they incapable of leadership? Or are they being blocked out by male self-interest? In 2006, it was remarked that 'most men – of course there are exceptions – still do not like reporting to or taking instructions from women'.

In 2018 there are female news editors, female editors and female chief executives, yet sexist attitudes persist. Women's decisions and actions are often questioned whereas male opinions and actions are more easily accepted. In meetings, the room might go silent while a male colleague is speaking, but a female colleague is interrupted and spoken over. Many women still buy into the belief that women are not capable of leading 'because they are emotionally driven' and are 'afraid of taking hard decisions'.

'Research shows that men are taken more seriously in the corporate world in general, so naturally this will also apply to men in media houses.'

'Men are seen as brave individuals who can always come up with good decisions.'

'Strong women are often seen as confrontational and troublemakers.'

Nonetheless, some women are making real inroads into high positions, especially in broadcasting – both commercial and community – and in some community newspapers. In most responses from women at community radio stations, they noted that they had risen through the ranks, their work ethic was stronger, and their sacrifices were greater than those of the men.

'I don't feel there is a problem with women in management positions at SABC News.'

In respect of beats, 'hard' beats like politics and economics still tend to go mainly to men, whereas softer beats such as lifestyle and fashion are still predominantly covered by women (see figure 6.1).

In 2006, beats like sport and politics went primarily to men. In figure 6.1, we see that only in general, entertainment and education did women surpass men.

Women still don't push for promotion

What do women do when they are not taken seriously, or are bypassed for good assignments and promotion? Do they fight for these positions? Rarely. In 2006

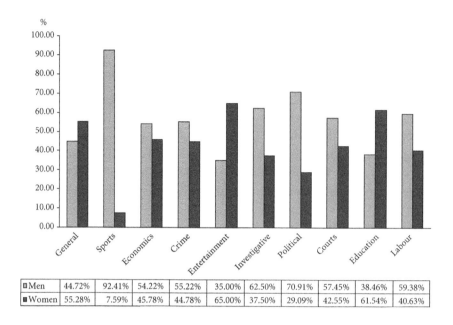

	General	Sports	Economics	Crime	Entertainment	Investigative	Political	Courts	Education	Labour
▣ Men	44.72%	92.41%	54.22%	55.22%	35.00%	62.50%	70.91%	57.45%	38.46%	59.38%
▪ Women	55.28%	7.59%	45.78%	44.78%	65.00%	37.50%	29.09%	42.55%	61.54%	40.63%

Figure 6.1: Top ten beats

Source: Daniels, Nyamweda and Nxumalo (2018)

and in 2018, they merely buckled down and worked harder – and received neither recognition nor respect. In 2006, one respondent said, 'I believe that women partly impose the glass ceiling on themselves by not pushing boundaries. Most women tend to be wallflowers regarding their careers; they expect people will just notice their dedication and hard work. Men learn very quickly about the value of networking and being vocal about their ambitions.'

Has it changed much in 2018? 'I never applied for senior positions until I was asked why I was not applying,' said one respondent. Ironically, adding to this reticence is the stigma attached to advancement policies for women. 'Some women don't participate because they do not want to be seen as quota appointments.' Once women do rise to the top, problems often surface. Some men refuse to take orders from a woman, and even junior women can be obstructive.

'I am often not taken seriously by my staff. There is no problem with the men but the women also don't want to be held accountable by another

> *woman. They expect constant concessions for not going out to cover stories which is sometimes unreasonable. This means more pressure is put on the male reporters to cover stories that require them to go out on the field. The female journalists prefer to sit in the office.'*

That is one side of the argument. The other is that once women climb the ladder to high positions, they pull the ladder up after them. 'Very senior women often pull down younger women, trip them up or otherwise make life hard for them,' wrote one respondent. 'Men often act as the best mentors,' said another.

Race still the priority

Issues of gender are generally pushed aside, or eclipsed by race-related issues. The instant backlash towards race transgressions within the corporate setting, although important, is never matched by a similar backlash surrounding gender.

> *'Race is front and centre of every discourse in South Africa at the moment.'*

> *'Race is still the most important issue we need to deal with, both as an industry and as a country.'*

> *'Racism is tackled first because it affects men.'*

Few women of colour are represented in top positions, even in 2018, and yet there are plenty of female candidates. 'If I look at my own newspaper, as well as the graduating class for my journalism diploma, there were more women than men in both. However, in my newspaper the top leadership positions were heavily skewed towards men,' said one respondent.

Journalism is risky

Respondents referred to a range of dangers and deterrents women faced in pursuing a career in journalism – in 2006, in 2009 and, still, in 2018. In the 2009 southern Africa survey, physical danger and discomfort were examined. The list of deterrents is long: erratic hours, night shifts, lack of maternity leave or flexi-time for family, lack of job security, covering dangerous situations. *The Namibian*'s editor-in-chief, Gwen Lister, could attest to serious dangers – she was jailed often, once while seven months' pregnant, and her offices were set alight. In 2018, covering stories where violence is involved was still dangerous.

> 'We often risk our lives while out on stories.'
>
> 'Women are not encouraged to be in the media industry because of threats and dangers.'

All media houses currently face financial pressure, with the concomitant risk of retrenchments and the diminishing prospect of decent salary increases or bonuses. Some women face extra risks. 'I have problems with the crew. They are all male and a lot of the time I feel unsafe around them because of intimidation and a lack of respect,' said one respondent in broadcasting.

> 'Women are subjected to sexist backlashing.'
>
> 'Women outside the newsroom are subjected to threats and victimisation.'

WHAT WOULD MAKE A DIFFERENCE?

Respondents in all the surveys noted that gender equality would be taken more seriously if women were in senior management positions, and most respondents agreed that female journalists were more likely to seek out female opinion than were male journalists. However, in 2018 respondents also took a wider view, commenting that gender balance is important because different sexes bring different perspectives in the media house. For the most part, respondents found women had certain gifts that bring value to a newsroom.

> 'Women have a good way of approaching people.'
>
> 'Everybody has the same capabilities, but men and women see things differently.'

121

POWER AND LOSS IN SOUTH AFRICAN JOURNALISM

> '*Women report sensitively on issues pertaining to rape and violence against women and children. There are narratives that are better presented and represented by the concerned gender.*'
>
> '*Different perspectives help a company thrive and avoid becoming stagnant.*'

As managers, women are perceived as more caring, and more professional. One respondent noted that 'it makes a big difference having a CEO who is a woman and who does not suffer fools. Golf and old-boys' clubs are scorned. Selections are self-explanatory, no elaboration necessary.'

Quotas

Respondents in the 2009 study had mixed reactions to quotas. Half of the men thought quotas were a fair way to achieve gender balance, an attitude shared by only one-third of female respondents. The researchers noted that men's belief in the use of quotas had, by then, had an effect – women were already better represented in media houses. Yet in 2018 the issue of quotas was again on the table because men still dominate top positions.

> '*Correcting structural imbalances cannot be left to the goodwill of men and women.*'
>
> '*Men's privileged positions have been established over a long period of time. Quotas will accelerate transformation.*'
>
> '*Historical bias and social conditioning cannot be undone without concentrated efforts.*'

Some respondents believed quotas would be acceptable, but with a time limit. 'Quotas should be used only to correct the current imbalance. Thereafter a better or fairer strategy should be used that allows for the advancement of both male and female employees,' said one respondent. Not everyone agreed. 'I don't like quotas. They create a negative environment,' wrote another respondent. 'It is people's outlook on life and how they regard women that should change,' said a third. The spectre of incompetence also entered the conversation in 2018.

'Quotas are fine as long as they do not result in placing incompetent people in roles.'

Training

In 2006, women wanted workshops in which they could be empowered to believe in themselves. Career planning and opportunities to expose them to all kinds of experiences would prepare them for leadership – and they wanted women as role models.

'Women are not empowered and mentored to believe in themselves, that they can fill a senior position, because women also buy into the perception that they cannot compete with men, cannot be as good as men, when they in fact can do things better than men.'

In 2009, when the study was extended to southern Africa, a male Mozambican journalist was quoted as saying that few women in his country train as journalists. 'The majority of students in the training institutions are men,' he said. 'I believe the cultural aspects continue to interfere in the decision to pursue a career in journalism, due to the working conditions.'

A young female editor in Swaziland noted that 'the lack of training is a major challenge'. 'You have to look for short courses yourself. In the media you are just thrown into the deep and you have to swim to the shore,' she said. In 2018, things have improved on several fronts. More and more women are enrolling for journalism degrees.

'Not only are the majority of my supervisors and colleagues women, but while I was studying journalism our classes were overwhelmingly female at both an undergraduate and postgraduate level.'

Several respondents also mentioned the importance of mentoring, and there was a call for gender forums, as well as training for women to mitigate the risks associated with journalism – everything from physical encounters to trolls. Better training could mean better chances of advancement, rising through the ranks, and earning better salaries as pay, noted one respondent, 'relates mostly to seniority, which is male dominant'.

Sexism

Some of the key findings in the Glass Ceilings 2018 were related to sexism. The 2018 research showed it was difficult to 'prove' sexism even though to those who experience it, women, it is blatant and painful. So much sexism relates to cultural practices, institutional culture, sexual harassment that no one else witnessed, jokes, innuendo, the old boys' network, being passed over for promotion, among other intangibles. However, this changes with the gender pay gap. Most respondents in the Glass Ceilings 2018 survey, nearly 80 per cent, said they knew there was gender salary disparity, and that women were paid less than men of the same experience and doing the same job. The comments section amplified this. The gender pay gap is a concrete measurable indicator of sexism, but human resources departments of media companies prefer to hide it.

The bigger media houses have all achieved the 50 per cent mark overall: of the media houses surveyed, 24 had between 50 per cent and 85 per cent women: Media24 had 57 per cent women, Tiso Blackstar (now Arena Holdings) 54 per cent; *Mail & Guardian* 52 per cent and the South African Broadcasting Corporation (SABC) 50 per cent.

Despite the increase there was still no parity at management level. Between 2009 and 2018 there had been an increase in women in senior management, from 35 per cent to 46 per cent and in top management from 25 per cent to 36 per cent. Women (47 per cent) and men (41 per cent) attributed the gender gap to men being taken more seriously than women. Women (39 per cent) and men (26 per cent) felt that women are bypassed in promotion processes. Women (35 per cent) and men (28 per cent) attributed this to the old boys' network.

The proportion of white men in top management has dropped but is still more than double that of white women. White men, who constituted 46 per cent of top media managers in 2006, have dropped to 14 per cent in 2018. White women in top management had dropped from 23 per cent to 6 per cent over the same period, but there was still more than double the proportion of white men (14 per cent) to white women (6 per cent) in top management in the media.

Black men are moving up the ranks at a much faster pace than black women. The proportion of black men in top management in the media had more than doubled from 22 per cent in 2006 to 50 per cent in 2018. The proportion of black women in top management had gone up five-fold, from 6 per cent in 2006 to 30 per cent in 2018, but this was still 20 percentage points lower than for black men. Black women (30 per cent in top management compared to 46 per cent of the population) were grossly under-represented. However, the gap was beginning to narrow for black women at senior management level, where they comprised 40 per cent of the total.

There has been an increase in women middle managers (assistant editors, news presenters/anchors, correspondents, designers and producers), but a decline in skilled professionals; although the number of women middle managers had increased from 47 per cent to 52 per cent, the number of women skilled technical and academically qualified workers (reporters and sub-editors) went down from 51 per cent to 38 per cent. This may reflect the general decimation of these core foot-soldiers as new media takes over the mainstream media.

The gender pay gap appears to be widening: In the three media houses that provided data, the pay gap between women and men in 2018, at 23 per cent, was higher than in 2009 (17 per cent). This may in part reflect the 'eroded middle' in which women tend to predominate in the new media era, with the structure of media increasingly dominated by a few top executives, and a large number of junior staff responsible for social media.

Policies do not promote the equal sharing of responsibilities in the home. Eighty-one per cent of the media houses said they gave maternity leave, compared to only 31 per cent with paternity leave policies.

Some respondents identified themselves as 'other' for the first time; 2 per cent comprised staff who identified their gender as 'other' (gender non-conforming persons). This was the first time that this indicator was measured in the Glass Ceilings study. That 2 per cent of staff are not identified as male or female is itself an indicator of progress over the last decade.

Sexual harassment is a daily reality for women in the media, but is not prioritised. In 2018, 87 per cent of media houses said they had sexual harassment policies, compared to 82 per cent in 2009. Almost all media houses (91 per cent) reported dealing with sexual harassment cases. Countless first-hand accounts in the report attest to sexist attitudes and practices at work and in the field. The SABC has set up a commission of inquiry into sexual harassment. Cyber misogyny is a growing threat. Although only 6 per cent of official respondents felt cyber misogyny is an issue in South Africa, 30 per cent of women and 9 per cent of men agreed that women journalists experience cyber violence. The first-hand account by Ferial Haffajee, former chair of Sanef, and one of South Africa's most senior women editors, is chilling testimony to gender violence in the media. Cyber misogyny may just be emerging, but like the speed of the social media that spawned it, is guaranteed to spiral out of control if not addressed seriously.

The gender pay gap

In 2017, the BBC conducted the first big study into the gender pay gap, surveying 10 000 large companies.[16] The survey found that 78 per cent of the companies paid men more than women; that fewer than one in seven paid women more than men; that men made up the majority of higher-paid jobs; that men were paid higher bonuses than women; that there was no sector paying women more; and that in some instances men were paid 50 per cent more than women, or twice as much.

The BBC's investigation into itself found a similar gap: that only a third of its top 96 earners were women, and the top seven are all men.[17] However, by July 2018, the BBC had reduced the gender pay gap to 8.4 per cent. The research also showed that the more conservative the media company, the bigger the wage gap, for example the *Telegraph's* wage gap was 35 per cent and the *Guardian's* was 11.3 per cent.[18]

The BBC said the main reason for its gender pay gap was that it had too few women in senior leadership roles and more women than men in the lowest-earning part of the workforce such as administrative staff. This appears to tally exactly with the findings and reasons in the 2018 Glass Ceilings report. Journalists in the South African newsrooms and media companies do not seem to know what the gender wage gap is, but they know it exists. One of the recommendations from the Glass Ceilings 2018 research is a call for transparency so that the exact gender wage gap is revealed and companies fix it. Companies should be required to publish annual gender pay gap data together with their annual profit and loss results.

CYBER BULLYING AND TROLLING

The newest threat to women in the newsroom, from the past decade of Glass Ceilings research, is cyber misogyny (hatred of women online), or trolling (online bullying and harassment) or social media bullying. Worldwide studies show that trolling affects women more than men. A recent UK study of Twitter abuse targeting celebrities by Demos found that 'journalism is the only category where women received more abuse than men, with female journalists and TV news presenters receiving roughly three times as much abuse as their male counterparts.'[19]

Cyber misogyny, expressed from online sexual harassment through to stalking and threats of violence, is a genuine psychological – and potentially physical – risk to safety of women journalists. It is also a threat to the active participation of women in civil society debate, fostered by news publishers, through online commenting platforms and their social media channels.

In 2018, added to the physical danger there is an electronic one, not imagined in earlier surveys: the prevalence of online trolls. Although only a few women reported cyber stalking, quite a few said they had been victims of unknown email or cellphone correspondents issuing violent threats, often of a sexual nature.

'When females do stories on certain issues that touch very close to home for certain males, the reaction is a very negative one on social media. Women have drawn a lot of flack on air for challenging the patriarchal perceptions in the past, and still do.'

Ways to deal with this new reality were addressed, with respondents to the Glass Ceilings 2018 research calling for media houses to support victims and even locate cyber bullies and stalkers. Suggestions from respondents include hiding the gender of the journalist (possible in print and online but not in broadcast), reporting cases to a senior journalist or to the police, and blocking the perpetrators, if one can identify them. One suggestion is to create a link, an online tracker that will report such incidents and follow the perpetrators.

'There needs to be some kind of way we can immediately report someone who we see is bullying or trolling us online.'

'The IT department should build strong defensive software that will protect all employees.'

Ferial Haffajee is one of South Africa's highest-profile black women editors, and among a few women in the country to have cracked the glass ceiling, having served as editor of two major newspapers, the *Mail & Guardian* and *City Press*. Haffajee's story, in her own words, of trolling and cyber bullying by the Guptas, is chilling.[20]

For months, I've looked at them when I'm alone. Quickly, like a dirty secret. The images make me wince with their distortions and insults. I snap my phone shut and move to another screen. Or make a cup of tea. Images are powerful and the designers have very specific messages. That I am a whore, a harridan, an animal and a quisling. I feel shame, and fear that my family will see them and not understand their genesis.

I thought I knew myself better than the crafters of these images do, and so sometimes I've laughed them off when asked about the score of images that have linked me to the hashtag decrying #whitemonopolycapital (white monopoly capital) and which have labelled me variously a presstitute (media prostitute) and a lapdog of the Richemont chairman and South African billionaire Johann Rupert. But upon reflection, the instinct to feel ashamed and to worry about what my less digitally savvy family might think means this kind of trolling works.

Rupert dropped Bell Pottinger as Richemont's public relations specialist, accusing them of running the campaign on white monopoly capital and making him the poster boy. Bell Pottinger was also working for the Gupta family on a hefty retainer. They are now widely believed to be the masterminds behind efforts to divert attention from the family's capture of the South African state.

Although I have never met Rupert and only spoken to him once or twice, the images had me (or a very badly Photoshopped version) in his lap. There is one of Rupert walking a dog with my face plastered on the pooch and another of him milking a bovine with human visage - mine. The attack is patriarchal and gendered: I am the woman as cow and bitch. The contrivers couldn't get more stereotypical if they tried.

Internationally, a study shows that female journalists face unbridled online harassment.[21] The following is an extract from a piece by Denise-Marie Ordway in the *Journalist's Resource*, published by the Harvard Kennedy School Shorenstein

Centre. Ordway wrote that in-depth interviews with dozens of female journalists from across the globe revealed that women in news face varied forms of harassment, from sexist remarks and inappropriate requests to threats of rape. Researchers, according to Ordway, also learned that the strategies women used to deal with such abuse can disrupt their newsroom routines, even prompting some to change the way they report the news. They described the harassment as 'rampant'.

'Consistently, the journalists we interviewed saw online gendered harassment as hampering their efforts to report the news, engage with the communities they cover, or have a voice in the digital sphere,' writes the research team led by Gina Masullo Chen, an assistant professor of journalism at the University of Texas at Austin. The study contains vivid descriptions of the abuses women said they faced, described in their own words. Some examples:

- An online editor from Germany said, 'The feedback [on this article] was not criticism, it was threats, it was death threats, it was calls for rape.'
- A veteran newspaper journalist in the US said she received hundreds of messages after writing about Donald Trump from the perspective of a Muslim woman. 'I was shocked by the dehumanisation and demonisation that exploded on Twitter and Facebook as well as direct email to the point to where I thought I should get security cameras,' she said.
- A broadcast journalist in the US explained that people leave misogynistic comments on her professional Facebook page so often that she blocks certain words. 'I have moderation on my page for the words "sexy", "hot" or "boobs"', she said.
- A video producer in the UK said, 'Now and then I'll get comments thrown at me, purely just about my hair colour. I will get comments about being [a] blonde and not being intelligent enough because of my hair.'

Reporters are often encouraged, and sometimes required, to promote their work and interact with audiences online, but audience engagement can have ugly consequences as some people use Twitter, Facebook and other online platforms to attack members of the press. Of the 75 female journalists interviewed for Chen's study, 73 said they had experienced gendered harassment online, or harassment that focuses specifically on their gender or sexuality. Television journalists reported experiencing harassment most often.

The journalists interviewed work or have worked in the US, Germany, India, Taiwan and the UK. Chen and her colleagues sought out women of different ages, races and experience levels, representing a variety of media outlets and newsroom types. While the small sample is not representative of female journalists as a whole, the researchers write that their goal was to 'find meaning through the female journalists' words, not make generalisable inferences'. 'The main takeaway for journalists and news organizations is that harassment of female journalists is a serious problem that needs to be addressed,' Chen told *Journalist's Resource*.

In another article, 'Trends in Newsrooms: Business of Gender Equality' published by *Media Online* in 2015, the gender activist and academic Julie Posetti said that important steps are being undertaken globally to provide training for women journalists to fight cyber misogyny. While highlighting the potential of social media channels to act as conduits for women's empowerment and solidarity, experts acknowledge the growing impact of cyber misogyny on women journalists.

The Australian Broadcasting Corporation (ABC) has begun 'social media defence' classes as an intervention, a strategy that media educator Jenna Price (who was threatened online with rape) welcomed, saying that media employers 'need to practise responsible corporate citizenship and ensure their staff have the social media skills *and* the emotional support required ... it needs policy, strategy and action'. However, if newsrooms themselves remain bastions of male domination, harassment and sexism, better management of the effects of cyber misogyny will not have a major impact on new moves to target women's empowerment in, and through, the media, Posetti wrote.[22]

Some of the recommendations for combating cyber bullying include:

- recognising the problem and the impact
- providing specific training for women journalists to help them deal with it
- stimulating senior management awareness of the issue; investing in community engagement management (including clear policies and guidelines for intervention, along with effective abuse reporting tools)
- devoting editorial resources to coverage of these issues; considering adding misogyny to moderation guideline definitions
- dedicating more staff to understanding and performing moderation; employing more senior women moderators/community managers
- advocating for the uptake of abuse-reporting tools like the Women Action Media initiative by social media companies.

These recommendations are from Australia but they can be applied in South Africa too. The Glass Ceilings 2018 showed signs of an anti-feminist backlash and also an increased anger and assertiveness by women in the media against sexism, which may be the result of the zeitgeist of the times, globally and nationally. Progress can be seen in the boldness of the comments and the speaking out against sexism and calling out of the gender pay gap, but, still, some things have not changed at all.

The research took place in a new era, with a heightened awareness and activism from women – globally, the #MeToo campaign, for example, and nationally, the #TotalShutDown march on 1 August 2018. Even though women in the newsroom are less militant in their assertiveness compared to their broader society, they could be finally taking their lead from here to say #TimeisUp. A speaking-out culture appears to be emerging. It is within this context that the recommendations are stronger than in any previous Glass Ceilings research.

WHAT IS TO BE DONE

- Call out sexism at every opportunity, say #TimeisUp. Name, shame and shun sexists, sexist behaviour and sexual harassment.
- Agitate for all companies to reveal their gender pay gap, following the example of the BBC, and insist on a timeframe.
- Institute diversity policies which must have a gender equality clause.
- Call out 'manels' (male-only panels) at media and journalism conferences.
- Measure yearly numbers of women in the newsroom, especially in the top rungs, and voices of women in the media/reportage itself.
- Mainstream gender equality initiatives and policies, and stop treating the gender equality conversation as peripheral.
- Build allies with other sectors, for example, non-governmental organisations and feminist bodies.
- Ban all sexist language in reporting and in the newsroom.
- Investigate the institutional practices and structural inequalities, and the cultural norms and values in different newsrooms that contribute to the discrimination of women.
- Enable talk sessions in newsrooms where women's voices can be heard and they can explain how they feel – and why, as women in the Glass Ceilings research over the past decade have been consistent in feeling patronised and demeaned.
- Spread knowledge of equity laws and gender policies through workshops.
- Change employment conditions to include parenthood time.

- Apply all of the above to diversity and inclusivity in general – which should include race, class, sexual orientation, religion and cultures, gender fluidity and transgenderism.

CONCLUSION: DECOLONIAL REFLECTIONS ON THE ANTI-FEMINIST BACKLASH

Ironically, the very same arena that allowed women to express their views, social media platforms, has been used to push back against women, as seen in Haffajee's story. In this chapter I have shown, in the words of women themselves, the struggles they face. They spoke out freely and fiercely. They appeared to have felt comforted by the anonymity of the survey. But the recommendations for women and media on how to deal with cyber bullying, cyber misogyny and other abuse is all very well – there must be consequences for the culprits.

A new breed of young media women are affirming their rights with increased anger and assertiveness, saying 'we refuse to be the wretched or the condemned of the earth'. At the heart of decolonial thinking is love for women, in the political sense, because they are at the bottom of the hierarchical structure. They are both racialised and sexualised in colonialism, and their bodies become part of the economy of sexual abuse and control.

This perpetuates in social media – in South Africa but also all over the world. In this chapter I have demonstrated both loss and power in the media: women gained power through expressing themselves on social media but the backlash was severe and the misogynistic powers pressed down harshly upon them. However, the speaking up and speaking out that was witnessed in the women journalists' comments in the research gives one hope that with the militancy that continues to grow, the strategies to combat this emotional violence also grows. This is at the heart of the decolonial turn, which is the subject matter for the next chapter.

7

Decolonial 'Green Shoots'

In a way, as modern subjects, we breath coloniality all the time and every day.
Nelson Maldonado-Torres, 'On the Coloniality of Being'

The media has power to think and act beyond the norms of everyday mainstream culture and thinking which would include, for example, the high value placed on middle- and upper-class thinking, speaking English, whiteness, maleness, heteronormativity, celebrity celebration, and more accumulation for the already wealthy. The media can also think and act beyond today's hysterical focus on more content on more platforms, chasing social media, more shiny new innovations, and the focus on combating 'fake' news which has always been in existence as misinformation, disinformation and political propaganda – but which is more serious than ever before in the digital age. In other words, journalists can use their media spaces to go beyond being reactive and combating the negatives, over-engaging on social media in 'Twars' (Twitter wars) and then enjoying the excess that comes with this: celebrity profiles and 'influencers' in that more exclusive rather than inclusive space.

In this chapter I examine whether there are new signs – or green shoots – in South Africa's media, beyond the breathing of colonialities' norms. The analysis here uses decolonial theory to peruse stories on black hair – as well as an examination of some new start-ups and investigative units – to examine if there are signs of detachments from past norms, from the usual liberal thinking in mainstream media. Mainstream media's treatment of the marginalised has been examined by other scholars, for example, Herman Wasserman on issues of listening and audiences,[1] and Sarah Chiumbu on how journalists frame social justice issues.[2] Journalists are almost always found wanting.

The theoretical argument here is also that black consciousness can exist in tandem with the 'decolonial turn', which is a shift in knowledge production to refocus the gaze that can render the invisible visible – indeed can bring the invisible to the centre. Black consciousness, like decolonial theory, argues to bring the *damnés*, or the wretched of the earth, to the centre. In this case and in most cases in the global South, it is blackness and woman that intersect with poverty, that constitute the wretched of the earth – for instance, the old woman on television (eNCA) in January 2019, who said: 'I have never seen water come out of a tap'. This, the bringing of the *damnés* into the centre, requires interventions of power.

One such force of power in the South African power ecosystem is the media. Nelson Maldonado-Torres has pointed out that because of its emancipatory goals and its suspension of method, the decolonial turn cannot be fully contained in single units of study, but what is at stake is the larger task of the very decolonisation of knowledge, power and being, including institutions such as the university.[3] Here, for this chapter we must add the institution of the mainstream media in South Africa to the above power matrix as an unfinished project that continues to unfold.

As discussed in the previous chapter on the anti-feminist backlash, associate professor of Chicana Studies at University of California Chela Sandoval conceptualised decolonial love not as a romantic love, but rather as 'invented love'.[4] It is love as a political technology, and it is political struggle against structures of dehumanisation and self-hate. Drawing on Sandoval's concept, South African black consciousness theorist Tendayi Sithole wrote as follows: 'As eloquently put by Sandoval, it is love that can access and guide over theoretical and political "*movida*" or revolutionary manoeuvres towards decolonised being.'[5] Indeed, love is the driving force. This is a revolutionary commitment steeped in the desire for genuine freedom and, for Sithole, a desire to be free must show in everything we do.

Twinned, decolonial theory and black consciousness become a political struggle against the structures of dehumanisation and, as Frantz Fanon said in *Black Skin, White Masks*, 'Yes to life, yes to love and yes to generosity.'[6] While drawing on these reflections, bearing media in mind, we can ask whether journalists can gaze anew to share some love for and with black consciousness in an integrated sincere way rather than the master signifier and passionate attachment to just freedom of expression, the watchdog role. Are there any kinds of *movidas* possible? It may be possible that Fanon's famous intervention 'Humanity is waiting for something other from us than such an imitation, which would be an almost obscene caricature' can be used to understand the media world that journalists inhabit.[7]

Stephen Bantu Biko was a philosopher poet, and his writings are inspirational and prophetic. 'Blacks are tired of standing at the touchlines to witness a game that they should be playing. They want to do things for themselves and by themselves,'[8] he wrote in his most famous work *I Write What I Like*. He also said, in the same book, that it becomes clear that as long as blacks are suffering from an inferiority complex – a result of 300 years of deliberate oppression, denigration and derision – they will be useless co-architects of a normal society.

Before this chapter turns to the 'case study' (for want of a better term) the theoretical concepts used here will be briefly explained. The background is that research, for example that of Media Monitoring Africa, shows how the voices of the powerful dominate in media coverage, including white male liberal ways of thinking. The 'case study' reveals how the media gazed at the story of a Pretoria Girls High School student, Zulaikha Patel, who began a protest in 2016 after her schoolteachers told her to cut, and/or or neaten and/or straighten her Afro hairstyle.

The above concepts will be used and blended with decolonial theory and black consciousness to make sense of the Afro hair saga of 2016, and how the media reacted and covered the stories. Ultimately, this leads on to the final chapter of this book in which I ask the questions: What is the media for, what is journalism in particular for, what power does it have and what power has it lost?

The next section looks at stories in the mainstream media about a saga that broke out at Pretoria Girls High School. In 2016, a thirteen-year-old girl, Zulaikha Patel, from Pretoria Girls High School (which was founded in 1902 and was all-white for most of its history), sported a big Afro hairstyle and was instructed by teachers to 'fix myself as though I was broken'.

I examine specifically what angles were taken, how the stories were framed, and who was supported – in a hysterical fight that showed an attachment by the authorities to old white normative values (the demand for straighter hair, to conform more closely to white hair) against the girl's right to express her black consciousness and self-love through her Afro. The underlying question is, what could be the alternative imagining that Fanon refers to when he warns against

Figure 7.1: Pretoria Girls High School student, Zulaikha Patel

Photograph courtesy of Alet Pretorius, *Beeld*

cheap imitations and caricatures of the West? Indeed, we recall Maldonado-Torres, in the epigraph to this chapter, 'In a way, as modern subjects, we breathe coloniality all the time and every day.'

Institutions and organisations all have rules, but sometimes the rules are old-school, and steeped in bias and prejudice – and sometimes or maybe even more often than not, the media reinforces the old normative thinking.

Patel led a silent demonstration against the school's hair policy. The protesting teenagers were threatened with arrest; Patel faced three armed security guards hired by the school management to stop the protest. The online video, which showed the subjection the girls faced, caused an outcry that went international. The demonstration inspired other protests in South Africa, in the Eastern Cape province at Lawson Brown High School in Port Elizabeth and in the Free State province at St Michael's School for Girls in Bloemfontein, where parents marched as well. The issue went viral on social media as people across the world shared pictures of their Afros. Panyaza Lesufi, the minister for education in Gauteng province, visited the school – and about more than hair policy. He had also heard about other prejudices. An online petition collected 25 000 signatures in one day in support of the girls' rights to wear Afros. After an investigation by the province's education department, the school was told to withdraw their hair policy. How did the South African media report on the local story, which received attention all over the world?

TRAUMA AND DECOLONIAL LOVE

Some of the important characterisations of the decolonial turn, which can be called democracy of a decolonial type, include these seven points: breaking the racist but also victimhood stereotypes; including decolonial love as a political technology; giving voice and visibility to the marginalised; being one *with* the subaltern, not *about* the subaltern; acknowledging diversity as well as local contexts and struggles; recognising that one size does not fits all and shifting the geography of reason. All these theoretical points have relevance for this Afro story.

The story headlines, and in some cases the introductions too, should be read with this summary of decolonial turn thinking in mind. The outlining, below, of the stories does not by any means signify a quantitative analysis. It is merely to highlight what was covered – and how. The analysis here remains a politico-philosophical one, hence its emphasis on decoloniality and black consciousness.

For the Pretoria Girls High School hair saga and the stories that it generated I gathered headlines from ten mainstream online newspapers.

News24

Black girls in tears at Pretoria school hair protest
29 August 2016
Tears flowed as black Pretoria High School for Girls pupils on Monday told of alleged racism and abuse suffered at the hands of white teachers. 'I have a natural Afro, but a teacher told me I need to comb my hair because it looks like a birds nest,' one girl told Gauteng education MEC Panyaza Lesufi, who visited the school on Monday morning.

School protest: 'We have failed our girls by relaxing our hair to please whites'
29 August 2016
Birds' nests, static hair, Afros that are too long – pupils at Pretoria High School for Girls are tired of these insults when they wear their hair natur-ally, and they are receiving support from others who have been through the same thing.

'Don't feel threatened by black pride'
13 September 2016
White South Africans should not feel threatened by or even be uncom-fortable with the surge of black consciousness and black pride. They – we, because I write this as a white South African male – should rather try to understand where it comes from and what it means.

Pretoria girls bring school to standstill amid racism allegations
29 September 2016
Pupils at Pretoria High School for Girls claim they have been subjected to racism and that their blackness has been discouraged.

'We're tired of being oppressed for our hair' – PGHS student
29 September 2016
Students at Pretoria Girls' High School (PGHS) have rallied the support of tertiary students from the University of Pretoria (Tuks).

Tuks students march in solidarity with Pretoria girls
29 September 2016
Pupils at Pretoria High School for Girls claim they have been subjected to racism and that their blackness has been discouraged.

Pretoria Girls High hair policy tops the news
4 October 2016
Protests against the Pretoria Girls' High School hair policy topped headlines in South Africa last week, a media monitoring organisation reported.

Mail & Guardian

Pretoria Girls High School pupil: I was instructed to fix myself as if I was broken
29 August 2016
It was a day when black students at Pretoria Girls High School were finally holding their school to account for racism … the pupils were the real leaders. 'They're ringing it [the bell] because they're afraid,' a student said.

Several state and private schools have bans on dreadlocks, Afros and braids
2 September 2016
A ban on learners sporting Afros, dreadlocks and braids is still in place at several state and private schools despite a fierce storm erupting on social

media this week over Pretoria High School for Girls' hair policy, which was described by some as racist.

Hair, white assimilation, and the girls who are rejecting it
30 September 2016
There's been an outpouring of support for the black girls at Pretoria Girls High School, but there's also been bafflement and more discrimination. It's just a school policy to straighten their hair, some have argued, but it's more than that: it is the protection of white standards at the expense of black identity.

Daily Maverick

Pretoria Girls High: A protest against sacrificed cultures and identities
30 August 2016
On Saturday, students at Pretoria High School for Girls stood against racism at the former white-only institution. As political leaders intervened, Greg Nicolson spoke to students and found that the issues spread across the country.

Racism row over S. Africa school's hair policy
29 August 2016
Pupils at Pretoria High School for Girls have said they were forced to chemically straighten their hair and not have Afros that were deemed untidy.

IOL (Independent Online)

Black hair, sharp scissors and the totality of white power
31 August 2016
The power of whiteness breeds itself through persuasion, coercion and fear, mediated by institutional power, writes Ayabonga Cawe: Andries Babeile stabbed a white pupil with a pair of scissors in the year 2000. Two years

earlier when a group of parents and pupils of Hoerskool Vryburg protested against alleged racism, the school governing body mobilised white parents to prevent the march. What followed was a violent spectacle similar to what we saw during a rugby match at the University of Free State last year. It was a typical case of the totality of white power flexing its muscles in a constitutional dispensation it neither respects nor appreciates, but reluctantly 'tolerates'.

Racism fury at Pretoria Girls High: MEC steps in
30 August 2016
On Monday anger vibrated across the country as footage of heavily armed security personnel patrolling the schoolyard appeared. They threatened to arrest the pupils. The pupils were protesting against the school's hair policy and for being questioned whenever they were in groups of two or more. They also claim they were barred from using their home languages in private discussions.

PE school in ethnic hair racism row
30 August 2016
Pupils from Lawson Brown High School in Port Elizabeth brought the school to a standstill on Tuesday when they protested over alleged racist verbal attacks concerning black authentic hair. The picket protest broke out on the streets in front of the school while learners were joined in solidarity with members from the Economic Freedom Fighters (EFF) who picketed in song and dance.

The Citizen

Uproar as Pretoria Girls' black pupils in 'untidy' hair protest
29 August 2016
Black learners at the school claim they were told to straighten their 'untidy' natural hair and stop speaking anything but English. Gauteng MEC of Education Panyaza Lesufi announced on Sunday he would be visiting Pretoria Girls' High School on Monday morning to address allegations of racism.

Afro hair horror story: It just 'had to be straight'
29 August 2016
When the comb becomes your great nemesis
There were two things I feared as a primary school pupil in the early 90s. It wasn't Okapi the bully, who always found it necessary to tease me about my bellbottom khaki trousers. The problem was also not Rigombo demanding to see what was in my school lunchbox. The real terror was the morning comb horror most black schoolchildren are familiar with. Your curly hair just had to be combed straight. It was a commonly agreed view that curly hair was not clean, and you had to comb the cleanliness into the curly 'untidiness'.

Lawson Brown pupils fight for natural hair
30 August 2016
EFF members joined the pupils in their picket protest against alleged racist verbal attacks about authentic black hair
Pupils from Lawson Brown High School in Port Elizabeth brought the school to a standstill on Tuesday when they protested over alleged racist verbal attacks concerning authentic black hair.

Apartheid-era journo's anti-Afro posts leave hair on end
31 August 2016
A man once described as 'a horror of the apartheid regime' has called the Pretoria girls 'whingers' with 'hair bushes' that need to be combed with a rake
Former SABC journalist Cliff Saunders waded into the debate about the black girls and their hair at Pretoria Girls High, taking to Facebook to launch a string of opinions directed primarily at the young woman who became the face of the protests against hair and language policy at the school.

Parent 'burns' teacher over natural hair dispute
19 August 2016
The father had a simple request: for the teacher to let his kid flourish like other kids

In a continued debate over natural hair on the Twitter streets, one user shared a screengrab of what appears to be a conversation between a school teacher and the pupil's father. In the conversation, the teacher apologises for sending the message late and continues to tell the parent, Mr Moremi, about the inappropriateness of his son's natural hair. This did not sit well with Mr Moremi.

How Zahara keeps her Afro on fleek
27 September 2016
Have you been struggling to maintain your natural hair? Perhaps Zahara's hair regimen will help you
Apart from Pearl Thusi, Bulelwa 'Zahara' Mkutukana's enviable Afro is probably the biggest we've seen. The *Country Girl* hitmaker's Afro is so big, some of us actually thought it was not real, but hey, it turns out all that rich, pitch-black hair is hers, she reveals in an interview with *Frochic*. Zahara tells the publication she always has had her hair natural, adding she doesn't like weaves but used to love braids. Apart from preferring to keep her hair natural, she says she has a sensitive scalp, which makes relaxing hair a bad idea for her.

Mayor Msimanga wants a dialogue after 'Afro-gate'
30 August 2016
Pretoria's leadership and provincial government are trying to find solutions after pupils were allegedly racially abused. Black pupils at Pretoria High School for Girls are accusing the institution of discrimination directed at their hair, language and dress code, telling Gauteng education MEC Panyaza Lesufi they were subjected to racial slurs from some teachers and white pupils.

I'm just black now, not Black Like Me, says Florence Masebe
29 August 2016
The actress says African women should take pride in their natural looks, not use the kinds of hair chemicals she was once the 'marketing face' of.
Award-winning South African actress Florence Masebe has urged black women to take pride in their natural looks and beauty, and to be assertive in claiming their rightful place in the rainbow nation.

The Daily Sun

WATCH: Black hair matters!
30 August 2016
Gauteng MEC for education Panyaza Lesufi has promised to get to the bottom of the controversy surrounding a Pretoria school's hair policy.

Top Afro salon opens in Kasi
2 September 2016
When it comes to hair, all women can relate. And for those who are going natural, the Ngemvelo Afro Only Specialist Salon in Vosloorus, Ekurhuleni, is the place to be. Two friends, Khethiwe Phakathi (30) and Mamsy Namane (30), launched their salon in Dindela section on Saturday. It specialises in products which are 100% from Mother Nature. Khethiwe said before they start working with their customers, they tell them about the importance of natural hair.

'Hands off our hair!'
31 August 2016
Like a wildly combed-out Afro, reaction to the hair protest has spread all around the country. 'We need action now, not later!' said Gauteng Cosas secretary Benedict Phalane in Tshwane yesterday. About 400 pupils from different schools marched to the Pretoria High School for Girls yesterday. This follows a visit by Gauteng MEC for Education Panyaza Lesufi to the school.

Afro lands cop in hot water!
13 December 2016
Beauty sometimes comes at a high cost – and possibly also a painful one! This was proved at the weekend when a policewoman, expected to uphold the law, neglected to follow the rules – all in the name of beauty. The officer, who looked beautiful in her Afro weave, was not wearing her police cap. Instead of wearing the cap, the cop, who had responded to a crime scene, opted to carry it tied at her waist.

It's your hair, it's your choice!
30 September 2016
The national outcry about what 'acceptable' black hair is has got Mzansi talking. Do we alter our hair with chemicals and hair pieces because we idealise the 'white' look? Do we think of our natural black hair as being scruffy or dirty because we've internalised our oppression?

Basetsana Kumalo's new look
15 October 2016
Businesswoman Basetsana Kumalo has got herself a new lease on life. The star is on a journey to declutter and heal her life, and in so doing, has decided to change up her look. Keeping it natural, Basetsana decided to go for a short afro, with a brand new colour – a big step for her considering she has never coloured her hair before.

eNCA

Black girls' hair a national debate
29 August 2016
Public figures and former pupils of Pretoria High School for Girls spoke out on Monday in support of scholars protesting the school's rules for black pupils.

Hair protest hits Cape Town school
1 September 2016
Pupils at a Cape Town school were barred from entering its premises after they protested against alleged racism. Black pupils at Sans Souci Girls High School in Newlands alleged that they were not allowed to have Afros and were punished for speaking their home languages.

Black girls' hair a national debate
29 August 2016
Public figures and former pupils of Pretoria High School for Girls spoke out on Monday in support of scholars protesting the school's rules for black

pupils. Shandukani Mulaudzi, a former Pretoria Girl's High pupil, said the issue was broader than hair.

Kinky, curly hair: a tool of resistance across the African diaspora
8 October 2016
Across the African diaspora, stigmatising kinky and curly hair was a central way that European colonisers and slave-owners subjugated black people. In many places, like Brazil and the US, hair texture later became a key marker of racial classification and social status. In apartheid South Africa, the 'pencil test' was used to determine proximity to whiteness, along with access to political, social and economic privileges. It involved inserting a pencil into the hair and testing whether it would hold or fall out.

School racism probe at Pretoria Girls High
29 August 2016
Education authorities are to probe Pretoria High School for Girls, after racism allegations surfaced against the institution.

Eye Witness News

Why SA is behind the Pretoria High School for girls protest
29 August 2016
Most South Africans have rallied behind girls from the Pretoria High School for Girls
Protests over the hair, as well as language policies and practices at Pretoria Girls' High School today sparked discussion around the experiences of black pupils who attend former 'Model C' schools.

Another WC school hit by protests over hair policies
10 September 2016
Some learners at Fairbairn College complained to the department about rules relating to hairstyles
The Western Cape Education Department has had to step in at yet another school where learners have protested against hair policies.

Opinion: kinky, curly hair: a tool of resistance across African diaspora
7 October 2016
Across the African diaspora, stigmatising kinky and curly hair was a central
way that European colonisers and slave-owners subjugated black people.

Times Live

Report: Teachers at Pretoria girls' school victimised black pupils over hair
3 December 2016
An investigative report has confirmed that teachers at the Pretoria High
School for Girls violated the dignity of black pupils by instructing black
school pupils to straighten their hair, ordered disciplinary action be taken
against them and made racist comments.

The Big Read: Kroes or not, hair is a race thing
1 October 2016
If only it were that simple, for hair has always been politics, economics and
social status. Even the absence of hair is a social statement, just as the abun-
dance of hair makes a political point.

Manaka Ranaka and Samkelo Ndlovu recount their own hair 'discrimination'
30 August 2016
In the midst of the controversy at Pretoria High School for Girls, two of
the biggest stars on SA TV screens, Manaka Ranaka and Samkelo Ndlovu,
spoke out about discrimination they once faced at school.

'Can we be BLACK in peace?' Celebs join #StopRacismAtPretoriaGirlsHigh
fight
29 August 2016
Some of the country's most famous faces have added their voices to the
calls of outrage at Pretoria High School for Girls, defending black students'
rights to wear their hair naturally in the classroom.

Herald Live

Pretoria Girls High faces fury after black pupils told to 'straighten hair'
29 August 2016
Pretoria Girls High School is facing a furious backlash after allegedly instructing black school pupils to straighten their hair. Gauteng Education MEC Panyaza Lesufi is due to visit the school on Monday to address the controversy as more than 4 500 people signed a petition calling for his intervention.

Sonia Sedibe loves her natural hair
8 October 2016
Actress Sonia Sedibe has proudly flaunted her cornrows, also revealing that she hasn't 'relaxed' her hair in eight years. Sonia's comments come just days after a raging debate around black pupils at Pretoria Girls High being asked to relax their hair captured the attention of the nation.

Opinions at Port Elizabeth schools split on school hair rules
3 October 2016
Collegiate Girls High School is one step ahead of the pack, having revised its code of conduct and rules regarding hair in June last year.

Solange Knowles joins #StopRacismAtPretoriaGirlsHigh fight
1 October 2016
It's no secret that American singer Solange Knowles has unwittingly become a muse for the rapidly growing, ever-engaged natural hair community. So, it comes as no surprise that she has added her voice to the thousands of messages of support for the girls at the Pretoria Girls High school.

Simphiwe Dana lashes out at Angie Motshekga for 'school hair policy'
31 August 2016
Outspoken musician Simphiwe Dana has launched a scathing attack on minister of basic education Angie Motshekga and the ANC, following comments by the minister defending the Pretoria Girls High school code of conduct.

> *School forced to step down over hair rules*
> *31 August 2016*
> A highly charged and emotional meeting between pupils, staff, parents and angry community members at Lawson Brown High School in Port Elizabeth yesterday has forced the school to review its policies and rules about hairstyles for black pupils.
>
> *Hair row breaks out at PE school*
> *30 August 2016*
> *Lawson Brown pupil defiant about changing afro style.*
> A defiant Port Elizabeth pupil has accused her school of racism amid threats of being barred from writing her first exam tomorrow if she does not get rid of her Afro hairstyle.

Can the subaltern speak? asked Gayatri Spivak in her seminal work of the same title.[9] She questioned whether intellectuals and ruling elites were going to continually speak for subalterns without acknowledging that knowledge is never fully known or complete. We cannot fully escape our location in power structures, for example, because racial hierarchies, and our knowledges too, are situated, as noted by Paula Moya's 'who we are and from where we speak', cited in Maldonado-Torres's work.[10] Hence the importance of the decolonial turn. More than this, it is an attitude that demands responsibility and willingness to take on the injustice of the hierarchies.

The Afro hair stories were affirming and celebratory, and chose diversity and democracy. They were indeed decolonial and black consciousness in their framing. A content analysis showed that 100 per cent of the stories were affirming of the girls' right to their naturally curly hair. The stories were evocative, with emotional language – for example: 'tears flowed', 'black pride', 'tired of being oppressed', 'protection of white standards at the expense of black identity', 'the power of whiteness breeds itself through persuasion, coercion and fear', 'hands off our hair' and 'can we be black in peace'. The stories did not affirm the conservative schoolteachers' injunction to a master colonial narrative of 'neaten' hair in their own image. An investigation found that the teachers at Pretoria Girls High had violated the girls' dignity by instructing them to have neat hair, the master signifier here being straight hair. Neat hair was fixed to the meaning 'straight' hair. The media played a role in highlighting this infringement.

Hysteria surrounded the mainstream and social media coverage of the Afro hair stories, but it raised consciousness. The gaze was black, and it emerged from the perspective of the marginalised. Those teachers who were subjecting black girls to adopting their norm – of straightening their hair in the image of whiteness – had to be stopped, to think, to pause, reflect, take a step back. After the teachers had interpellated the girls by naming and shaming them for their Afros, the world and its media appeared to step in to shame them in turn, by calling them racist. The media showed some beginnings of decolonial and black consciousness which had hardly been visible in the past. This is not definitive but, rather, it suggests that there may be possibilities for decolonial green shoots in the media; that there may be a growing consciousness, and that decolonial love may be possible.

This chapter now takes a small tangent, to media that may be considered 'alternative' to the mainstream. In some cases, these are 'start-ups', and in others they are investigative units. Could these also be considered decolonial green shoots in South African media? What must be borne in mind when considering this possibility is that at the heart of decolonial theory is social justice – for all races, genders, sexualities, classes and ages, not only a select few who have always enjoyed privileged status.

Who are the green shoots? For more than a decade after apartheid ended there was no alternative press such as in the days before the political change in 1994, when the *Weekly Mail, South, New Nation* and *Vrye Weekblad* provided a deeper probing, leftist-leaning line of coverage than the mainstream media.

In recent times, however, green shoots have emerged that are – more than being alternative – virtually the only investigative journalism units acting as bulwarks against rank corruption and abuse of power. GroundUp is an independent online news agency, donor funded, established in 2012; it specialises in public-interest news, particularly in legal issues. *Spotlight* is a print and online publication focusing on South Africa's health system especially in respect of TB and HIV. The amaBhungane Centre for Investigative Journalism is an independent, non-profit newsroom that develops investigative journalism in the public interest. Previously the M&G Centre for Investigative Journalism, amaBhungane (isiZulu for 'the dung beetles') was launched in 2010. Scorpio is the official investigative unit of the *Daily Maverick*, launched in May 2017. It was the Scorpio team that exposed South African Revenue Service (SARS) commissioner Tom Moyane's shady dealings with Gupta company Oakbay, which got him fired by President Cyril Ramaphosa three days after Scorpio's revelations. The Daily Vox is an independent media organisation with no political affiliation.

It was launched in 2014; news about and for the young citizen is its priority. New Frame is a not-for-profit social justice media project with a primary focus on news rather than opinion. *The Conversation Africa* is an independent source of news and views from the academic and research community.

These organisations and the journalists who work with them attempt to make a contribution to a deepening democracy by tackling issues that the marginalised suffer. Frequently relying on donorship (private and public, local and international), the organisations have a different kind of funding model from the mainstream media of the big conglomerates such as Media24 (owned by Naspers), Tiso Blackstar (now Arena Holdings) and Independent Media. Sometimes, mainstream media can resignify from past norms.

CONCLUSIONS: MEDIA AND DEMOCRACY OF A DECOLONIAL TURN

In the particular case of black hair, the mainstream media resignified from past norms. It rejected the subjectivising authoritarian gaze to use, instead, an empathetic and loving black gaze, when it supported the Pretoria Girls High students. There was a detachment from past norms that oppressed. The schoolteachers expressed significant hysteria, calling in private security when the girls protested. The girls exercised agency, called on the Constitution, and showed power in their protest march against the colonial norm. The media exercised its power by supporting the protests in the way it reported them. By 2019, girls were sporting Afros with pride, if they so wished, all over South African government schools.

There is a certain enjoyment attached to hysteria. Enjoyment is usually identified with *surplus* enjoyment or excitation. If you subtract the excess, you will lose the enjoyment. Enjoyment as such emerges only in this surplus because it is constitutively an 'excess'. There was an excess in this hair saga on the part of teachers who were trying to make black girls more like white girls.

Fanon argued that we must not desire to catch up with Europe but strive to find a different path to advance humanity. The decolonial turn theorists highlight both the big gaps and the assumptions inherent in these old grand narratives of universal truths, which tend to cover up and conceal particular struggles and, importantly, show the racist stereotypes.

We cannot completely escape our location in power structures such as racial hierarchies – and our knowledges too are situated. Paula Moya's words 'who we are and from where we speak' highlight the importance of the decolonial turn, an attitude that demands responsibility and willingness to take on the injustice of the hierarchies.

From this perspective, which consists of acknowledging diversities and multi-plicities of methods of knowledge, there can never be one universal truth and knowledge that is privileged above all else, that is centred – with everything and everyone else hanging on to the periphery – the poor, the transgendered, woman in the global South (the last-named in itself too large a category to make assumptions about).

Coloniality survives colonialism, and as modern subjects, 'we breathe coloniality all the time and every day'. These words, at the beginning of this chapter, are appropriate for the black hair stories, which in turn disrupted this 'colonial breathing'.

Some of the important characterisations of the decolonial turn are breaking down stereotypes including love; giving voice and visibility to the marginalised; with the subaltern and not about the subaltern; acknowledging diversity as well as local contexts and struggles; recognising that one size does not fits all; and shifting the geography of reason. All of these issues came to light in the Afro hair saga. The stories show a new kind of growing consciousness, which did not exist a decade ago. In addition, some reporters sported doeks at a mainstream televi-sion station in defiance of the dress code.

The same argument can be made for the growth of new media outside the mainstream media, tackling angles and stories from a different perspective and bringing the marginalised closer to the centre.

As we look at the balance of forces between power and loss in the media, the hair stories and the new green shoot media organisations cannot be ignored. They could be signs of new power. It is fashionable to analyse the mainstream media as not fulfilling its mandate to serve all, to be so obsessed with uncovering corruption (especially public sector corruption), to be captivated only by the voices of the powerful that they ignore blackness, suffering and poverty. These criticisms are often valid but we should be wary of ignoring or even burying green shoots and not acknowledging the kinds of consciousness raising that does happen, and can happen.

Black consciousness activists and decolonial theorists criticise mainstream media for affirming the already powerful by centralising the same old elite voices. It may be, in some odd way, that the media heard the shaming and injunction and that, when the Pretoria schoolgirl started the protest by speaking out and raising her fist with the black power sign, the media decided to do its bit too. This raised consciousness led to the intervention of the government. The media, in raising the voices of the girls and centralising their struggle, enabled the Othering to stop. The media itself inscribed itself in its own gaze, showing that you cannot completely escape yourself and your subjectivities in your own gaze – you can put your blackness back into your gaze. This is what was beginning to happen in 2016–2018, albeit slowly. Reflexivity is a bending back on itself, a turn, an individual shaping of own norms and reactions. And, as Maldonado-Torres interpreted Fanon's love, it is about giving and receiving love, towards a world of non-sexist conviviality and reciprocal recognition. Decoloniality and black consciousness cannot be separated. They move in tandem.

In this way, the media can acknowledge the gaze or the stain that prevents it from looking at the picture from a safe objective distance. Its own view is subscribed in the content of its gaze. It is accepting the fact of blackness and it is showing signs of resignifications.

This chapter also raises another question for the media and for its own subjectivities.

Must people be reminded of misery, wretchedness and damnation every day and all the time? Some decolonial thought, not explored here, would say that this is indeed the lived experience. However, another imaginary, away from wretchedness and victimhood, is possible – a celebratory one. The hair stories, it can be suggested, were a decolonial turn of a liberatory kind. If this is the case, then this could be the citings of green shoots of decolonial self-love. The media's complicity in reiterating white norms and values may be slowly ending on some level. But is it love? It may be the beginnings of love.

The media, in its own way, appeared to be detaching from past signifiers; resignifications unsettle past passionate attachments. Decolonial turn and black consciousness theorists have analysed how the formerly oppressed can and do appropriate and imitate the culture, ethics and greed of their former oppressors through power, language and – of course – corruption. The formerly oppressed can reproduce conditions of power to suit them, they can breathe coloniality all the time, instead of striving for a more humane world. The media can exercise its power and it can show more humanity, equality, and healthy doses of decolonial love. Part of this humanity is also exposing greed and corruption. The background question to this chapter, in a sense, is: what is journalism for, and what kind of power does it have? This leads on to the last chapter, an analysis of power and loss in media in South Africa.

8

Power, Loss and Reimagining Journalism

True power does not need arrogance, a long beard and a barking voice. True power strangles you with silk ribbons, charm and intelligence.
Oriana Fallaci, cited in Slavoj Žižek, *First as Tragedy, Then as Farce*

The conundrums of power and loss this book has discussed include the increasingly populist nature of politics and the concomitant information disorder causing trust in journalism to erode. Social media usage proliferates. Women journalists are targeted in brutal cyber attacks. Job losses in newsrooms are severe. Important beats, such as courts, labour and books, have all but disappeared from mainstream media, and community media has largely moved to Facebook – while the big tech companies are now under scrutiny over their unregulated power. In essence, a crisis in journalism exists, which should also then present the craft with opportunities for change.

The power gains include that investigative journalism has increased, and collaborations – intracountry, continentally and internationally – rather than competition characterise the new genre of working. There are new start-up media companies that are doing journalism differently, from the ground up, and there are also, in mainstream media, green shoots in thinking, as in the framing and the coverage of the Afro hair saga. The gaze in this instance emanated purely from the perspective of the black woman's experience, or a decolonial lens. There is some evidence of reflection in action.

Could it be the time for professional journalists and owners of the news media to press the pause button, to slow down, to take three steps backwards in order to take two steps forward? Is it time to stop chasing social media, likes, clickbaits, algorithms, innovation and, indeed, all 'bright, shiny new things' (to use Julie Posetti's phrase)?[1] Some media analysts argue that the only way forward is to demand Facebook pay for journalism. But that would increase Facebook's grip on journalism, its owning the public space even more.

Much of the content of this book has illustrated the losses for journalism over the period that the internet has marginalised the traditional news media, and the social and political price paid. Nevertheless, there is much good that remains, located in investigative journalism, collaboration (as opposed to competition) including cross-border or international public donor funding, new ways of reporting in some start-ups, and a greater assertiveness by women in the media.

THEORETICAL GAZES THAT ASSISTED THIS ANALYSIS

A few like-minded theoretical lenses have been used to make sense of journalism's conundrums of power and loss in South Africa, with overlap and reference to the international situation – radical democracy combining the use of psychoanalytical concepts, decoloniality blended with black consciousness, and feminist theory.

Radical democracy argues for the greatest possible inclusion of voices to enable diversity in the many public spaces – arguments, robust contestations, differences or dissension, but with a minimal consensus. In South Africa, this minimal consensus could be those values espoused in the Constitution. The role of journalism is to acknowledge and to keep these multiplicities of public spaces open. The radical democracy theorist Chantal Mouffe proffered that the role of journalism is to keep the spaces open within which different groups struggle for hegemony.[2] It should contribute to the creation of agonistic (as opposed to enemy opposition) public spaces where alternatives to what is current could be put forward. Currently on the table is the liberal capitalist political paradigm which has proved not to create a more humane world for all. Indeed, democracy has not deepened, but inequality has expanded.

Theoretical concepts from political philosophy of power, loss, trauma, master signifier, passionate attachment and ambivalence have been useful in this book for many of the chapters. For example, the job losses in traditional journalism have constituted a trauma for the journalists who were passionately attached to their identities. There was deep ambivalence about 'moving on', having experienced a massive sense of loss of power. There are many forms that power takes: dominated by an outside force as in pressing down upon one, and then also, internalised, as in one can participate in one's own subjection. There can be reflexive turns towards the voice of power, after being hailed and shamed and labelled, on which Frantz Fanon also theorised when he started one of his chapters with 'Look, a Negro!', to talk about 'the fact of blackness'.

DECOLONIALITY AND BLACK CONSCIOUSNESS

The theoretical argument here is that black consciousness exists in tandem with the 'decolonial turn'. The latter is a shift in the production of knowledge. It refocuses the gaze to render the invisible visible. There is a need for the invisible to be brought to the centre. Black consciousness argues, as does decolonial theory, for the bringing of the *damnés*, or the wretched of the earth, to the centre. In the global South, it is blackness and women that intersect with poverty, constituting the wretched of the earth. These theories were valuable in the discussions about community media going online, as well as the anti-feminist backlash chapter, the Afro hair saga, and the green shoots in media in chapter 7.

'Whenever you hear anyone abuse the Jews, pay attention, because he is talking about you,' Fanon's philosophy professor said to him. Fanon acknowledged that the professor was 'universally right'. The kind of denunciation, of shaming and othering that is central to decoloniality and black consciousness theory was important for several chapters in this work. Central to this was also 'decolonial love', which Chela Sandoval called a political technology, a political struggle against the structures of dehumanisation.[3] At the epicentre of this has to be love for those at lowest rung of power: woman, black woman, poor woman.

FEMINIST THEORY

There are several different feminisms, as well as robust contestations between feminists. In this book, feminism (simplified) has meant equality between women and men. Women have the right to choose whoever and whatever they want to be without the constriction of patriarchal domination bearing down upon them, monitoring and censoring them. Feminist theories have been used to discuss how media companies discriminated against women and the backlash that women experienced in social media. A pattern emerged: a backlash occurs when it seems that women have made substantial gains in their efforts to obtain equal rights. A backlash is a counter-assault, a conservative response to the achievements of feminism.

BEYOND THEORY GAZES: THE POLITICAL CLIMATE

The political temperature in South Africa in 2018–2019 was searingly hot. There have been several commissions of inquiry headed by retired judges, including the Zondo commission of inquiry into state capture, the Nugent commission into the South African Revenue Service (SARS), the Mpati commission into the Public Investment Corporation, and the Mokgoro commission into the National Prosecuting Authority. These commissions unearthed, in breathtaking detail, the bribery and corruption at the nexus between the private and public sectors. Within this context senior women, political and investigative journalists, were attacked by the Economic Freedom Fighters (EFF), most specifically and vividly after the VBS Mutual Bank exposure. The backlash against women has been harsh and misogynistic. The EFF is the very same party that claimed it wished to 'decolonise' South Africa. The message was populist – either devoid of a solid understanding of decolonisation or deliberately and cheaply twisting the meaning of decolonisation to suit its ideological agenda. Social media was a central medium for the party's vitriol against women. In October 2018, the EFF's leader, Julius Malema, listed several journalists' names for his party's supporters to 'deal with decisively'. Following his comments, some of the journalists were physically accosted, and abused on social media. One journalist was verbally threatened outside the Parktown, Johannesburg venue of the Zondo commission, where Malema had made some of these threats. In another incident, a senior editor was accosted by three men who shouted her surname and mocked her while she was out shopping. The threats online were racially abusive. This had a ripple effect in the newsroom, young women journalists feeling nervous and fearful, and led them to withdraw from beats that were previously the domain of males: political reporting and investigative journalism. In response to the attacks on women journalists, the *Daily Maverick* editor Branko Brkic reflected in a column that it was an extraordinary act of cowardice to attack women journalists in this way, merely for doing their jobs, particularly in a society plagued with violence against women. It showed a party that was 'weak but vicious'. Brkic wrote that the suppression of free media, racism and violence against women was taken to a 'Trumpian' level when they were wrapped in one continual vicious attack. It had a just sufficient legal caveat: should something horrible happen to the targets of their attack, those responsible would claim innocence and then 'throw one's own supporters under the legal bus instead', Brkic wrote.[4] These attacks on women journalists were the loud, barking voice of power, a bullying voice, showing weakness and viciousness, the opposite of true power.

What is the future of news and where does the good power lie? It is trite, a homily, a cliché perhaps, to say that in crisis lies an opportunity. It remains true, nonetheless. We have seen, in myriad ways, that journalism is in a crisis and that the public suffer from a lack of access to reliable news. Ideas on how to emerge from the crisis, to something better, are needed. This chapter started with the conundrums that social media has presented for journalism. Let us turn now to ideas related to that issue.

Social media and journalists

It is possible that news could be saved if journalists disengaged, at least to some extent, from social media. It is good for journalists to post links to their stories, but they could also avoid reactiveness and refrain from presenting a contrary position as if all social truth can be reduced to binary oppositions. Needless provocation merely stirs more unhelpful noise. What, for example, is the good of tweeting something like this before the election: 'Malema or Maimane? Vote now, polls close in 24 hours'. It is binary, but as a question it makes unstated, fallacious assumptions upon which nothing useful can be built. Posted on social media for people to vote on, it presents an artificial, indeed ridiculous, false dichotomy.

There has to be some level of involvement by journalists in social media. There is value in watching, lurking and imbibing, perhaps, the mood and the debates. But it should not be forgotten that Twitter, Instagram and Facebook do not represent the whole of South Africa – or even half of its population. The toxicity of Twitter resides in the binary oppositions it presents, and there is a danger in too much excitation, or Jacques Lacan's *jouissance*, attached to one or the other view. The more journalists contribute to this divisiveness, and the 'shouty' nature of social media, the more journalism loses. The multiple views they are supposed to reflect, the nuance that could be offered and the analyses of these views is not found on social media, reliance on which merely does the opposite to creating a radical democracy with a diversity of opinion. Dissonance is not to be confused with democracy, and social media tends to feed war-like 'enemy positions'. As we are seeing in the politics of the world at large, so we are seeing in South Africa.

None of this criticism of social media denies that it has a positive role to play in social discourse, apart from 'finding friends' or sharing pictures of one's breakfast. Social media has enabled real-life dramas such as weather disasters to be shared instantly, even though sometimes this, too, is constructed with fake pictures. It can be an outstanding avenue for activism. For example, during the #MeToo campaign, publics could amass quickly, and journalists could pick up on the issue and run with it. They could interview people on podcasts and highlight the plights of many affected by sexual violence.

Media companies need imagination

Media-owning companies have shown insensitivity and clumsiness in the way they have retrenched in droves, cutting the professional journalist workforce in the past ten years. The functioning of the news media has never recovered from the 2008 global financial crisis, when companies hired 'content producers' to replace journalists. Content producers produce content, and content can be anything that fills an empty receptacle.

Newsrooms today have a few tech-savvy young content producers, who work long hours, days on end, earning low wages. Instead of discarding older journalists there could have been – and there remains – room for a more imaginative scheme to retain both the older and the younger. For example, the previously high-earning senior journalists could work fewer hours, coaching the young content producers to write, encapsulating the context that is so often missing in the 'content'. In turn, the content producers could coach the older on, for instance, how to make videos and podcasts and then upload them. In this way, technology becomes demystified, and skills are passed on in both directions. In the chapter on job losses, we saw that none of the media companies asked the senior journalists, including sub-editors (whom they unceremoniously cast aside without so much as even the farewell party of the past) whether they would be prepared to accept lower salaries, or whether they would work half days or half weeks, so that their skills could be retained and passed on. This has been one of the biggest power losses to journalism.

Regain trust

The more the idea of 'fluid journalism' is touted by the techno determinists and techno optimists, the more journalism loses. The more that journalism is conflated with social media, and the more that 'fake news' appears on social media, the more trust is lost in journalism. Opinion making or analysis by experts in their particular fields is not journalism. Journalists have to stop chasing social media and technology and shift the focus to fair reporting, good long-form pieces, analysis and investigations. Those brands that prove themselves tend to survive, irrespective of what platform they publish on. Public interest journalism can survive.

What I referred to as the 'green shoots' in chapter 7 are signs of hope. There is some reimagining of what public interest journalism could be. Many of these agencies are non-profit, relying on crowd-sourced funding and philanthropy (*Daily Maverick* and amaBhungane, for instance) as well as alliances with academia, as exemplified by *The Conversation*.

Collaborations

Collaborations and alliances is the international and local investigative journalism trend to catch the crooks. Alliances between civil society advocacy groups such as the Right2Know, community-based organisations and non-governmental organisations (NGOs) may be useful, especially for the feminist struggle against violence and for other issues such as climate change. However, advocacy journalism should be marked as such. This would apply to groups involved in improving the position of the poor, the marginalised and unemployed, as well as those supporting LGBTIQ (lesbian, gay, bisexual, transgender/transsexual, intersex and queer/questioning) concerns.

I sat in a South African National Editors' Forum (Sanef) meeting in 2018 with women's groups and LGBTIQ groups and was struck at how many expressed frustrations with mainstream newspapers: they told how they wrote analyses and opinion for op-eds which got 'dumped' or, in newsroom jargon, 'spiked'. 'That's mainstream media for you,' they said. If our world is to become a kinder place, as it would be with a decolonial-turn type of thinking, this ought to change. What is the point of hearing the same old ways of being, when there are new views, reflecting new times, landing on editors' desks? Who benefits when new views are cast aside? For the first time in the Glass Ceilings research, a small proportion of respondents referred to themselves as 'other' rather than male or female. Those asserting a right to have fluid identity and sexuality testify to changes in the times. This must be accommodated in the surveys we do, in the content we write, who we interview and how we do so, if true diversity is to be reflected and accommodated in the media.

Audiences will continue to be platform-agnostic

The business of sustainable models is not the main thrust of this book. However, we know that advertisers, and classifieds, by and large, have abandoned print, and the prices of newspapers have rocketed. Some readers left print for online, some remained, continuing to pay the high prices. Then, some, a middle layer if you like, abandoned daily newspapers to acquire their news from a variety of sources and platforms: television, podcasts, online sites, radio, the weekend papers only. The third layer, those born in the middle and upper class, in the smartphone era (as well as in the age where trees must be saved, the twenty-one-year-old) would almost certainly not buy legacy media, having started off their lives getting news free on social media and online.

The digital transition remains a messy and random one, with no obvious option for news organisations to choose. No one has cracked the code to make money from digital, although the *New York Times* which now gathers about 40 per cent of its revenue from digital subscriptions, and the *Washington Post* have reported on and off over the last few years that they are climbing to new heights. In other parts of the world, the public has become accustomed to the 'silky ribbon' of obtaining news for free online, also finding it on social media, where it is mixed up with 'fake news' – the latter travelling faster than any other.

By 2019, the *New York Times*, interestingly enough, had slightly more women users (than men) amid its 3.4 million paid subscribers: could this be the result of hiring a gender editor in 2017, inspired by the #MeToo movement? This book has pointed to the significance of diversity and gender equality throughout its chapters – it also seems to make business sense.

A role for governments

The government-funded Media Development and Diversity Agency (MDDA) has not been a huge success. The community newspaper sector is dying. The news groups resorted to Facebook instead of forming independent online digital news products. The general expectation was that social media and the internet would allow for more diversity but, instead, more power than ever before has been relocated to the international technology companies. Journalism moved from one set of large corporate entities to another.

Facebook's valuation was estimated to be above $470 billion, while Google's market value rose from $200 billion in 2012 to almost $800 billion in 2018. The imposition of fair and effective tax on large media entities such as Facebook and Google has become an urgent campaign but it will require a concerted international effort and considerable political will to be seriously effective. Some countries are already leading the charge, and the idea has been mentioned in a few recent reports. An example is Harry Dugmore's journalism research project on the sustainability of media.[5]

Is there a role for the government in the conundrum now urgently pressing upon journalism? The answer is both yes and no. The ruling party has been deeply embedded in the public broadcaster, the South African Broadcasting Corporation (SABC). It has held a firm grip on the appointment of the board, resulting in censorship and editorial interference. The public broadcaster has been used like a football, as contending factions within the ruling party have tried to score goals. The MDDA, which the government has funded inadequately, should be overhauled.

The information disorder and 'fake news'

The phenomenon of 'fake news' will continue and will worsen in an age of growing nationalism, populism and the onslaught against democracy. The media researchers Claire Wardle and Hossein Derakhshan advocate that we stop using the term 'fake news'.[6] In the age of information disorder in the media landscape, the term 'fake news' glibly glosses over misinformation, disinformation, mal-information (deliberately malicious, intended to harm) and political propaganda. Fake news is enabled by technology, and in particular social media, although this is not the same as saying technology and social media are responsible. They merely make it easier.

Fake news is also on the increase where job losses are severe in journalism and many have turned to public relations. There are more communications specialists and experts, public relations and spin doctors than there are journalists. Ironically, we need more technological innovation to combat what technology enabled. We need to find ways to catch the trolls. We could also discourage the 'likes' and 'follow me' culture. People see something 'juicy' and retweet, thinking they will get more retweets and likes, and followers. Then we could sanction, by naming and shaming, those on social media (including mainstream media) who spread falsities that cause harm. Media and academics should inform the public about the depth and scale of this trend in the disordered and chaotic information landscape.

The master signifier in 'fake news' is power and politics. That is fixed whereas everything else floats, and journalism is now on the back foot because the publics are confused about where the fake news comes from. When members of the public jump in to spread information they know may be fake, they are engaging in *Schadenfreude* (joys of misfortune or malicious joy).

More investigations

Investigative journalism is an area of great power in the media and should be further capacitated. As a result of its plethora of stories over the past two decades, it helped bring down a corrupt president. This book ends at a time, in 2019, when the Zondo commission was revealing how tender manipulation took place, how many millions were paid in bribes (including cash stuffed in Louis Vuitton handbags), when again we saw that Jacob Zuma and many of his supporters were at the heart of the witnesses' testimonies. But sight must not be lost of the fact that, for instance, investigative journalists had revealed the links between Bosasa and government corruption more than a decade ago. The Zondo commission was now hearing it directly from witnesses, blowing the whistle. However, there was also an allegation that some journalists (on a list of names) had been bribed by Bosasa, which resulted in speculation. Journalists and others began looking for clues about 'the list', through favourable stories written about Bosasa. But they could not be found. What could be found was that those journalists who had uncovered corruption about Bosasa years ago had been vilified, which included death-threatening phone calls.

The state of the newsroom

Calling public relations personnel journalists attests to the problem (enhanced by digital media) of a new term, 'fluid journalism'. There are many people putting out 'facts', 'information' or 'opinion' in the media, but are they journalists? In this context fact-checking and verification, which is what journalists are supposed to do, has become more important than ever.

Independent fact-checking entities such as *Africa Check*, based in Johannesburg, are widespread worldwide. This is good news but fact-checking entities are needed in newsrooms too. A cry for 'back to basics' may seem cur-mudgeonly in the digital age in which we operate, but it is one way to save the craft. Verification and fact-checking gives reliability and credibility to the news, and adds value to it. The ranks of the journalist fact-checkers have been almost depleted but at great cost to the value of news.

There should be greater awareness of the Press Code in our newsrooms. The regulation system is a voluntary one, a system that relies on a code of ethics and persuasion, and refresher training on the Press Code should be introduced.

Imagination and diversity in reporting

Political reporting could incorporate rigorous policy analysis and fatuous claims and promises could be exposed for what they are. The chaos in the UK that has followed Brexit has shown that for almost every plausibly attractive political idea there is a price to be paid. There is likely to be a market for the expert scrutiny of political policy, written in terms that everyone can understand.

There are many political parties in South Africa, although only about a quarter of them contest elections. Still, what do they stand for, who funds them and why should we care or vote for them? Is it really democratic to have so many parties contesting an election? I ask the same questions of myself and of the media, at every election, but I do not get answers. I am keen to know where the different parties stand on unemployment, poverty, feminism and climate change. This is one way to reimagine, a move away from reporting how many 'lengths' this or that of the three main parties is ahead of the other in the race. Reporters could think in terms other than the same formulaic reporting during elections.

In an era of globalisation, technology is moving faster than most could have anticipated. It is simultaneously both hard to find the truth and dangerous to reveal it. There are populists, internationally and nationally, who describe journalists as enemies of the people when they reveal the truth. There are many ways for journalists to do things differently from those who are arrogant and bark loudly, but who have no real power. Among the ways to regain trust and good power is to be true to professional codes and ethics, to do stories in the public interest and to use social media more judiciously, instead of the usual and common 'knee-jerk' reactions which merely feed the inherently polarising nature of social media.

Then, the big tech companies could be tackled on issues of social responsi-bility. And note should be taken of what is happening in the community media sector, now gasping its last breaths. Perhaps tax reforms could release funds to revive the sector. More pressure has to be put on government to decrease the cost of broadband, and increase spectrum, a key for participatory democracy. The backlash against feminism must be combated, and ways sought to catch the trolls, then name and shame them. Media companies could really have done with, and can still do with, more imagination and humanity, in their execution of the journalists' job losses bloodbath. Reporting could be given a different slant by recruiting other voices in the stories journalists do, in order to enhance diversity. We could also add empathy to the mix, as we saw with the Afro hair stories. The media has power to think and act beyond the norms of everyday mainstream culture and perceptions.

This book has performed an interrogation of power (of media, of journalists, of media companies, of politicians and corruption) and – side by side with the power – the losses. It asks and answers the question of whether journalism is capable of rising to the challenge – in this era of populism, of black and white or binary oppositions, of fake news and misinformation, of crisis of trust – of performing its role in a democracy. It acknowledges and notes that there is something afoot: old norms are shifting and structures of power are challenged more than ever before as there is more pushback against the greed of corporates, corrupt politicians, patriarchy, racism – but also mainstream media which came as part of the old norms and elitist establishments.

What this means, then, is that there is an opportunity for change to finally serve audiences. This book has shown that investigative journalism continues to be lauded (but also interrogated) but I have argued that journalists can do more than expose the corrupt; they can also expose the media companies for their lack of humanity. Those still in the profession could do journalism with more compassion, empathy and diversity of voices. With artificial intelligence apparently round the corner (or here already), the space for empathy and compassion in journalism is more crucial than ever. Journalists can seek out the subtleties in stories and move away from 'he said, she said' binary oppositions imitating social media's vapidity. But social media norms and mores are not to blame; this lack of nuance has always been there. Journalism can find humanity itself amid the noise and silky ribbons of social media, of the binary oppositions of us and them, male and female, black and white, left and right, for climate change or not, feminist or sexist. I have suggested in this book that all this seems possible when we examine the mainstream coverage of the Afro saga, and the start-ups such as New Frame, GroundUp, *The Conversation* and the *Daily Maverick*.

As Fanon said in *Black Skin, White Masks*, 'yes to life, yes to love, yes to generosity' (and no to degradation, scorn, indignity, inhumanity). We could reflect on this as we reimagine media and journalism in the 'battle for the creation of a human world – a world of reciprocal recognition'. We could also reflect on his reflection that humanity is waiting for something different from us, instead of obscene imitations, by which he meant the excesses experienced in the colonial past. This must apply to journalism as much as to politics and life itself. In this book we have seen the mechanics of power and how it acts. Power is quirky, slippery and paradoxical. It shifts and slides, depending on where you are standing, your position and your gaze. It can be horizontal among equals, and it can be internal when we subject ourselves to compliance, as we do in a reflexive turn. It can enable insecurities, trauma and passionate attachments. Power can also strangle like a silk ribbon. Power also lies in reimagining.

EPILOGUE

Wherever there is too much power and a lack of accountability, may there continue to be an oppositional consciousness to resist abuse, and may this be highlighted by independent, credible and trustworthy news media.

This book ends in 2019. At the beginning of the year South Africans were struggling with electricity blackouts and the state-owned enterprise, the energy supplier Eskom, was being bailed out – again – by the government (R23 billion a year for the next three years, to continue over ten years, amounting to a total of R150 billion). Techno optimists were preparing for the 'Fourth Industrial Revolution'. Two irreconcilable things. There was no mention of how to deal with the media tech monopolies, Facebook, Google and Twitter.

In February 2019, a few months before the national election when politics was likely to get uglier than ever and misinformation likely to spread like wildfire, neither President Cyril Ramaphosa's State of the Nation speech nor Finance Minister Tito Mboweni's budget speech referred to the crisis in news media – but they did make vague references to rendering access to digital information more affordable. There also appeared to be a commitment to ending the scourge of corruption, with a focus on Eskom. The contribution that high-impact public interest and investigative journalism has made to outing the corrupt at Eskom and in state-owned enterprises in general has been enormous. (The contribution that journalism has made is the focus in this book, but that is not to underplay the role of whistleblowers, at Eskom for example and in opposition parties, unions, civil society and non-governmental organisations (NGOs) such as Corruption Watch.)

By August 2019, Eskom's debt was revealed to be about R500 billion, and it was interpellated and shamed as responsible for plunging South Africa's economy into a crisis, with more downgrades imminent. The official unemployment figure rose to 29 per cent, the highest in post-apartheid South Africa. The rand weakened, the price of petrol went up. The *Mail & Guardian* announced it would serve section 189 notices to retrench staff, citing the challenges faced by traditional media, including the migration of readers from print to digital platforms. In addition, Sekunjalo Independent Media, which owns the Independent Newspapers group, owed the Public Investment Corporation (PIC, which controlled the country's pension funds) R1.5 billion rands and by November 2019 there were calls at the PIC inquiry to liquidate the company (as reported by Jackie Cameron in 'Lies, damned lies and Sekunjalo statistics' on Biznews). If the group collapsed then about 600 more journalists would be out of jobs.

Local news is dying fast, and this is not just evident from the research I have undertaken but from my experience too. For four years, I have struggled to find out what the new development was in my neighbourhood in Houghton, along Louis Botha Avenue in Johannesburg. Yet every night on the news I found out what US President Trump was tweeting about. I joined the Houghton Heritage Society at a substantial annual fee in the hope of getting some news about my neighbourhood. I still haven't found out.

The writing for this book also ended at a time when findings of the inquiry into editorial interference at the South African Broadcasting Corporation (SABC) were released. The report noted that the public broadcaster had suffered from the capricious use of authority and power to terrorise staff and to deflect the corporation from its mandate. Its editorial policies affirm the issues covered in chapter 2.

In the same month, South African National Editors' Forum's (Sanef's) inquiry into media ethics and credibility, headed by former judge Kathy Satchwell, began. This came from the impetus of the number of incorrect stories and apologies made by the *Sunday Times* after the 'rogue unit' and the Cato Manor death squad stories, as discussed in chapter 3. At the time, Sanef welcomed *Sunday Times* editor Bongani Siqoko's acknowledgement, but stated that this was just the first step in rebuilding and regaining the public trust. The forum stated that this was a moment for individual media houses to introspect seriously and review editorial systems with a view to enhancing media credibility. To strengthen this process, it began the independent investigation into issues of editorial integrity, across the industry as a whole, with the *Sunday Times* merely the impetus. These interventions, through inquiries, were clear indications that large parts of the industry wanted to change journalism for the better.

What else can be done? I have ten main points, findings and questions to be raised for discussion, from this book's research but also my own experience:

1. Accept that the old media ecosystem is dead. People read today's news today, immediately, and not in a newspaper tomorrow. This is digital disruption. In 2008, for example, there were 234 million websites in the world and by 2018 this grew to a billion and a half, as wrote Alan Rusbridger, former editor of the *Guardian* in London, in his book *Breaking News: The Remaking of Journalism and Why it Matters Now*. Accept also that the old business model for the sustainability of news media is dead and cannot be resurrected, and that journalism is a public good. But, then, journalism must really serve the publics – all the publics. For example, no one reported on what the demands were of the Khoi San protesting outside the ANC's policy conference in 2018. None of the publics are aware of what they wanted, as far as I am aware. They are the first people of South Africa, and yet they remained marginalised.

2. The not-for-profit model appears to be the only option, but publics, governments, the state, philanthropists, NGOs and perhaps corporate incentive schemes could support journalism if they could recognise the importance of it and the need for it. As the famous writer Toni Morrison, who died at the time of writing, in August 2019, said, we should make a difference for something other than ourselves. The irony is that supporting good not-for-profit journalism makes a difference to us all if we consider the contribution investigative journalism has made to bringing down a corrupt president.

3. To win back credibility, the news media has to have alliances with communities, individuals and civil society groupings. To listen, to hear and to be self-reflexive would work. The stand-alone, stand-afar, pretend objectivity must end.

4. There should be one all-encompassing and comprehensive media code for all media platforms, given that convergence rules the day. For example, a radio station does an interview with an analyst then puts the interview on its online news; then that same item gets tweeted; then it's in the newspaper the next day – redundantly so, but already there are four platforms involved. The Press Council has begun work to amalgamate all media under one basic umbrella code of ethics.

5. Journalists, media organisations and social media junkies could consider pressing the pause button, reflect and think before tweeting and chasing

tails. Mistakes happen, and your credibility is lost, often forever. You get remembered for that mistake, again and again. Related to this is that the training of journalists by media companies themselves needs to happen again. If it doesn't, we will continue to get news that lacks context and relies on being sensational.

6. For journalism to succeed and win credibility, journalists have to be under less pressure from news desks, editors and media companies to work 24 hours a day and seven days a week, and to perform on so many platforms – with broadcast, video, online, Twitter and Facebook.

7. Women journalists all over the world, including in South Africa, are suffering from threats of rape and murder – and some have been murdered already. This is for me one of the most important and urgent issues of our time. Women journalists are being bullied and interpellated as 'cabal', 'slut' bitch' and 'whore', and law enforcement agencies are not acting against it.

8. Some more empathy and compassion, anyone? There are now bots in China reading the news, even smiling in appropriate places and looking slightly downcast at sad news. These bots are already working 24/7; they don't need time to stop to reflect, to think, eat, bath, take maternity, or paternity, or sick, or holiday leave, among other human things. The attempt to run journalists to the ground and treat them as bots has created trauma, as we saw in this book's chapter on job losses.

9. Journalists must also tell their own stories and be self-reflexive, acknowledging positionality, their race, class, gender and other multiple subjectivities. Many in this book said they had never had the chance in their 25-year careers to speak about what journalism meant to them.

10. Only international alliances could regulate Facebook (which owns Twitter and now WhatsApp too) and Google. It is as if the genie of internet and social media news is out of the bottle. South Africans on their own can't save journalism from the ravages of the tech giants, both a blessing and a curse, except by pressing for a worldwide law.

Meanwhile, journalists will have to continue shining the spotlight on the corrupt and unaccountable. But they also need to have more empathy and compassion, and listen from the ground up, pay attention to diverse audiences, and not focus exclusively on the elites. Democracy needs powerful and independent journalism working in the public interest and, besides investigations into corruption, this includes increasing diversity, gender equality, local media, stemming job losses in journalism, alliances and partnerships with civil society – as well as philanthropic encouragement, and public and private funding. Journalism, in turn, needs democracy to survive and thrive. This combination would be the ultimate silky ribbon of power. In an ideologically riven world, of populism characterised by binary oppositions, the flaky silk ribbon of social media complicates this power.

This book began with a quote from Michel Foucault: 'Wherever there is power there is resistance'. May this continue to be true in South Africa – where there is power abuse, may journalism continue to be an oppositional consciousness of resistance.

Press Code of Ethics and Conduct for South African Print and Online Media (effective from 1 January 2016)

1. Gathering and reporting of news

1.1. The media shall take care to report news truthfully, accurately and fairly.

1.2. News shall be presented in context and in a balanced manner, without any intentional or negligent departure from the facts whether by distortion, exaggeration or misrepresentation, material omissions, or summarisation.

1.3. Only what may reasonably be true, having regard to the sources of the news, may be presented as fact, and such facts shall be published fairly with reasonable regard to context and importance. Where a report is not based on facts or is founded on opinion, allegation, rumour or supposition, it shall be presented in such manner as to indicate this clearly.

1.4. News should be obtained legally, honestly and fairly, unless public interest dictates otherwise.

1.5. The gathering of personal information for the purpose of journalistic expression must only be used for this purpose.

1.6. Media representatives shall identify themselves as such, unless public interest or their safety dictates otherwise.

1.7. Where there is reason to doubt the accuracy of a report or a source, and it is practicable to verify the accuracy thereof, it shall be verified. Where it has not been practicable to verify the accuracy of a report, this shall be stated in such report.

1.8. The media shall seek the views of the subject of critical reportage in advance of publication; provided that this need not be done where the institution has reasonable grounds for believing that by doing so it would be prevented from reporting; where evidence might be destroyed or sources intimidated; or because it would be impracticable to do so in the circumstances of the publication. Reasonable time should be afforded the subject for a response. If the media are unable to obtain such comment, this shall be reported.

1.9. Where a news item is published on the basis of limited information, this shall be stated as such, and the reports should be supplemented once new information becomes available.

1.10. The media shall make amends for presenting information or comment that is found to be inaccurate by communicating, promptly and with appropriate prominence so as to readily attract attention, a retraction, correction or explanation.

1.11. An online article that has been amended for factual accuracy should indicate as such. In the event of an apology or retraction, the original article may remain, but the publisher must indicate in a prominent manner that it has led to an apology or retraction – and should link to both the apology/retraction and the original article.

1.12. No person shall be entitled to have an article removed which falls short of being defamatory, but is alleged by such person to be embarrassing.

1.13. Journalists shall not plagiarise.

2. Independence and conflicts of interest

2.1. The media shall not allow commercial, political, personal or other non-professional considerations to influence or slant reporting. Conflicts of interest must be avoided, as well as arrangements or practices that could lead audiences to doubt the media's independence and professionalism.

2.2. The media shall not accept a bribe, gift or any other benefit where this is intended or likely to influence coverage.

2.3. The media shall indicate clearly when an outside organisation has contributed to the cost of newsgathering.

2.4. Editorial material shall be kept clearly distinct from advertising and sponsored content.

amaBhungane Stories in the Past Two or Three Years

5 February 2016	Guptas conquer state arms firm Denel
5 February 2016	Gupta ties are Zuma's undoing
19 February 2016	Zuma Jnr hits the big time with Optimum deal
18 March 2016	The president who tossed away the rule book
24 March 2016	The 'Gupta owned' state enterprises
24 March 2016	Evidence of state capture mounts
1 May 2016	Guptas 'backed' Maine's R140k-a-month bond
15 May 2016	Guptas sue for 27.5% of Independent Media
30 May 2016	How Denel was hijacked
6 June 2016	Guptas media bid rebuffed
19 June 2016	Guptas R51bn train grab
24 July 2016	Gupta-linked company set to score R800-million in Transnet IT solution tender deal
28 August 2016	Gupta-linked firm's R167m Transnet bonanza
30 August 2016	Tegeta coal quality hopelessly noncompliant, says report
1 September 2016	Treasury blocks Eskom's Tegeta contract
18 September 2016	Transnet's shady Gupta loan deal
19 September 2016	Questions over new Denel partner
15 October 2016	Gordhan blows whistle on Guptas R6.8bn 'suspicious and unusual payments'
21 October 2016	R587m in six hours – How Eskom paid for Gupta mine
29 October 2016	State capture – The Guptas and the R250 million 'kickback laundry'

3 November 2016	Zwane and his new appointment go way back
4 November 2016	State approved Guptas' raid on mine rehab fund
8 December 2016	From Zuma Inc to the Zuptas – A story of perseverance
8 December 2016	Video: amaBhungane explain the explosive Gupta money-laundering allegations
8 December 2016	Analysis by Sam Sole: Zuma's treasonous alliance with the Guptas
8 December 2016	Exclusive: Guptas 'laundered' kickback millions – here's the evidence
15 February 2017	Gupta owned newspaper in line of fire of new Nielsen report
19 February 2017	The Guptas and the 'box of gems'
22 April 2017	R10 billion in 15 days – Another massive Eskom boost for the Guptas
16 May 2017	How Brian Molefe 'helped' Gupta Optimum heist
18 May 2017	AmaB wins access to information battle over Gupta Waterkloof Landing
19 May 2017	Gupta mine grab: How Brown misled parliament
1 June 2017	Guptas and associates scores R5.3 billion in locomotive kickbacks
1 June 2017	Guptas pushed Eskom for R1.68 billion pre-payment
9 June 2017	How Eskom was captured
30 June 2017	Mckinsey caught up in Trillian lies
30 June 2017	Key findings from Budlender's damning Trillian dossier
5 July 2017	Gupta leaks: Working for the Guptas where sexual harassment was part of the job
11 July 2017	Gupta leaks: Software giant SAP paid Gupta from R100 million kickbacks for state business
15 July 2017	Gupta leaks: Bell Pottinger PR campaign unpacked
20 July 2017	How Gupta associates fleeced Cosatu
21 July 2017	Eskom admits lying on Trillian
22 July 2017	The Gupta microsite your one stop shop

24 July 2017	Gupta leaks: Spin machine commissioned BLF's Mngxitama
8 August 2017	How the Guptas paid for Zuma's home
9 August 2017	Why you should care about the #GuptaLeaks – An international view
5 October 2017	How McKinsey and Trillian milked billions from South Africa Inc
23 October 2017	The McKinsey Dossier: How Transnet cash stuffed Gupta letter boxes
19 January 2018	#GuptaLeaks: Meet the money launderers
19 January 2018	#GuptaLeaks: Liverpool company owns 49% of Indian firm implicated in kickback scheme
19 January 2018	#GuptaLeaks: Indian politician's deal with Gupta partner
7 February 2018	#GuptaLeaks: How Bank of Baroda's misadventures dragged it into SA's political crisis
6 March 2018	Mediosa management mum, on the run
8 March 2018	SAP's #GuptaLeaks investigation finds 'irregularities' and 'question marks'
9 March 2018	The great train robbery part 1 – The Zurich tryst
23 March 2018	The great train robbery part 2 – The choo-choo switcheroo
28 March 2018	The Nkonki pact part 1: How the Guptas bought themselves an auditor
29 March 2018	The Nkonki pact part 2: Eskom's new billion-rand consulting deal for Essa & Co
13 April 2018	Nkonki CEO resigns after we expose Gupta fronting deal
23 April 2018	The Nkonki pact part 3: Eskom funded Essa's capture of audit firm
20 May 2018	Gupta link in R647m train deal
3 June 2018	A total train-smash: The R16bn 'Gupta premium'

NOTES

CHAPTER 1

1   The media encompasses more than news media and investigations. It includes, for example, advertising, marketing, online content, social media and blogging, and citizen journalism. This book's focus is on the news media, or 'journalism'.

2   The Guptas, an immigrant Indian business family, befriended former president Jacob Zuma. In the #GuptaLeaks, the nexus was found to be at the heart of corruption between the public and private sector.

3   'The Global Slump in Press Freedom', *The Economist,* 23 July 2018.

4   BBC News, 'Khashoggi Death: Saudi Arabia Says Journalist Was Murdered', *BBC News*, 22 October 2018. Accessed 20 January 2020, https://www.bbc.com/news/world-middle-east-45935823.

5   Achille Mbembe, *On the Postcolony* (Johannesburg: Wits University Press, 2015).

6   South African National Editors' Forum (Sanef), Institute for the Advancement of Journalism (IAJ), Press Council of South Africa, South African Communications Association (Sacomm), Media Workers Association of South Africa (Mwasa), Media Development and Diversity Agency (MDDA), Freedom of Expression Institute (FXI), Save Our SABC (SOS), Media Monitoring Africa (MMA), Media Institute of Southern Africa (Misa), Association for Independent Publishers (AIP), Broadcast Complaints' Commission of South Africa (BCCSA), PEN South Africa, National Press Club, Southern African Freelancers' Association (Safrea), Cape Town Press Club, Gender Links, Right2Know, National Association of Broadcasters and amaBhungane.

7   Chela Sandoval, *Methodology of the Oppressed: Theory Out of Bounds, Volume 18* (Minneapolis, MN: University of Minnesota Press, 2000), 3.

8   See Francis B. Nyamnjoh, '"Potted Plants in Greenhouses": A Critical Reflection on the Resilience of Colonial Education in Africa', *Journal of Asian and African Studies*, 47:2 (2012), 148.

9   Viola C. Milton, 'A Kind of Blue: Can Communication Research Matter?' Paper presented at the University of South Africa, Pretoria, 20 March 2019.

10 Tendayi Sithole, *Steve Biko: Decolonial Meditations of Black Consciousness* (New York: Lexington Books, 2016).

11 Pier Paolo Frassinelli, 'Decolonisation: What it is and What Research Has to do with it', in *Making Sense of Research*, ed. Keyan G. Tomaselli (Pretoria: Van Schaik, 2018), 3–10.

12 Sabelo J. Ndlovu-Gatsheni, 'Why Decoloniality in the 21st Century?', *The Thinker*, 48 (2013): 10–15. See also Sithole, *Steve Biko*.

13 Helge Rønning and Tawana Kupe, 'The Dual Legacy of Democracy and Authoritarianism', in *De-Westernizing Media Studies*, ed. James Curran and Myung-Jin Park (London: Routledge, 2000), 138–156.

14 Winston Mano and Viola C. Milton, 'Citizen Journalism and the Ebola Outbreak in Africa', in *Participatory Politics and Citizen Journalism in a Networked Africa*, ed. Bruce Mutsvairo (London: Palgrave Macmillan, 2016), 244–261.

15 Colin Chasi, 'Violent Communication is Not Alien to Ubuntu: Nothing Human is Alien to Africans', *Communicatio*, 40:4 (2014), 287–304.

16 Herman Wasserman and Arnold de Beer, 'Which Public? Whose Interest? The South African Media and Its Role during the First Ten Years of Democracy', *Critical Arts*, 19:1–2 (2005), 36–51.

17 Keyan G. Tomaselli, 'Ownership and Control in the South African Print Media: Black Empowerment after Apartheid, 1990–1997', *Ecquid Novi: African Journalism Studies*, 18:1 (1997), 67–68.

18 Lynette Steenveld, 'Transformation of the Media: From What to What?' *Rhodes Journalism Review*, 16 (1998), 1–4.

19 See Guy Berger, 'Towards an Analysis of South African Media and Transformation 1994–1999', *Transformation*, 38 (1999), 82–116.

20 Pieter J. Fourie, ed., *Media Studies: Social (New) Media and Mediated Communication Today, Volume 4* (Cape Town: Juta, 2017).

21 Harry Dugmore, *Paying the Piper: The Sustainability of the News Industry and Journalism in South Africa in a Time of Digital Transformation and Political Uncertainty.* (Rhodes University, Grahamstown: Digital Journalism Research Project, 2018). Accessed 15 February 2019, https://themediaonline.co.za/wp-content/uploads/2018/05/PAYING-THE-PIPER-The-sustainability-of-the-news-industry-and-journalism-in-South-Africa-in-a-time-of-digital-transformation-and-political-uncertainty.pdf.

22 Jane Duncan, 'South African Journalism and the Marikana Massacre: A Case Study of an Editorial Failure', *The Political Economy of Communication*, 1:2 (2013), 65–88.

23 Sarah Chiumbu, 'Media, Race and Capital: A Decolonial Analysis of Representation of Miners' Strikes in South Africa', *African Studies*, 75 (2016), 417–435.

24 Glenda Daniels, Tarisai Nyamweda and Collin Nxumalo, *Glass Ceilings: Women in South African Media Houses 2018* (Johannesburg: Gender Links, 2018). *Glass Ceilings* was launched on Black Wednesday/Media Freedom Day, 19 October 2018, in Johannesburg.

25 Lizette Rabe, 'Glass Ceiling, Concrete Ceiling', *Rhodes Journalism Review*, 26 (2006): 20–21.

26 Ylva Rodny-Gumede, 'Male and Female Journalists' Perceptions of Their Power to Influence News Agendas and Public Discourses', *Communicatio*, 41:2 (2015), 206–219.

27 Pat Made and Colleen Lowe Morna, eds, *Glass Ceilings: Women and Men in Southern Africa Media* (Johannesburg: Gender Links, 2009).

28 Oriana Fallaci, cited in Slavoj Žižek, *First as Tragedy, Then as Farce* (London: Verso, 2009), 50.

29 Gayatri Spivak, 'Can the Subaltern Speak?', in *Marxism and the Interpretation of Culture*, ed. Carry Nelson and Lawrence Grossberge (Champaign, IL: University of Illinois Press, 1988), 271–313.

30 Sandoval, *Methodology of the Oppressed*, 4.

31 Sandoval, *Methodology of the Oppressed.*

32 Judith Butler, *The Psychic Life of Power: Theories in Subjection* (Palo Alto, CA: Stanford University Press, 1997).

33 Committee to Protect Journalists, 'Record Number of Journalists Jailed as Turkey, China and Egypt Pay Scant Price for Repression', *Committee to Protect Journalists Reports,* 13 December 2017. Accessed 30 July 2018, https://cpj.org/reports/2017/12/journalists-prison-jail-record-number-turkey-china-egypt.php.

34 ANC, 'Policy Conference Resolutions about the Media', paper presented at the ANC's 52nd National Conference, Polokwane, 20 December 2007; 'Communications and the Battle of Ideas', paper presented at the ANC's 53rd National Conference on resolutions adopted in 2012, Mangaung, 31 January 2013; 'Media Transformation, Ownership, and Diversity', paper presented at the ANC's 50th National Conference, Mafikeng, 16 December 1997.

35 Launch of the Print and Digital Media Transformation Task Team (PDMTTT) media release on 27 September 2012.

36 Reg Rumney, 'Towards a Policy on Media Diversity and Development', Government Communication and Information Service (GCIS) discussion document, 2017.

37 See www.marklives.com.

38 Glenda Daniels, *State of the Newsroom, South Africa 2014: Disruptions Accelerated* (Johannesburg: Wits Journalism Department, University of the Witwatersrand, 2014). Accessed 28 August 2019, https://journalism.co.za/new/wp-content/uploads/2018/03/State-of-the-newsroom-2014.pdf.

39 Glenda Daniels, 'Left Out in the Cold', in *State of the Newsroom, South Africa Structured/Unstructured*, ed. Alan Finlay (Johannesburg: Wits Journalism Department, University of the Witwatersrand, 2018), 17–26.

40 Daniels, Nyamweda and Nxumalo, *Glass Ceilings*. The book arose from a research project conducted by Gender Links and Sanef to ascertain the status of women in the newsroom and media companies.

41 Claire Wardle and Hossein Derakhshan, 'One Year On, We're Still Not Recognising the Complexity of the Information Disorder Online', *First Draft*, 31 October 2017. Accessed 11 December 2018, https://firstdraftnews.org/coe_infodisorder/.

42 The New Beats research, 2018. The New Beats research is an international project based in Melbourne, Australia, and focuses on job losses in the journalist industry. I lead the South African wing of the research.

CHAPTER 2

1 Dale McKinley, *South Africa's Corporatised Liberation: A Critical Analysis of the ANC in Power* (Johannesburg: Jacana, 2017).

2   In September and October 2018 many *Sunday Times* stories, especially on the SARS rogue unit, the Cato Manor death squad and the Zimbabwe renditions, were found to be untrue. This is discussed in more detail in the next chapter on journalism's loss of credibility and power.

3   I was the chairperson of the Sanef ethics and diversity subcommittee at the time of conducting the survey in Johannesburg newsrooms in 2016.

4   Judith Butler, *The Psychic Life of Power: Theories in Subjection* (Palo Alto, CA: Stanford University Press, 1997).

5   See amaBhungane, 'The McKinsey Dossiers Parts 1–5', *Daily Maverick*, 14 September–23 October 2017.

6   Slavoj Žižek, *The Sublime Object of Ideology* (London: Verso, 1989), 107.

7   Butler, *The Psychic Life of Power*, 101.

8   'Coconut' is a term used to describe black journalists who are critical of the ruling party – black on the outside but white on the inside. See Glenda Daniels, *Fight for Democracy: The ANC and the Media in South Africa* (Johannesburg: Wits University Press, 2012).

9   Frantz Fanon, *Black Skin, White Masks*, trans. Charles Lam Markmann (New York: Grove Press, 1967), 106.

10 Butler, *The Psychic Life of Power*, 3.

11 Guptagate refers to the landing of a private jet bringing people to a wedding in the family of Zuma's friends, the Guptas, at the Waterkloof Air Force Base in Pretoria. Sibusiso Ngalwa, 'Zuma's Name Secured Gupta Landing', *Sunday Times*, 5 May 2013.

12 The 'media' in this research refers to the news media, as in journalism, and more specifically, to investigative journalism, which is most under attack by the ruling party. The media are also split into two: those who believe that the ANC as ruling party deserves a sympathetic press, and those who believe that independence from political parties should be maintained as part of the critical and professional codes of conduct in the Press Code.

13 Raymond Louw, *So This is Democracy? State of Media Freedom in Southern Africa, 2017* (Windhoek, Namibia: Misa/Fesmedia, 2018).

14 Louw, *So This is Democracy?* Reproduced by permission of the late Raymond Louw.

15 Before 2012 the media was self-regulated, but since the Press Freedom Commission inquiry headed by Justice Pius Langa, it is now co-regulated with more members of the public sitting in on hearings than members of the press, hence 'co' rather than 'self'.

16 ANC, 'Communications and the Battle of Ideas', paper presented at the ANC's 53rd National Conference on resolutions adopted in 2012, Mangaung, 31 January 2013.

17 Glenda Daniels, 'Delay in the Fight against Secrecy Not a Final Victory', *Mail & Guardian*, 24 June 2011.

18 Žižek, *The Sublime Object of Ideology*, 87–128.

19 'Zuma: ANC Not Trying to Control the Media', *Mail & Guardian*, 15 August 2010.

20 Chris Roper, 'The Day We Broke Nkandla', *Mail & Guardian*, 4 December 2013.

21 Zuma in a television interview with eNCA on 10 September 2013.

22 *News24*, 'Media to Blame for Nkandla Perceptions – Zuma', *News24*, 13 February 2015. Accessed 12 July 2018, https://www.news24.com/SouthAfrica/News/Media-to-blame-for-Nkandla-perceptions-Zuma-20150213.

23   See Emily Corke's reportage of the presidential lunch in her article 'Protection of State Information Bill Still Under Consideration,' *EWN*, 18 October 2015. Accessed 10 January 2019, https://ewn.co.za/2015/10/18/ Protection-of-state-information-bill-still-under-consideration.

24   Jeff Wicks, 'SABC 8 Press on with ConCourt Battle', *News24*, 13 September 2016. Accessed 20 January 2018, https://www.news24.com/SouthAfrica/News/ sabc-8-press-on-with-concourt-battle-20160913.

25   See Maggs on Media debate with the COO of the SABC and me. *eNCA*, 'Debate: SABC Won't Revisit "Self-Censorship" Decision: Motsoeneng', *eNCA*, 6 June 2016. Acessed 20 July 2018, https://www.enca.com/south-africa/ debate-sabc-wont-revisit-self-censorship-decision-motsoeneng.

26   Thando Kubheka and Dineo Bendile, 'SABC Refuses to Back Down on its New Editorial Polices', *EWN*, 12 July 2016. Accessed 9 June 2018, https://ewn. co.za/2016/07/12/SABC-refuses-to-back-down-on-its-new-editorial-policies.

27   Kubheka and Bendile, 'SABC Refuses to Back Down'.

28   Glenda Daniels, Tarisai Nyamweda and Collin Nxumalo, *Glass Ceilings: Women in South African Media Houses 2018* (Johannesburg: Gender Links, 2018).

29   Qama Qukula, 'Top SABC Journalists Applauded for Brave Testimony', *Cape Talk*, 13 December 2016. Accessed 15 February 2019, http://www.capetalk.co.za/ articles/236151/top-sabc-journos-applauded-for-brave-testimony.

30   Jenna Etheridge, 'Broken Heart Syndrome Kills "SABC 8" Journalist Suna Venter', *News24*, 29 June 2017. Accessed 22 January 2020, https://www.news24.com/ SouthAfrica/News/sabc-8-journalist-suna-venter-dead-20170629.

31   Žižek, *The Sublime Object of Ideology*.

32   The two discourses often overlap but are not always the same.

33   In 2017 the big other was 'white monopoly capital', which was not discussed in this chapter, so it is a point in passing, but needs to be mentioned.

CHAPTER 3

1   Branko Brkic won the Nat Nakasa award for courageous journalism in 2018, with special mention also being made of the #GuptaLeaks team from amaBhungane, *News24* and Scorpio – Pauli van Wyk, Lester Freamon, Adriaan Basson, Richard Poplak, Adi Eyal, Micah Reddy, Susan Comrie, Angelique Serrao, Stefaans Brummer, Antoinette Muller, Marianne Thamm, Sam Sole, Tabelo Timse, Pieter-Louis Myburgh, Craig McKune, Lionel Faull, Rebecca Davis and Sally Evans.

2   Judith Butler's concept of performativity in her book *The Psychic Life of Power: Theories in Subjection* (Palo Alto, CA: Stanford University Press, 1997), 95.

3   Herman Wasserman, 'Why Journalists in South Africa Should do Some Self-Reflection', *The Media Online*, 31 October 2018. Accessed 10 November 2018, https://themediaonline. co.za/2018/10/why-journalists-in-south-africa-should-do-some-self-reflection/.

4   Niren Tolsi spoke about journalism and race and class at the Ruth First lecture at the University of the Witwatersrand on 18 October 2019.

5   Steven Friedman, 'Political Journalists Are Often Pawns in Factional Fights', *Business Day*, 24 October 2018. Accessed 15 February 2019, https://www.

businesslive.co.za/bd/opinion/columnists/2018-10-24-steven-friedman-political-journalists-are-often-pawns-in-factional-fights/.

6   Sanef press statement, accessed 24 October 2019, https://sanef.org.za/sanef-celebrates-courageous-journalism-and-elects-new-leadership-25-june-2018/.

7   Nic Dawes, former editor of the *Mail & Guardian*, gave an address at the Duke Menell Media Exchange in August 2017.

8   The sources of the comments in the following section are from the author's attendance at the Global Investigative Journalism Conference on 17 November 2017, Wits University, Johannesburg, and subsequent notes.

9   Jacques Pauw, 'Why the *Sunday Times* Should Go to the Zondo and Nugent Commissions', *Daily Maverick*, 27 September 2018. Accessed 10 January 2019, https://www.dailymaverick.co.za/opinionista/2018-09-27-why-the-sunday-times-should-go-to-the-zondo-and-nugent-commissions/

10   Pearlie Joubert, interview by Kieno Kammies, Cape Talk breakfast show. Omny.fm, 2 October 2018. Accessed 10 January 2019, https://omny.fm/shows/the-kieno-kammies-show/pearlie-joubert-on-sunday-times-handling-of-sars-r.

11   Anton Harber, 'Celebrate the Best of Our Investigative Reporters, but Remember the Worst as Well', *The Harbinger*, 15 February 2018. Accessed 2 July 2019, http://www.theharbinger.co.za/wordpress/2018/01/19/celebrate-the-best-of-our-investigative-reporters-but-remember-the-worst-as-well/.

CHAPTER 4

1   By this I mean journalists that are trained to gather information from multiple sources, verify information by checking and double checking, write or broadcast fair and balanced stories for the public through traditional (as opposed to social) media such as newspapers, radio and television.

2   Interviews with managers in different media companies who spoke off the record and unions all attested to this halving.

3   Glenda Daniels, *State of the Newsroom, South Africa 2014: Disruptions Accelerated* (Johannesburg: Wits Journalism Department, University of the Witwatersrand, 2014). Accessed 28 August 2019, https://journalism.co.za/new/wp-content/uploads/2018/03/State-of- the-newsroom-2014.pdf.

4   The New Beats survey is an international research project based in Melbourne, Australia and involves countries from many parts of the world, including South Africa. It tracks what happens to journalists when they leave the newsroom.

5   Glenda Daniels, *State of the Newsroom, South Africa 2013: Disruptions and Transitions* (Johannesburg: Wits Journalism Department, University of the Witwatersrand, 2013). Accessed 17 January 2020, https://journalism.co.za/new/wp-content/uploads/2018/03/State_of_the_newroom_ 2013.pdf.

6   In the famous story of the slave and lord, the slave was not as happy as you would expect once he was freed; there was a stubborn attachment of conditions to his past, which gave him reason for being. He fell into 'unhappy consciousness' once freed. See Judith Butler, *The Psychic Life of Power: Theories in Subjection* (Palo Alto, CA: Stanford University Press, 1997), 31–61.

7   Butler, *The Psychic Life of Power*, 58.
8   Butler, *The Psychic Life of Power*, 61.
9   Neil Coetzer, 'Alternatives to Retrenchment – Are Employers Obliged to Save Jobs?' *De Rebus*, (July 2016), 31–32.
10   See Butler, *The Psychic Life of Power*, 58.
11   See Michel Foucault in James Faubion, *Power: Essential Works of Foucault, 1954–1984, Volume 3* (London: Penguin, 2002), 331.

CHAPTER 5

1   The MDDA was set up by an Act of Parliament in 2002 to create an enabling environment for media to develop, to encourage diversity of content and media, and to develop and support community media efforts.
2   A 'knock and drop' is a local newspaper that is delivered free to your door, without your ordering it.
3   Gayatri Spivak, the postcolonial Indian-born philosopher, borrowed the term 'subaltern' from Gramsci to discuss oppressed subjects, and the marginalised who have no voice.
4   Musa Sishange from the MDDA explained at a World Press Freedom Day seminar in Johannesburg on 2 May 2017 that 'one size does not fit all', and warned against making assumptions about communities without being on the ground to know what their struggles are.
5   Nelson Maldonado-Torres, 'On the Coloniality of Being', *Cultural Studies* 21:2–3 (2007), 243.
6   Tina Dyakon, 'More Americans Trust the Media Than They Did Last Year and the Majority Trust Local News', *Poynter*, 22 August 2018. Accessed 11 November 2019, https://www.poynter.org/ethics-trust/2018/more-americans-trust-the-media-than-they-did-last-year-and-the-majority-trust-local-news/.
7   Amanda Meade, 'Philanthropist Judith Neilson to Fund a R100m Institute for Journalism in Sydney', *The Guardian*, 28 November 2018. Accessed 11 November 2019, https://www.theguardian.com/media/2018/nov/28/philanthropist-judith-neilson-to-fund-a-100m-institute-for-journalism-in-sydney.
8   Joshua Benton, 'What Will Happen When Newspapers Kill Print and Go Online Only?' *Nieman Lab*, 26 September 2018. Accessed 11 November 2019, https://www.niemanlab.org/2018/09/what-will-happen-when-newspapers-kill-print-and-go-online-only-most-of-that-print-audience-will-just-disappear/.
9   SASSA stands for South African Social Security Agency, a national agency of the government created in April 2005 in order to distribute social grants on behalf of the Department of Social Development.
10   Benton, 'What Will Happen When Newspapers Kill Print'.
11   Benton, 'What Will Happen When Newspapers Kill Print'.
12   Print and Digital Media Transformation Task Team, *Report on the Transformation of Print and Digital Media* (Johannesburg: Print and Digital Media South Africa, 2013).
13   Deaths through initiation are a common occurrence in South Africa, when unsafe practices for circumcisions take place.

CHAPTER 6

1   The term 'backlash' gained popularity in 1991 with Susan Faludi's explanation that after gains in feminism there is a backlash from the traditionalists and establishment against such gains.

2   Amnesty International and Element AI, 'Troll Patrol Findings: Using Crowdsourcing, Data Science and Machine Learning to Measure Violence and Abuse against Women on Twitter' 2018. Accessed 9 January 2019, https://decoders. amnesty.org/projects/troll-patrol/findings.

3   A book project by Sanef and Gender Links written by Glenda Daniels, Tarisai Nyamweda and Collin Nxumalo, and edited by Colleen Lowe Morna. *Glass Ceilings: Women in South African Media Houses 2018* (Johannesburg: Gender Links, 2018).

4   Glenda Daniels, *State of the Newsroom South Africa 2014: Disruptions Accelerated* (Johannesburg: Wits Journalism Department, University of the Witwatersrand, 2014). Accessed 28 August 2019, https://journalism.co.za/new/wp-content/ uploads/2018/03/State-of-the-newsroom-2014.pdf.

5   *Mail & Guardian*, 'Who Runs SA's Media is a Black and White Issue', *Mail & Guardian*, 4 January 2019.

6   Julie Reid, 'Conceptualising a New Understanding of Media Diversity', in *New Concepts in Media Diversity: A View from South Africa* (Pretoria: Unisa Press, forthcoming 2020).

7   Caitlin Tucker, 'Women Journalists in the Newsroom: A Conversation about What's Changed and What Needs to Change', *Northwestern Now*, 7 February 2014. Accessed 18 September 2018, https://news.northwestern.edu/stories/2014/02/ women-journalists-in-the-newsroom#sthash.nlfGUaUk.dpuf.

8   International Women's Media Foundation, *Global Report on the Status of Women in News Media* (Washington: Knight Foundation, 2011).

9   Susan Faludi, *Backlash: The Undeclared War against American Women* (New York: Crown, 2006).

10   Angela McRobbie, 'Post-Feminism and Popular Culture', *Feminist Media Studies*, 4:3 (2004), 255.

11   Nelson Maldonado-Torres, 'On the Coloniality of Being', *Cultural Studies*, 21:2–3 (2007), 240–270.

12   Chela Sandoval, *Methodology of the Oppressed: Theory Out of Bounds Volume 18* (Minneapolis, MN: University of Minnesota Press, 2000).

13   Maldonado-Torres, 'On the Coloniality of Being', 225.

14   'Motherhood penalty', sometimes called 'family penalty', is a sociological term that refers to systematic disadvantages in pay, perceived competence, benefits of working mothers, relative to childless women. The term can also refer to an unspoken reality that women are paid less because of their *potential* to fall pregnant – for example, a female employee being overlooked for a promotion to a senior position because she got engaged or married.

15   'Mansplaining' a combination of the two words 'man' and 'explaining' is a term used by feminists to refer to the action of a man explaining something to a woman in a tone

that is condescending or patronising. The 'explanation' is spoken with an undertone of assumed poor competence of the person being spoken to, and is usually unsolicited.

16   Clara Guibourg, 'Gender Pay Gap: Six Things We've Learnt', *BBC News*, 7 April 2018. Accessed 30 June 2018, https://www.bbc.com/news/business-43668187.

17   Graham Ruddick, 'BBC Facing Backlash from Female Stars after Gender Pay Gap Revealed', *The Guardian*, 20 July 2017.

18   Jim Waterson, 'BBC Reduces Gender Pay Gap', *The Guardian*, 4 July 2018.

19   DEMOS, 'Male Celebrities Receive More Abuse on Twitter Than Women', 24 August 2014. Accessed 17 January 2020, https://demos.co.uk/press-release/demos-male-celebrities-receive-more-abuse-on-twitter-than-women-2/.

20   Ferial Haffajee and Marc Davies, 'Ferial Haffajee: The Gupta Fake News Factory and Me', *HuffPost SA*, 6 June 2017. Accessed 22 January 2020, https://www.huffingtonpost.co.uk/entry/ferial-haffajee-the-gupta-fake-news-factory-and-me_uk_5c7eaa44e4b078abc6c24e7f.

21   Denise-Marie Ordway, 'Study Shows Female Journalists Face "Rampant" Online Harassment', *Journalist's Resource*, Harvard Kennedy School Shorenstein Centre, 2 August 2018. Accessed 5 December 2018, https://journalistsresource.org/studies/society/news-media/female-journalists-harassment-online-research/.

22   Julie Posetti, 'Trends in Newsrooms: Business of Gender Equality', WAN-IFRA blog, 4 August 2018. Accessed 10 January 2019, https://blog.wan-ifra.org/2015/08/04/trends-in-newsrooms-business-of-gender-equality.

CHAPTER 7

1   Herman Wasserman, 'Journalism in a New Democracy: The Ethics of Listening', *Communicatio*, 39:1 (2013), 67–84.

2   Sarah Chiumbu, Vasu Reddy and Narnia Bohler-Muller, 'Social Justice for the Poor: The Framing of Socioeconomic Rights in Selected South African Newspapers', *Journalism*, 19:7 (2016), 959–975.

3   Nelson Maldonado-Torres, 'On the Coloniality of Being', *Cultural Studies*, 21:2–3 (2007), 240–270.

4   Chela Sandoval, *Methodology of the Oppressed: Theory out of Bounds, Volume 18* (Minneapolis, MN: University of Minnesota Press, 2000).

5   Tendayi Sithole, *Steve Biko: Decolonial Meditations of Black Consciousness* (New York: Lexington Books, 2016), 140.

6   Frantz Fanon, *Black Skin, White Masks*, trans. Charles Lam Markmann (New York: Grove Press, 1967), 222.

7   Frantz Fanon, *The Wretched of the Earth*, trans. Charles Lam Markmann (New York: Grove Press, 1963), 315.

8   Steve Biko, *I Write What I Like* (Johannesburg: Picador Africa, 2004), 15.

9   Gayatri Spivak, 'Can the Subaltern Speak?', in *Marxism and the Interpretation of Culture*, ed. Carry Nelson and Lawrence Grossberge (Champaign, IL: University of Illinois Press, 1988), 271–313.

10   Nelson Maldonado-Torres, 'Thinking Through the Decolonial Turn: Post-Continental Interventionism Theory, Philosophy, and Critique - An Introduction',

Transmodernity: Journal of Peripheral Cultural Production of the Luso-Hispanic World, 1:2 (2011), 1–15.

CHAPTER 8

1   Julie Posetti, *Time to Step Away from the 'Bright, Shiny Things'? Towards a Sustainable Model of Journalism Innovation in an Era of Perpetual Change.* (Oxford University, Reuters Institute for the Study of Journalism, 2018). Accessed 10 January 2019, https://reutersinstitute.politics.ox.ac.uk/sites/default/files/2018-11/Posetti_Towards_a_Sustainable_model_of_Journalism_FINAL.pdf.

2   Chantal Mouffe, *The Democratic Paradox* (London: Verso, 2000).

3   Chela Sandoval. *Methodology of the Oppressed: Theory Out of Bounds, Volume 18* (Minneapolis, MN: University of Minnesota Press, 2000).

4   Branko Brkic, 'Weak but Vicious – EFF Edition', *Daily Maverick*, 26 November 2018. Accessed 17 January 2020, https://www.dailymaverick.co.za/article/2018-11-26-weak-but-vicious-eff-edition/.

5   Harry Dugmore, *Paying the Piper: The Sustainability of the News Industry and Journalism in South Africa in a Time of Digital Transformation and Political Uncertainty.* (Rhodes University, Grahamstown: Digital Journalism Research Project, 2018). Accessed 15 February 2019, https://themediaonline.co.za/wp-content/uploads/2018/05/PAYING-THE-PIPER-The-sustainability-of-the-news-industry-and-journalism-in-South-Africa-in-a-time-of-digital-transformation-and-political-uncertainty.pdf.

6   Claire Wardle and Hossein Derakhshan, 'One Year On, We're Still Not Recognising the Complexity of the Information Disorder Online', *First Draft*, 31 October 2017. Accessed 11 December 2018, https://firstdraftnews.org/coe_infodisorder/.

anti-feminist backlash: the swing against gains that women have made in their struggle for equality.

cyber misogyny: hatred of women expressed online.

damnés: the wretched of the earth.

decolonial turn: a shift in knowledge production to refocus the gaze (from the liberal mainstream agenda) to render the invisible, visible – indeed, to bring the invisible to the centre.

'fake news': a broad and inadequate term, encapsulating propaganda, misinformation, disinformation and mal-information.

feminism: in this book the term refers broadly to equality between the genders and, more than this, means bringing women right to the centre of the political and media matrix.

glass ceiling: an invisible barrier that obstructs a woman's progress in the workplace.

loss: having something that then disappears – through death or trauma, through losing employment, or through losing an ideal.

mansplaining: a man explaining something to a woman in a condescending and patronising way.

#MeToo: a movement/campaign for all those who say, or support 'I have also been sexually violated, I now speak up'.

power: a force that presses down upon the subject externally (and that subjection can also be what forms the subject internally).

radical democracy: a deeper, more inclusive and robust democracy than what is current in the Western liberal world today.

social media: websites and technologies that enable the sharing of social networks, information, news, gossip, and the creation of brands such as Twitter, Facebook, Instagram, YouTube, WhatsApp and LinkedIn.

The concepts below are Lacanian, adapted by Slavoj Žižek in *The Sublime Object of Ideology* and further interpreted and used in my book *Fight for Democracy: The ANC and the Media in South Africa*.

enjoyment: Like Lacan's *jouissance*, enjoyment is usually identified with surplus enjoyment or excitation. If you subtract the excess, you will lose the enjoyment. Enjoyment in this context is surplus, because it is an 'excess'. It is where ideology resides.

excess/surplus: something more in the object than the object itself. For example, 'Coke' standing in for 'America' and 'freedom', signifying more than sugar and carbonated water.

interpellation: naming, hailing, labelling, calling, shaming and subjecting that person to that name – for example, lesbian, black, racist or (as in chapter 7) 'hey, you with the Afro, neaten up'.

jouissance: is surplus excitation, even violent intrusion, bringing more pain than pleasure; it may mean enjoyment (as in being a voyeur in a juicy story) but it is also experienced as pain or suffering (as in paranoia or persecution) and is identified in 'the Other'.

master signifier: something that takes on a fixed, rigid meaning, to which all other meanings are tied to the point of being circulatory. A 'floating signifier' is a signifier with no fixed meaning, whose meaning is not closed off and is not attached or linked to another signifier.

passionate attachment: a self-colonising path that some forms of identity can take, such as victimhood, and being attached to the shackles, where the subjects are attached to their subordination.

resignification: to not reiterate norms that oppress, or to detach from past signifiers. Resignifications could unsettle past passionate attachments; this is a form of resistance, as in not accepting the name or the labelling.

the gaze from where am I looking: the stain preventing me from looking at the picture from a safe objective distance. My own view is subscribed in the content of my gaze. In today's 'woke' generation parlance, you are asked to 'check your privilege', or acknowledge your position, or gaze.

BIBLIOGRAPHY

AIP Conference. *The Future Starts Now: Role of the Independent Media in the Current South African Context*. Notes and attendance by author, September 2013, Johannesburg.

Althusser, Louis. 'Ideology and Ideological State Apparatuses, Essays on Ideology', in *Mapping Ideology*, ed. Slavoj Žižek (London and New York: Verso, 1984), 100–140.

amaBhungane, 'McKinsey Dossiers Parts 1–5', *Daily Maverick*, 14 September–23 October 2017.

Amnesty International and Element AI. 'Troll Patrol Findings: Using Crowdsourcing, Data Science and Machine Learning to Measure Violence and Abuse against Women on Twitter'. 2018. Accessed 9 January 2019, https://decoders.amnesty.org/projects/troll-patrol/findings.

ANC (African National Congress). 'Communications and the Battle of Ideas'. Paper presented at the ANC's 53rd National Conference on resolutions adopted in 2012, Mangaung, 31 January 2013.

ANC. 'Policy Conference Resolutions about the Media'. Paper presented at the ANC's 52nd National Conference, Polokwane, 20 December 2007.

ANC. 'Media, Transformation, Ownership and Diversity'. Paper presented at the ANC's 50th National Conference, Mafikeng, 16 December 1997.

BBC News. 'Khashoggi Death: Saudi Arabia Says Journalist Was Murdered', *BBC News* 22 October 2018. Accessed 20 January 2020, https://www.bbc.com/news/world-middle-east-45935823.

Benton, Joshua. 'What Will Happen When Newspapers Kill Print and Go Online Only?' *Nieman Lab*, 26 September 2018. Accessed 11 November 2019, https://www.niemanlab.org/2018/09/what-will-happen-when-newspapers-kill-print-and-go-online-only-most-of-that-print-audience-will-just-disappear/.

Berger, Guy. 'Towards an Analysis of South African Media: Transformation 1994–1999', *Transformation*, 38 (1999): 82–116.

Bezuidenhout, Jessica. 'Zuma Pals Score First Nuke Deal', *Mail & Guardian*, 16–22 September.

Biko, Steve. *I Write What I Like* (Johannesburg: Picador Africa, 2004).

Bosch, Tanja. 'Twitter and Participatory Citizenship: #FeesMustFall in South Africa', in *Digital Activism in the Social Media Era: Critical Reflections on Emerging Trends in Sub Saharan Africa*, ed. Bruce Mutsvairo (London: Palgrave Macmillan, 2016), 159–173.

Brkic, Branko. 'Weak but Vicious – EFF Edition', *Daily Maverick*, 26 November 2018. Accessed 17 January 2020, https://www.dailymaverick.co.za/article/2018-11-26-weak-but-vicious-eff-edition/.

Butler, Judith. *The Psychic Life of Power: Theories in Subjection* (Palo Alto, CA: Stanford University Press, 1997).

Butler, Judith, Ernesto Laclau and Slavoj Žižek. *Contingency, Hegemony and Universality: Contemporary Dialogues of the Left* (London: Verso, 2000).

Cameron, Jackie. 'Lies, Damned Lies and Sekunjalo Statistics'. *Biznews*, 19 November 2019. Accessed 27 March 2020, https://www.biznews.com/undictated/2019/11/19/lies-sekunjalo-statistics-independent-media.

Chabalala, Jeanette. '#GuptaLeaks Team Scoops Another Award For Courageous Journalism'. *News24*, 25 June 2018. Accessed 20 January 2020, https://www.news24.com/SouthAfrica/News/guptaleaks-team-scoops-another-award-for-courageous-journalism-20180625.

Chasi, Colin. 'Violent Communication is Not Alien to Ubuntu: Nothing Human is Alien to Africans', *Communicatio*, 40:4 (2014), 287–304.

Chiumbu, Sarah. 'Media, Race and Capital: A Decolonial Analysis of Representation of Miners' Strikes in South Africa', *African Studies*, 75 (2016), 417–435.

Chiumbu, Sarah, Vasu Reddy and Narnia Bohler-Muller. 'Social Justice for the Poor: The Framing of Socioeconomic Rights in Selected South African Newspapers', *Journalism*, 19:7 (2016), 959–975.

Coetzer, Neil. 'Alternatives to Retrenchment – Are Employers Obliged to Save Jobs?' *De Rebus*, (July 2016), 31–32.

Committee to Protect Journalists. 'CPJ Recognizes Global Press Oppressors Amid Trump's Fake News Awards', *Committee to Protect Journalists Reports*, 8 January 2018. Accessed 17 August 2018, https://cpj.org/2018/01/cpj-recognizes-global-press-oppressors-amid-trumps.php.

Committee to Protect Journalists. 'Record Number of Journalists Jailed as Turkey, China and Egypt Pay Scant Price for Repression', *Committee to Protect Journalists Reports*, 13 December 2017. Accessed 30 July 2018, https://cpj.org/reports/2017/12/journalists-prison-jail-record-number-turkey-china-egypt.php.

Corke, Emily. 'Zuma: I Am a Victim of Unregulated Media', *EWN*, 19 October 2015. Accessed 22 January 2020, https://ewn.co.za/2015/10/19/Zuma-I-am-a-victim-of-unregulated-media.

Corke, Emily. 'Protection of State Information Bill Still Under Consideration', *EWN*, 18 October 2015. Accessed 10 January 2019, https://ewn.co.za/2015/10/18/Protection-of-state-information-bill-still-under-consideration.

Cowan, Kyle. 'SARS Takes Jacques Pauw to Court', *TimesLIVE*, 19 December 2017. Accessed 2 February 2018, https://www.timeslive.co.za/news/south-africa/2017-12-19-sars-takes-jacques-pauw-to-court/.

Daniels, Glenda. 'Left Out in the Cold', in *State of the Newsroom: Structured/Unstructured*, ed. Alan Finlay (Johannesburg: Wits Journalism Department, University of the Witwatersrand, 2018), 17–26.

Daniels, Glenda. 'Why the Demise of Specialist Reporters is a Loss For Any Democracy', *The Conversation*, 28 November 2018. Accessed 20 January 2020, https://theconversation.com/why-the-demise-of-specialist-reporters-is-a-loss-for-any-democracy-107196.

Daniels, Glenda. *State of the Newsroom, South Africa 2014: Disruptions Accelerated* (Johannesburg: Wits Journalism Department, University of the Witwatersrand, 2014).

Accessed 28 August 2019, https://journalism.co.za/new/wp-content/uploads/2018/03/State-of-the-newsroom-2014.pdf.

Daniels, Glenda. *State of the Newsroom, South Africa 2013: Disruptions and Transitions* (Johannesburg: Wits Journalism Department, University of the Witwatersrand, 2013). Accessed 17 January 2020, https://journalism.co.za/new/wp-content/uploads/2018/03/State_of_the_newroom_2013.pdf.

Daniels, Glenda. *Fight for Democracy: The ANC and the Media in South Africa* (Johannesburg: Wits University Press, 2012).

Daniels, Glenda. 'Delay in the Fight against Secrecy Not a Final Victory', *Mail & Guardian*, 24 June 2011.

Daniels, Glenda. 'Open Season on Media', *Mail & Guardian*, 17 June 2011.

Daniels, Glenda, Tarisai Nyamweda and Collin Nxumalo. *Glass Ceilings: Women in South African Media Houses 2018* (Johannesburg: Gender Links, 2018).

DEMOS. 'Male Celebrities Receive More Abuse on Twitter Than Women', 24 August 2014. Accessed 17 January 2020, https://demos.co.uk/press-release/demos-male-celebrities-receive-more-abuse-on-twitter-than-women-2/.

De Waal, Mandy. 'Manyi vs the Media: The Ad Budget Battle Begins', *Daily Maverick*, 13 June 2011. Accessed 17 January 2020, https://www.dailymaverick.co.za/article/2011-06-13-manyi-vs-the-media-the-ad-budget-battle-begins/.

Dugmore, Harry. *Paying the Piper: The Sustainability of the News Industry and Journalism in South Africa in a Time of Digital Transformation and Political Uncertainty.* (Rhodes University, Grahamstown: Digital Journalism Research Project, 2018). Accessed 15 February 2019, https://themediaonline.co.za/wp-content/uploads/2018/05/PAYING-THE-PIPER-The-sustainability-of-the-news-industry-and-journalism-in-South-Africa-in-a-time-of-digital-transformation-and-political-uncertainty.pdf.

Duncan, Jane. 'South African Journalism and the Marikana Massacre: A Case Study of an Editorial Failure', *The Political Economy of Communication*, 1:2 (2013), 65–88.

Dyakon, Tina. 'More Americans Trust the Media Than They Did Last Year and the Majority Trust Local News', *Poynter*, 22 August 2018. Accessed 11 November 2019, https://www.poynter.org/ethics-trust/2018/more-americans-trust-the-media-than-they-did-last-year-and-the-majority-trust-local-news/.

eNCA Maggs on Media. 'Debate: SABC Won't Revisit "Self-Censorship" Decision: Motsoeneng', *eNCA*, 6 June 2016. Accessed 20 July 2018, https://www.enca.com/south-africa/debate-sabc-wont-revisit-self-censorship-decision-motsoeneng.

eNCA. 'Zuma Takes a Swipe at Media over Xenophobia Coverage', *eNCA*, 24 May 2015. Accessed 17 January 2020, https://www.enca.com/south-africa/zuma-takes-swipe-media-over-xenophobia-covera.

Escobar, Arturo. 'Worlds and Knowledges Otherwise: The Latin American Modernity/Coloniality Research Program', *Cultural Studies*, 21:2–3 (2007), 197–210.

Etheridge, Jenna. 'Broken Heart Syndrome Kills "SABC 8" Journalist Suna Venter', *News24*, 29 June 2017. Accessed 22 January 2020, https://www.news24.com/SouthAfrica/News/sabc-8-journalist-suna-venter-dead-20170629.

Eyoh, Dickson. 'African Perspectives on Democracy and the Dilemmas of Post-Colonial Intellectuals', *Africa Today*, 45:3 (1998), 281–306.

Faludi, Susan. *Backlash: The Undeclared War against American Women* (New York: Crown, 2006).

Fanon, Frantz. *Black Skin, White Masks*, trans. Charles Lam Markmann (New York: Grove Press, 1967).

Fanon, Frantz. *The Wretched of the Earth*, trans. Charles Lam Markmann (New York: Grove Press, 1963).

Faubion, James. *Power: Essential Works of Foucault, 1954–1984, Volume 3* (London: Penguin Books, 2002).

Flueckiger, Simone. 'Practical Advice For Tackling Gender Imbalance in News Media from #WINSummit1800', WAN-IFRA blog, 12 June 2018. Accessed 22 January 2020, https://blog.wan-ifra.org/2018/06/12/practical-advice-for-tackling-gender-imbalance-in-news-media-from-winsummit18.

Foucault, Michel. *The History of Sexuality Volume 1: An Introduction* (New York: Vintage, 1990).

Foucault, Michel. 'The Subject and Power', *Critical Inquiry*, 8:4 (1982), 777–795.

Fourie, Pietered, *Media Studies: Social (New) Media and Mediated Communication Today, Volume 4* (Cape Town: Juta, 2017).

Frassinelli, Pier Paolo. 'Decolonisation: What it is and What Research Has to do with it', in *Making Sense of Research*, ed. Keyan G. Tomaselli (Pretoria: Van Schaik, 2018), 3–10.

Freedom of Expression Institute (FXI). *The Media and the Law: A Handbook for Community Journalists* (Johannesburg: Freedom of Expression Institute, 2007).

Friedman, Steven. 'Political Journalists Are Often Pawns in Factional Fights', *Business Day*, 24 October 2018. Accessed 15 February 2019, https://www.businesslive.co.za/bd/opinion/columnists/2018-10-24-steven-friedman-political-journalists-are-often-pawns-in-factional-fights/.

Friedman, Steven. 'Whose Freedom? South Africa's Press, Middle-Class Bias and the Threat of Control', *Equid Novi: African Journalism Studies*, 32:2 (2011), 106–121.

Gillwald, Alison, Onkokame Mothobi and Broc Rademan. 'The State of ICT in South Africa'. Policy Paper No. 5, Series 5: After Access (Cape Town: Research ICT Africa, 2018).

Guibourg, Clara. 'Gender Pay Gap: Six Things We've Learnt', *BBC News*, 7 April 2018. Accessed 30 June 2018, https://www.bbc.com/news/business-43668187.

Haffajee, Ferial and Marc Davies. 'Ferial Haffajee: The Gupta Fake News Factory and Me', *HuffPost SA*, 6 June 2017. Accessed 22 January 2020, https://www.huffingtonpost.co.uk/entry/ferial-haffajee-the-gupta-fake-news-factory-and-me_uk_5c7eaa44e4b078abc6c24e7f.

Harber, Anton. 'Celebrate the Best of Our Investigative Reporters, but Remember the Worst as Well', *The Harbinger*, 15 February 2018. Accessed 2 July 2019, http://www.theharbinger.co.za/wordpress/2018/01/19/celebrate-the-best-of-our-investigative-reporters-but-remember-the-worst-as-well/.

Hunter, Qaanitah. 'Nkandla Fall Guy Hits Out at Zuma', *Sunday Times*, 27 March 2016.

Hunter, Qaanitah and Thanduxolo Jika. 'Operation Exit Zuma: Top ANC Leaders Driving Secret Plan', *Sunday Times*, 17 April 2016.

International Women's Media Foundation. *Global Report on the Status of Women in News Media* (Washington: Knight Foundation, 2011).

Jika, Thanduxolo, Jan-Jan Joubert and Qaanitah Hunter. 'For the Sake of Your Country, Mr President, GO NOW!' *Sunday Times*, 3 April 2016.

Joubert, Pearlie. Interview by Kieno Kammies, *Cape Talk* breakfast show, Omny.fm, 2 October 2018. Accessed 10 January 2019, https://omny.fm/shows/the-kieno-kammies-show/pearlie-joubert-on-sunday-times-handling-of-sars-r.

Kubheka, Thando and Dineo Bendile. 'SABC Refuses to Back Down on Its Editorial Policies', *EWN*, 12 July 2016. Accessed 9 June 2018, https://ewn.co.za/2016/07/12/SABC-refuses-to-back-down-on-its-new-editorial-policies.

Kruger, Theuns. 'Hlaudi Motsoeneng's Controversial Tenure at the SABC', *Graphics24*, 6 October 2016. Accessed 19 January 2020, https://www.grafika24.com/hlaudi-motsoeneng-controversial-tenure-at-the-sabc-timeline/.

Louw, Raymond. *So, This is Democracy? State of Media Freedom in Southern Africa, 2017* (Windhoek, Namibia: Misa/Fesmedia, 2018).

Mabweazara, Hayes, Okoth F. Mudhai and Jason Whittaker. 'Introduction: Online Journalism in Africa: Trends, Practices and Emerging Culture', in *Online Journalism in Africa: Trends, Practices and Emerging Culture* (London and Oxford: Routledge, 2014) 1–13.

Made, Pat and Colleen Lowe Morna. *Glass Ceilings: Women and Men in Southern Africa Media* (Johannesburg: Gender Links, 2009).

Mahlase, Mahlatse. 'Sanef Statement on the Treatment of Journalists at the 54th ANC Elective Conference', South African National Editors Forum, media statement, 17 December 2017.

Mail & Guardian. 'Who Runs SA's Media is a Black and White Issue', *Mail & Guardian*, 4 January 2019.

Mail & Guardian. 'Zuma at the Precipice', *Mail & Guardian*, 4 November 2016.

Mail & Guardian. 'Zuma's Hit List', *Mail & Guardian*, 26 August 2016.

Mail & Guardian. 'Concourt Klap: What Next for JZ?' *Mail & Guardian*, 1 April 2016.

Mail & Guardian. 'Zuma: ANC Not Trying to Control the Media', *Mail & Guardian*, 15 August 2010.

Makinana, Andiswe. 'Zuma Condemns "Opposite of the Positive" South African Media', *Mail & Guardian*, 10 September 2013.

Makinana, Andiswe, Setumo Stone and Hlengiwe Nhlabathi. 'Zuma Tells MPs to Vote against Motion or Else', *City Press*, 13 November 2016.

Maldonado-Torres, Nelson. 'Thinking Through the Decolonial Turn: Post-Continental Interventionism Theory, Philosophy, and Critique – An Introduction', *Transmodernity: Journal of Peripheral Cultural Production of the Luso-Hispanic World*, 1:2 (2011), 1–15.

Maldonado-Torres, Nelson. 'On the Coloniality of Being', *Cultural Studies*, 21:2-3 (2007), 240–270.

Mano, Winston. 'Racism, Ethnicity and the Media in Africa', in *Racism, Ethnicity and the Media in Africa: Mediating Conflict in the Twenty-First Century*, ed. Winston Mano (London: I.B. Tauris, 2015), 1–27.

Mano, Winston. *Racism, Ethnicity and the Media in Africa: Mediating Conflict in the Twenty-First Century* (London: I.B. Tauris, 2015).

Mano, Winston and Viola C. Milton. 'Citizen Journalism and the Ebola Outbreak in Africa', in *Participatory Politics and Citizen Journalism in a Networked Africa*, ed. Bruce Mutsvairo (London: Palgrave MacMillan, 2016), 244–261.

Mbembe, Achille. *On the Post Colony* (Johannesburg: Wits University Press, 2015).

McKinley, Dale. *South Africa's Corporatised Liberation: A Critical Analysis of the ANC in Power* (Johannesburg: Jacana, 2017).

McRobbie, Angela. 'Post-Feminism and Popular Culture', *Feminist Media Studies*, 4:3 (2004), 255–264.

Meade, Amanda. 'Philanthropist Judith Neilson to Fund a R100m Institute for Journalism in Sydney', *The Guardian*, 28 November 2018. Accessed 11 November 2019, https://www.theguardian.com/media/2018/nov/28/philanthropist-judith-neilson-to-fund-a-100m-institute-for-journalism-in-sydney.

Milton, Viola C. 'A Kind of Blue: Can Communication Research Matter?' Paper presented at the University of South Africa, Pretoria, 20 March, 2019.

Mokone, Thabo, Caiphus Kgosana, Bobby Jordan and Stephan Hofstatter. 'Three Damning Blows For Zuma', *Sunday Times*, 1 December 2013.

Mouffe, Chantal. *The Democratic Paradox* (London: Verso, 2000).

Moya, Paula. 'Who We Are and from Where We Speak', *Transmodernity: Journal of Peripheral Cultural Production of the Luso-Hispanic World*, 1:2 (2011), 79–94.

Mutsvairo, Bruce. *Digital Activism in the Social Media Era: Critical Reflections on Emerging Trends in Sub Saharan Africa* (London: Palgrave, 2016).

Ndlovu-Gatsheni, Sabelo J. 'Why Decoloniality in the 21st Century?' *The Thinker*, 48 (2013), 10–15.

News24. 'Media to Blame for Nkandla Perceptions – Zuma', *News24*, 13 February 2015. Accessed 12 July 2018, https://www.news24.com/SouthAfrica/News/Media-to-blame-for-Nkandla-perceptions-Zuma-20150213.

Ngalwa, Sibusiso. 'Zuma's Name Secured Gupta Landing', *Sunday Times*, 5 May 2013.

Ngcukana, Lubabalo and S'Thembile Cele. 'Calls for Zuma to Resign Increase', *City Press*, 4 September 2016.

Nhlabathi, Hlengiwe, S'Thembile Cele, Setumo Stone and Andisiwe Makinana. 'Zuma's ANC Leadership Left Hanging by a Thread', *City Press*, 27 November 2016.

Nicolson, Greg. 'High Court on Zuma's Corruption Charges: Not the End, But Damning', *Daily Maverick*, 27 April 2016. Accessed 22 January 2020, https://www.dailymaverick.co.za/article/2016-04-29-high-court-on-zumas-corruption-charges-not-the-end-but-damning/.

Nyamnjoh, Francis B. '"Potted Plants in Greenhouses": A Critical Reflection on the Resilience of Colonial Education in Africa', *Journal of Asian and African Studies*, 47:2 (2012), 129–154.

Ordway, Denise-Marie. 'Study Shows Female Journalists Face "Rampant" Online Harassment', *Journalist's Resource*, Harvard Kennedy School Shorenstein Centre, 2 August 2018. Accessed 5 December 2018, https://journalistsresource.org/studies/society/news-media/female-journalists-harassment-online-research/.

Pauw, Jacques. 'Why the *Sunday Times* Should Go to the Zondo and Nugent Commissions', *Daily Maverick*, 27 September 2018. Accessed 10 January 2019, https://www.dailymaverick.co.za/opinionista/2018-09-27-why-the-sunday-times-should-go-to-the-zondo-and-nugent-commissions/.

Posetti, Julie. *Time to Step Away from the 'Bright, Shiny Things'? Towards a Sustainable Model of Journalism Innovation in an Era of Perpetual Change* (Oxford University, Reuters Institute for the Study of Journalism, 2018). Accessed 10 January 2019,

https://reutersinstitute.politics.ox.ac.uk/sites/default/files/2018-11/Posetti_
Towards_a_Sustainable_model_of_Journalism_FINAL.pdf

Posetti, Julie. 'Trends in Newsrooms: Business of Gender Equality', WAN-IFRA blog, 4 August 2018. Accessed 10 January 2019, https://blog.wan-ifra.org/2015/08/04/trends-in-newsrooms-business-of-gender-equality.

Print and Digital Media Transformation Task Team. *Report on the Transformation of Print and Digital Media* (Johannesburg: Print and Digital Media South Africa, 2013).

Qukula, Qama. 'Top SABC Journalists Applauded for Brave Testimony', *Cape Talk*, 13 December 2016. Accessed 15 February 2019, http://www.capetalk.co.za/articles/236151/top-sabc-journos-applauded-for-brave-testimony.

Rabe, Lizette. 'Glass Ceiling, Concrete Ceiling', *Rhodes Journalism Review*, 26 (2006), 20–21.

Radcliff, Damian. 'How Local Journalism Can Upend the "Fake News" Narrative', *The Conversation*, 27 November 2018. Accessed 17 January 2020, https://theconversation.com/how-local-journalism-can-upend-the-fake-news-narrative-104630.

Reid, Julie. 'Conceptualising a New Understanding of Media Diversity', in *New Concepts in Media Diversity: A View From South Africa* (Pretoria: Unisa Press, forthcoming 2020).

Reid, Julie. 'Media Freedom Debacles Aside, the Press is Failing Us', *Daily Maverick*, 24 October 2012. Accessed 17 January 2017, https://www.dailymaverick.co.za/opinionista/2012-10-24-media-freedom-debacles-aside-the-press-is-failing-us/.

Ricketson, Matthew. 'What Has Been Lost in Legacy Media's Job Losses? What Can Be Re-instated in Digital Newsrooms?' Discussion paper presented at the New Beats Seminar at the Australia Media Traditions conference, University of Melbourne, 28 November 2018.

Ries, Brian, Meg Wagner, Sophie Tatum and Jessie Yeung. 'Supreme Court Nominee Faces Sexual Assault Allegation', *CNN*, 21 September 2018. Accessed 20 January 2020, https://edition.cnn.com/politics/live-news/kavanaugh-sexual-assault-allegation-dle/index.html.

Rodny-Gumede, Ylva. 'Male and Female Journalists' Perceptions of Their Power to Influence News Agendas and Public Discourses', *Communicatio*, 41:2 (2015), 206–219.

Rønning, Helge and Tawana Kupe. 'The Dual Legacy of Democracy and Authoritarianism', in *De-Westernizing Media Studies*, ed. James Curran and Myung-Jin Park (London: Routledge, 2000) 138–156.

Roper, Chris. 'The Day We Broke Nkandla', *Mail & Guardian*, 4 December 2013.

Ruddick, Graham. 'BBC Facing Backlash from Female Stars after Gender Pay Gap Revealed', *The Guardian*, 20 July 2017.

Rumney, Reg. 'Towards a Policy on Media Diversity and Development', Government Communication and Information Service (GCIS) discussion document, 2017.

Rusbridger, Alan. *Breaking News: The Remaking of Journalism and Why it Matters Now* (London: Canongate Books, 2018).

Sandoval, Chela. *Methodology of the Oppressed: Theory Out of Bounds, Volume 18* (Minneapolis, MN: University of Minnesota Press, 2000).

Schmidt, Christine. 'Canada Introduces a $595 Million Package in Support of Journalism', *Nieman Lab*, 26 November 2018. Accessed 17 January 2020, https://www.niemanlab. org/2018/11/canada-introduces-a-595-million-package-in-support-of-journalism/.

Siqoko, Bongani. 'We Got it Wrong and for That We Apologise', *TimesLive*, 14 October 2018. Accessed 17 January 2020, https://www.timeslive.co.za/sunday-times/news/2018-10-13-we-got-it-wrong-and-for-that-we-apologise/.

Sishange, Musa. 'Media Development and Diversity Agency (MDDA)'. Presentation at World Press Freedom Day Seminar, Johannesburg, 2 May 2017.

Sithole, Tendayi. *Steve Biko: Decolonial Meditations of Black Consciousness* (New York: Lexington Books, 2016).

Smith, David. 'South Africa Secrecy Law Surprise as Zuma Rejects Controversial Bill', *The Guardian*, 12 September 2013.

Sole, Sam. 'Journalism in the Age of the Zuptas', *Politicsweb*, 12 September 2017. Accessed 17 January 2020, https://www.politicsweb.co.za/opinion/journalism-in-the-age-of-the-zuptas.

Spivak, Gayatri. 'Can the Subaltern Speak?', in *Marxism and the Interpretation of Culture*, ed. Carry Nelson and Lawrence Grossberge (Champaign, IL: University of Illinois Press, 1988), 271–313.

Steenveld, Lynette. 'Transformation of the Media: From What to What?' *Rhodes Journalism Review*, 16 (1998), 1–4.

Stone, Setumo. 'State Capture Investigation: Kill Zuma's Deal', *City Press*, 13 November 2016.

The Economist. 'The Global Slump in Press Freedom', *The Economist*, 23 July 2018.

The Media Online. 'Zuma Likes the Idea of "Patriotic" Media', *The Media Online*, 11 September 2013. Accessed 20 January 2020, https://themediaonline.co.za/2013/09/zuma-likes-the-idea-of-patriotic-media/.

Tolsi, Niren. 'Fire and Media: Towards a New Journalism in South Africa'. Ruth First Memorial Lecture, Johannesburg, 18 October 2018.

Tomaselli, Keyan G. 'Ownership and Control in the South African Print Media: Black Empowerment after Apartheid, 1990–1997', *Ecquid Novi: African Journalism Studies*, 18:1 (1997), 67–68.

Tucker, Caitlin. 'Women Journalists in the Newsroom: A Conversation about What's Changed and What Needs to Change', *Northwestern Now*, 7 February 2014. Accessed 18 September 2018, http://www.northwestern.edu/newscenter/stories/2014/02/women-journalists-in-the-newsroom.html#sthash.nlfGUaUk.dpuf.

Wardle, Claire and Hossein Derakhshan. 'One Year On, We're Still Not Recognising the Complexity of the Information Disorder Online', *First Draft*, 31 October 2017. Accessed 11 December 2018, https://firstdraftnews.org/coe_infodisorder/.

Wasserman, Herman. 'Why Journalists in South Africa Should do Some Self-Reflection', *The Media Online*, 31 October 2018. Accessed 10 November 2018, https://themediaonline. co.za/2018/10/why-journalists-in-south-africa-should-do-some-self-reflection/.

Wasserman, Herman. 'Journalism in a New Democracy: The Ethics of Listening', *Communicatio*, 39:1 (2013), 67–84.

Wasserman, Herman and Arnold de Beer. 'Which Public? Whose Interest? The South African Media and Its Role During the First Ten Years of Democracy', *Critical Arts*, 19:1–2 (2005), 36–51.

Wasserman, Herman, Wallace Chuma and Tanja Bosch. 'Voices of the Poor are Missing from South Africa's Media', *The Conversation*, 22 January 2016. Accessed 5 February 2018, https://theconversation.com/voices-of-the-poor-are-missing-from-south-africas-media-53068.

Waterson, Jim. 'Facebook Gives £4.5m to Fund 80 Local Newspaper Jobs in UK', *The Guardian*, 19 November 2018.

Waterson, Jim. 'BBC Reduces Gender Pay Gap', *The Guardian*, 4 July 2018.

Wicks, Jeff. 'SABC 8 Press on with ConCourt Battle', *News24*, 13 September 2016. Accessed 20 January 2018, https://www.news24.com/SouthAfrica/News/sabc-8-press-on-with-concourt-battle-20160913

Women in the World. 'Women Politicians, Journalists Abused Every 30 Seconds on "Toxic" Twitter', *Women in the World*, 27 December 2018. Accessed 22 January 2020, https://womenintheworld.com/2018/12/27/women-politicians-journalists-abused-every-30-seconds-on-toxic-twitter/.

Žižek, Slavoj. *First as Tragedy, Then as Farce* (London: Verso, 2009).

Žižek, Slavoj. *The Sublime Object of Ideology* (London: Verso, 1989).

INTERVIEWS

Clay, Paddi: email interview, 31 July 201

Flanagan, Louise: email interview, 24 July 2018

Joseph, Raymond: email interview, 11 July 2018

Kemp, Yunus: email interview, 12 July 2018

Louw, Chris: personal interview, Johannesburg, 16 October 2018

Ludman, Barbara: personal interview, Johannesburg, 22 July 2018

Mathews, Charlie: email interview, 25 July 2018

Mkhabela, Mpumelelo: email interview, 3 August 2018

Monare, Moshoeshoe: personal interview, Johannesburg, 20 July 2018

Moyo, Thembi: personal interview, Johannesburg, 11 December 2018

Orderson, Crystal: email interview, 16 July 2018

Reynolds, Seamus: personal interview, 24 July 2018

Robertson, Heather: email interview, 13 July 2018

Sepotokele, Themba: email interview, 5 July 2018

Vale, Louise: personal interview, 8 August, 20 August and 25 September 2018

INDEX

Page numbers in *italics* indicate figures and tables.

Printed and bound by CPI Group (UK) Ltd, Croydon, CR0 4YY

13/04/2025

14656580-0004